Gaining Freedoms

Gaining Freedoms

CLAIMING SPACE IN ISTANBUL AND BERLIN

Berna Turam

Stanford University Press
Stanford, California

Stanford University Press
Stanford, California

©2015 by the Board of Trustees of the Leland Stanford Junior University. All rights reserved.

Printed in the United States of America on acid-free, archival-quality paper

Library of Congress Cataloging-in-Publication Data

Turam, Berna, author.
  Gaining freedoms : claiming space in Istanbul and Berlin / Berna Turam.
    pages cm
  Includes bibliographical references and index.
  ISBN 978-0-8047-9362-9 (cloth : alk. paper)--ISBN 978-0-8047-9448-0 (pbk. : alk.)
  1. Political participation--Turkey--Istanbul. 2. Social conflict--Turkey--Istanbul. 3. Public spaces--Political aspects--Turkey--Istanbul. 4. Istanbul (Turkey)--Politics and government--21st century. 5. Istanbul (Turkey)--Social conditions--21st century. 6. Turks--Germany--Berlin--Politics and government. 7. Social conflict--Germany--Berlin. 8. Public spaces--Political aspects--Germany--Berlin. 9. Kreuzberg (Berlin, Germany) I. Title.
  JQ1809.A15T827 2015
  306.20089'9435043155--dc23
                    2014044592

  ISBN 978-0-8047-9452-7 (electronic)

Typeset by Bruce Lundquist in 10/14 Minion

To the freedom-loving youth of my country—
the passionate Gezi protestors

To my mother, Sevim Turam,
the first and fiercest freedom-defending woman in my life

To my father, Batur Turam,
who showed me how to trust and respect freedoms

To my sister, Esra Turam,
who has always generously shared her free-spirited universe with me

To John A. Hall,
my friend and mentor, who taught me the
primacy of and passion for freedom

And to my son, Sean Whitney,
who gave me wings to fly

CONTENTS

ACKNOWLEDGMENTS

This book is the result of a long journey, throughout which both I and the people studied in it practiced, learned, and enjoyed gaining freedoms and claiming space in our lives. I thank all my friends, family, and colleagues in Istanbul and Berlin, who were great hosts, company, and sources of intellectual support.

My first teacher of freedom was John A. Hall, who against the backdrop of the prevalent pejorative approach to the defenders of liberties in Turkey—where they are dismissively called "liboş"—helped me to understand how freedom works and its unique, indispensable value in our lives. This book is in his debt in many ways. He read and commented on the entire manuscript, and his encouragement and support never stopped during the research and writing process until the final titling of the book. Similarly, my great friend and colleague Yeşim Bayar was always at the center of my thinking, analysis, and revisions. She read several drafts of many chapters and discussed the book passionately with me for years. Her friendship, kindness, and empathy kept me going during long periods of writing in isolation, especially when I was inflamed by the ups and downs of Turkey's explosive politics.

I was blessed with my colleagues' and friends' invaluable comments, critiques, and questions. Valentine Moghadam, Phillip Brown, and Suzanna Walters engaged with the introduction both critically and constructively, and Kathrin Zippel and Tim Creswell shared their precious comments on the part about Kreuzberg. I benefitted from their wisdom immensely. My former departmental chair Steve Vallas and my friend and colleague Esra Özyurek were always there, both as good friends and as sources of academic rigor, whenever I needed their advice. I cannot sufficiently thank Liza Weinstein, Tom Vicino, Hande Ramazanoğulları, and Mehmet Cemalcılar for their time, detailed comments, and enthusiastic engagement with different chapters. Cem Sertoğlu, Esra Sertoğlu, Mehmet Cemalcılar, Yiğit Ersu, and Erika Koss generously shared their suggestions at different stages of the book, from deciding on the book cover and the title to the blurbs. I am grateful to Zeynep Gambetti, Ali Kazma, Emir Tan, Jens Krabel, İpek İpekçioğlu, Neco Çelik, Koray Yılmaz-Günay, Fatih Abay, and many others in Istanbul and Berlin, whose names I will not reveal for confidentiality's sake, for helping me in the field, facilitating contacts, and scheduling interviews.

Working with my editor, Kate Wahl, has yet again been a precious and very pleasant experience. I benefitted from her ideas, suggestions, and invaluable editing throughout the writing process. The anonymous reviewers of SUP provided very constructive comments. I am grateful for the teamwork of this distinguished group.

I am deeply indebted to my great friend Amilcar Barreto, an Enlightenment intellectual with a rare mind for details, who laboriously prepared the index and added the Turkish symbols. I thank him for his time, precision, and patience, but most of all for his generous friendship. I also thank all my friends in different cities for taking good care of me when writing was depleting and deflecting all my energies from cooking, shopping, and living, particularly the great chefs Mark Sutherland, Denise Garcia, Jeremy Lapon, and Ayşe Porcaro and the fashionista in my life, Hande Ramazanoğulları. Thanks for being you and always there.

I am grateful for the startup research fund in 2009-10, for the research grant from the Center for Emerging Markets at Northeastern University in 2011–12, and for support from the College of Social Sciences and Humanities' Faculty Research Development Fund in 2012–13. During my numerous field trips funded by these generous grants, several undergraduate and graduate students accompanied me and gave me inspiration for analysis. My special thanks go to Betül Balkan Ekşi, Cihan Tekay, Behice Pehlivan, and Fatih Abay, who not only visited some of my field sites in Istanbul and Germany but also shared my enthusiasm for the subject matter. Rachel Gorab read the entire first draft of the book and made corrections to the English.

I presented earlier drafts of different chapters at annual meetings of major academic associations: for the Middle East Studies Association, the International Political Psychology Conference in Istanbul, and the Association for the Study of Nationalities in New York, and twice for the American Sociological Association. At different stages of writing the book, I gave talks at many universities, including the London School of Economics, Yale University, Columbia University, the University of Chicago, the University of Michigan at Ann Arbor, Boston College, and Bilkent University in Ankara. I was invited to deliver the

Annual Campagna-Kerven lecture at Boston University. Among many colleagues who invited me and/or commented on my work in my lectures and conference and panel presentations, my special thanks goes to Augustus Richard Norton, Alfred Stepan, Nathan Brown, Amy Mills, Diane Davis, Liza Wedeen, Terry Karl, Ellen Lust, Mine Eder, Monica Ringer, Peter van der Veer, Jonathan Laurence, Ahmet Kuru, Jenny White, Deniz Kandiyoti, Ziya Öniş, Metin Heper, Alev Çınar, Elisabeth Özdalga, Manal Jamal, Zeynep Gambetti, Murat Güneş, Murat Somer, Nicole Watts, Reşat Kasaba, Irvin Schick, Nilüfer Isvan, Kerem Öktem, İştar Gözaydın, Karen Barkey, Ateş Altınordu, and Yeşim Arat.

I am deeply indebted to the locals of the three sites, Teşvikiye, Kreuzberg, and the University of Freedom (a pseudonym used to protect privacy and confidentiality of the campus and its members). Their cooperation was the key to the completion of the field research.

Finally, I could not have done the fieldwork and written this book without the unconditional support of my wonderful family and my son's warmth, wit, and love.

ACRONYMS

AKM	Atatürk Kültür Merkezi (Atatürk Cultural Center)
AKP	Adalet ve Kalknma Partisi (Justice and Development Party)
AM	Autonomous Movement
BDP	Barış ve Demokrasi Partisi (Peace and Democracy Party)
CDU	Christlich Demokratische Union Deutschlands (Christian Democratic Party)
CHP	Cumhuriyet Halk Partisi (Republican People's Party)
DİTİB	Diyanet İşleri Turk İslam Birliği (Turkish-Islamic Religious Association)
FDP	Freie Demokratische Partei (Free Democratic Party)
FID	Forum fur Interkulturellen Dialog (Forum for Intercultural Dialogue)
GM	Gülen Movement
LGBT	lesbian, gay, bisexual, and transgender
MGK	Milli Güvenlik Konseyi (National Security Council)
PKK	Partiya Karkerên Kurdistan (Kurdistan Workers' Party)
ODTÜ	Orta Doğu Teknik Üniversitesi (Middle East Technical University)
RP	Refah Partisi (Welfare Party)
SPD	Sozialdemokratische Partei Deutschlands (Social Democratic Party)
TOKİ	Toplu Konut İdaresi (Public Housing Administration)
TÜBİTAK	Turkish Scientific and Technological Research Council of Turkey
UF	University of Freedom
YÖK	Yüksek Öğretim Kurulu (Higher Education Council)

INTRODUCTION

The City and the Government

The city is a space where the powerless can make history. That is
not to say it is the only space, but it is certainly a critical one.

Saskia Sassen, "The Global Street: *Making* the Political"

ON MONDAY, MAY 27, 2013, some seventy peaceful demonstrators organized a sit-in at Gezi Park in downtown Istanbul's Taksim Square.[1] Their goal was to oppose the demolition and replacement of the park with a mall. At first the Gezi demonstrations, initiated by urban activists who wanted to save the trees, did not appear much different from the numerous Occupy movements that had developed in cities around the world. But in less than a week, as harsh police retaliation attracted wider circles of supporters,[2] the Gezi demonstrations triggered large-scale resistance across the nation and throughout the Turkish diaspora.[3] The protest rapidly turned into an uprising against Prime Minister Tayyip Erdoğan's increasingly authoritarian rule. Most important, the Gezi protests brought together ordinary people, mostly non-activists, university students, artists, intellectuals, and academics, who had long been divided by ancient ideological hostilities.[4] In their defense of freedom and rights, the demonstrators formed new alliances that rose above these deep-rooted old antagonisms.

Muted by Erdoğan during the weeks of the protest, the Turkish television channels showed documentaries of penguins, while the world condemned the extreme use of tear gas, tanks, and police beatings. *The Economist* published a cover depicting Erdoğan in the robe and headdress of an Ottoman ruler, and asked "Erdogan: Democrat or Sultan?"[5] The *New York Times* displayed images of police brutality toward unarmed protestors on its front page and published the protestors' charges. A passive protestor, the "Standing Man" whose image was quickly spread around the world, was given a major German human rights award for his "courageous commitment to freedom of expression and human rights."[6] Divan Hotel in Taksim, which opened its doors to protesters and the wounded, was awarded the "Hospitality Innovation Award" by an organization based in Munich.[7]

In the new world politics, government violations of freedom and rights co-exist with democratic alliances and practices in many nations that are vaguely referred to as democracies. Cosmopolitan cities like Istanbul in particular have increasingly experienced deep conflict with ethnic or religious claims seemingly replacing struggles over "Enlightenment ideals of universal citizenship."[8] As urban space generated pro-democratic alliances out of deep divides, Erdoğan's government lost its initial (2002–7) enthusiasm for political reform and sank deeper and deeper into authoritarianism. Does this then suggest an inherent relationship between identitarian clashes and urban space? On the contrary, the Turkish case shows that the violation of basic codes of civility in the city has everything to do with political institutions that seek to control and "govern urban life."[9]

This book explores the link between contested urban sites and government without reducing this relation exclusively to the global forces of neoliberalism. More specifically, it reveals and analyzes opposite political transformations in the realm of the city and the government. As urban space generated more democratic practices and alliances, the government sank deeper into authoritarianism.

In *The Spaces of Democracy*, Richard Sennett asks: "what is urban about democracy?"[10] He answers that certain urban sites, such as squares, bring differences together and enable various identities to interact and mingle. As opposed to this view that emphasizes the cohabitation of differences, others have highlighted the clash of identities in the city as the core of a new global urban politics.[11] By studying highly contested urban sites from Istanbul to Kreuzberg, Berlin's so-called Turkish neighborhood, my ethnography suggests that neither festive cohabitation nor clash of differences renders the city central for democracy. Then, why and under which conditions does urban space take on an imperative role in democratic contestation? More specifically, in which ways and why does urban space become pivotal in unifying a previously divided opposition in defending freedoms and rights?

The predominant explanation of why urban space matters comes from the critics of neoliberalism, who often prioritize socioeconomic factors over political ones. Most urban studies view the city critically as a primarily neoliberal space. Notwithstanding the fact that cities have become hotbeds of class inequalities, this ethnography shifts the focus of analysis from strictly socio-economic to primarily political dimensions.[12] On the basis of in-depth empirical evidence, the defense of freedoms and rights comes to the forefront of analysis in this study. It is significant that among these political matters, the "spatiality of freedom"[13]—the fact that freedom pertains to and is constituted by space—has probably been the least explored subject.

In the aftermath of the so-called Arab Spring, another prevailing approach to urban space is centered on the presumed discord between democracy and Islamism, which largely flourished in cities. Over the preceding decade, Erdoğan had been perceived in the West as the epitome of a much-applauded "moderate Islam," acquiring the image of a "democratic leader of the Islamic world." Yet, seemingly overnight, he crushed this image when the police brutally evacuated Gezi Park. Major world powers, particularly the United States, hinted at withdrawing support for Erdoğan, while Germany sent warning messages to the government. Within Turkey, Erdoğan and his Justice and Development Party (Adalet ve Kalkınma Partisi, henceforth AKP) lost the support of secular circles of various political orientations. Moreover, Muslim democrats, such as pious feminist and anti-capitalist groups, joined the Gezi protestors condemning AKP's policies. Despite these remarkable new bonds between Muslim and secular residents, many associated the Gezi protests with AKP's, and thereby Islam's, incompatibility with democracy.

The concurrent explosion of urban protests across the world from Latin America and the United States to Europe and the Middle East suggests a new trend in world politics that cannot be reduced to the clash between Islam and secular democracy. Globally, more and more people express their anti-government feelings by claiming and occupying urban spaces, as the formal official channels no longer suffice to represent people's sociopolitical needs and grievances. Hence, indexing the Gezi protests to the politics of class, ethnicity, or religion fails to situate the urban contestation in Turkey in the larger geopolitics of space. Rather than pointing to the defeat of secular democracy by "pious Muslims"[14] or the "Islamist" government, urban contestation in Turkey speaks to a sharpening polarization between the supporters and opponents of a deeper democracy that accommodates the rights and liberties of all, including minorities and dissenters, regardless of their differences of ideology or identity.[15] When the parliament is dominated by an overempowered government and/or when political institutions fail to accommodate dissent or minorities, the city becomes the prime hub of democratic contestation over freedoms and rights.

Looking beyond the *seeming* ideological clash and polarization on the surface, we actually see more and more urbanites demanding and collaborating for civic rights and freedoms to live, talk, think, dress, and act as they choose.

THE URBAN PUZZLE

Two major urban protests have defined contemporary Turkish politics: the Republican Marches (Cumhuriyet Mitingleri) in 2007 and the Taksim-Gezi Protests in 2013. Both developed in Turkey's major cities. But beyond a superficial similarity in a shared anti-government stance against the AKP, they did not have much in common. In fact, their political agendas, methods, and vision were polar opposites. The Republican Marches divided the secular discontents of the AKP and split urban space into hostile zones, whereas the Gezi Protests unified an already divided urban opposition to the government over the defense of freedoms and rights. So what changed in such a short time in the political arena and the city that culminated in a drastic change in the nature of political opposition? The main goal of this ethnography is to answer this question.[16]

During the Republican Marches in April–May 2007, more than a million people poured into the streets of Istanbul, Izmir, and Ankara. In the aftermath of these demonstrations, I found myself in a zone of discontent that was divisive and infused with anxiety and fear in Istanbul. Offensive language, discriminatory behavior, and even physical confrontations in neighborhoods, university campuses, and streets were common. I had a hunch then that something important, something with long-term effects, was taking place in urban space. Now in retrospect, it became clear that 2007 was the start of fault lines in urban space and political divides between the governing branches of the state. Conflicts at both levels have deepened since then, as the AKP expanded its political supremacy and alienated large numbers of state actors and urbanites, all of which amounts to half of Turkish society living in despair.

The Republican Marches in 2007 were largely a "secularist backlash," an outcry against the increasing popularity and successive victories of the pro-Islamic AKP government.[17] Capitalizing on and fuelling the clash along the Islamist-secularist axis, the demonstrations condemned the increasing visibility of religion in the public sphere, as well as the socioeconomic and political empowerment of pious Muslims. The secularist protestors acted out in support of their commitment to protect the laicism (state control of religion) that has been one of the main pillars of the Turkish Republic since its founding in 1923. A considerable number of protestors even had sympathies for military tutelage over politics as an ultimate guard against the "Islamic threat."[18] Clearly, the agenda of the Republican Marches did not have much to do with democracy or freedoms and rights. On the contrary, they were mostly motivated by sheer power struggle between the new Islamist elite and the old secularist elite. Therefore, these protests not only deepened identitarian fault lines, such as religious versus secularist cleavage, but they also estranged genuine democrats, who refused an *unconditional* defense of laicism at the cost of freedoms and rights for all.

Neither disorder nor contestation is of the essence of the city life. Urban contestation is closely linked to and shaped by the competing "territorialities of the institutions."[19] Put differently, the disputes in the city are largely molded by the use or intrusions of political institutions, such as the government, that claim "ownership" of space or control conduct of urban life. In the years leading up to the 2007 Marches, Turkey had gone through major structural transformations of class and social status.[20] The gradual replacement of the secularist political elite by the new pious Muslim elite had created deep-rooted power struggles between the two groups. The structural change was accompanied by major political transitions. In its first term (2002–7), the AKP conducted efficient economic and political reform, such as putting an end to military control of politics and passing laws that protected women against violence. However, AKP's political reforms slowed down during its second term (2007–11) with the demise of Turkey's EU dream, and ultimately stagnated during the third term (2011–present).[21]

The slowing down of the political reforms followed AKP's nomination of Abdullah Gül from within the ruling party to become the first pious president of the secular Turkish Republic. Most secular democrats perceived this move as contradictory to the separation of powers between the legislative and executive branches of the state. The ensuing presidential crisis marked the beginning of a power struggle between the branches of the government. The military issued a warning (*muhtıra*) on its website directed at the AKP and reminded the AKP of its power and domination over the political realm.[22] Following the presidential crisis, the AKP became increasingly confrontational and aggressive in its politics against the military.[23] After being elected for the third time in free and fair elections in 2011, the pro-Islamic AKP gradually adopted undemocratic patterns of rule, some of which were inherited from the early Republican era,[24] such as violation of rights and freedoms of minorities and political opponents.[25]

Efficient negotiation and cooperation with the increasingly hegemonic AKP failed in the parliament and other branches of the state, and urban space generated dissent. Vocal contestations occurred, primarily in major cities. When pious Muslims gradually integrated into more inclusive urban sites, and began sharing bourgeois lifestyles in the city, longtime secular residents became alarmed and started to act in defense of "their sphere" of freedom and privacy. Bitterly contested issues included, but were not limited to, freedom of lifestyle,[26] dress, privacy, sexuality, expression, and thought. A *new territoriality* emerged in Istanbul, which was largely symptomatic of urban residents' rising fears of losing their intimate space—space that people often associate with their individual freedom and rights.

Unlike some other large cities, such as Izmir and Eskişehir, where the secularists have an uncontested monopoly of power and control, Istanbul has become increasingly difficult to share between pious and secular urbanites. More specifically, the weakness of formal political channels in encountering AKP's supremacy culminated in spontaneous daily quarrels over lifestyle, and heated bickering over freedoms.[27] As AKP increasingly picked on and interfered with "un-Islamic" ways of life, Istanbul has turned into a zone of clashes and confrontation. Drinking alcohol, wearing revealing outfits, such as showing cleavage,[28] and displaying intimacy and sexuality in public spaces became charged symbols of political contestation over freedoms.

From 2011 on, the political situation in Turkey grew more alarming: arrests and unsubstantiated detentions of journalists, academics, and university students peaked. Jails were full of people accused of terror-related activities and denied a trial. A considerable number of people convicted of terrorist activities in Turkey had "never taken up a gun" or committed violence.[29] By 2013, the government had changed its position on judicial reform, stepping back from earlier commitments and placing the judiciary under the control of the prime minister. In this way, Turkey's traditional Kemalist judicial tutelage, often referred to as "a juristocracy," was replaced by judicial control by the new pro-Islamic elite.[30]

In sharp contrast to the weakening of democratic credentials and rising authoritarianism under AKP's rule, urban space prominently generated pro-democratic contestation, along with democratic alliances. Six years after the Republican Marches, the Gezi protests erupted. In contrast to the divisive Republican Marches, Gezi had a remarkably unifying effect on oppositional forces and voices. As Erdoğan's political supremacy politicized the state, new urban alliances seeking freedoms and rights developed in squares, parks, and streets across the country, bridging the traditional ideological fault lines within the opposition.

Gezi was the culmination of a long-term transformation that had simmered over the years in major cities, particularly Istanbul. The AKP distrusted city life in general, particularly profane art, un-Islamic or liberal lifestyles, and nightlife, and it developed explicit antipathies to secular sites in the unruly yet very pivotal city of Istanbul, which was capable of escaping the government's grab (unlike Ankara, for example). Subsequently, the AKP has thus launched a process of encroachment upon the city's urban space, green areas, forests and parks, art centers, and iconic historical places loaded with meaning and intimacy for the locals, hastily building new malls, expensive residences, public housing, and roads with no regard for aesthetic sensibilities. In line with the AKP's capitalist ambitions, and at the expense of the historical city, the government has championed aggressive forms of neoliberalism. Meanwhile, nepotism has led to rivalry among its inner cadres and followers, who compete over contracts for new construction.

The AKP's obsession with controlling and cashing in on urban space has gone hand in hand with violation of civil rights, specifically the rights of expression, press, assembly, and protest. During its third term, more than one thousand cases were brought to the European Court of Human Rights. In turn, the deterioration of individual liberties and civic rights reinforced the prioritization of the use of urban space for resistance and opposition to the government.

Ironically, AKP's disproportionate encroachment on city life provoked new expressions of love of freedom in urban space. For example, residents of what had been a rather homophobic city started to paint their streets, doorsteps, sidewalks and squares in LGBT rainbow colors. AKP's increasing supremacy triggered a new urban search for freedom,[31] manifested in mundane living rather than strategic organizing and mobilization. This new urban politics cannot be explained by the rich existing literature on organized collective action, social movements, or political mobilization,[32] mainly because these blossom and flourish in strikingly spontaneous, creative, often humorous, and mostly unintentional aspects of everyday life.[33] As a "non-movement," to use Asef Bayat's terminology, it manifests itself in the way city dwellers live their lives—their urban lifestyles, consumption patterns, tastes, and so on. Different from collective upheavals in history or current contentious politics,[34] this politics of everyday life informs the rise of a new form of urbanism as the major resistance to the authoritarian government.

This new urbanism simply opposes political supremacy by demanding, claiming control, and "ownership" of urban space. This is more than utilizing the city to organize or protest. This claim of space has a direct effect on power dynamics through shaping ways of life in neighborhoods, campuses, and streets.[35] Facing an increasingly unresponsive, discriminating, and repressive government, urban residents carve their space of rights and freedoms out of cities, where they can and feel entitled to contest politically. Paradoxically, as urbanites defended their doorsteps, streets, and neighborhoods against an increasingly authoritarian government, pro-democratic sensibilities and alliances grew across groups, which were historically divided and antagonized, particularly since the Republican Marches.

Spatial defiance and urban anxieties are fortified by people's decreasing trust in, and increasingly unfulfilled demands from, the government. When urban residents feel that their rights and liberties are not protected and their life world is attacked, their discontents are manifested in various forms of *territorialities*, such as claims over neighborhoods, campuses, parks, squares, and so on. In the absence of a reliable institutional protection of rights and freedoms, residents tend to hold on to their immediate space as the base of their rights and freedoms. Intimate spaces take on a primary value under these conditions of weakening democracy and revived authoritarianism, since these places are associated with a sense of spatial belonging, intimate familiarity, and territorial entitlement.

Briefly, during the short period between the Republican Marches and the Gezi Protests, Turkey went through major urban and political transformation in the opposite directions, democratization in the city and authoritarianism by the government. The power of the contested urban space came from its ability to stand above the identitarian or ideological fault lines in the defense of universal values of democratic liberties and rights.

This book is an ethnographic analysis of this shift, which "liberated" and united pro-democratic urbanites from the cages of ideological divides and urban fault lines between Islamism and secularism. In sharp contrast to this liberating trend in the city, Erdoğan and his government have become increasingly trapped by these old, polarizing cages, which impede capacities of cooperation between the political elite in the government and opposition. While the urban trend deepened and strengthened democracy, the government capitalized on the idea of the "deep state," implicated in illegality, illegitimacy, unaccountability, and corruption.

THE SECULAR DIVIDE: NEW URBAN ALLIANCES

During the earlier phases of my fieldwork, while looking for something else, I landed on an eye-opening finding. In the aftermath of the Republican Marches and the presidential crisis, deep polarization made me dig into conflicts *between* Muslim and secular(ist) actors. To my surprise, however, I found deep cleavages *among* the secular locals on the streets. As I followed the sites of high contestation, I realized that the secular residents were divided over increasing presence of devout Muslims. More specifically, they were falling into conflict over the terms of the entrance and accommodation of Muslim piety in "secular spaces."[36] In divided Istanbul, the association of these sites with secular life-styles and politics was taken for granted, and they had previously seemed un-assailable by pious Muslims. More recently, some of these secular "fortresses" have turned into increasingly disputed zones, inasmuch as they have become more capable of inclusion and opened up to the pious Muslims.

What exactly attracted pious Muslims to these areas, which were previ-ously the domain of an uncompromising secularist urbanism? "I feel *invisible* in Beyoğlu," said Sümeyye, a head-scarved young woman, to describe her feel-ing of comfort in a neighborhood noted for leisure activities, nightlife, and even a scattered red-light district. When I asked where else she felt similarly, she enthusiastically compared this mixed downtown neighborhood to Gezi Park during the protests. She added adamantly: "I never feel like that in Ankara or Izmir." She explained further that her head scarf made it difficult for her to feel anonymous outside "certain places" in Istanbul. I asked what differentiated these "certain places" from others for her? Was it the secularity or religiosity of the place? Sümeyye shook her head. Apparently, she felt free or anonymous nei-ther in Fatih, Istanbul's well-known Islamic neighborhood, nor in sterile secu-lar places. She was talking about a new kind of inclusion and accommodation, which reduced the feelings of self-consciousness caused by public symbols of piety or secularity.

Three Contested Sites

The three secular sites analyzed in this book reveal nuanced patterns of spatial and political transformation. These sites were picked according to their different but striking ways of attraction and inclusion of "devout Muslims."[37] The first one, Teşvikiye, an upscale downtown Istanbul neighborhood, attracted Muslim high-spenders to its high-end consumption venues and haute-couture boutiques. On the basis of their economic privilege, devout high-spenders not only felt tempted but also entitled to participate in Teşvikiye's daily life through high consumption and leisure. My other research site, the University of Freedom (henceforth UF) in Istanbul is one of the top-ranking universities of Turkey, noted for offering a "liberal education."[38] Hence, the UF attracted high-achieving Muslim students, who scored in the top percentile in the national university placement exam.

In 2010, I moved my fieldwork[39] to the third site of my research, Kreuzberg-Berlin, which is the largest and densest Turkish neighborhood outside Turkish borders. Built up gradually as the hub of Turkish immigrants since the 1960s, both the city of Berlin and the district of Kreuzberg have accommodated an increasing number of pious and head-scarved Turkish-descent residents in the past decade. My goal in moving the research from a homeland urban neighborhood to an ethnically concentrated "Turkish neighborhood" in Germany was to discover whether similar dynamics could be found on the international level. Put differently, I was interested in the international reach of the fault lines and political divides from the neighborhoods of Istanbul. Accordingly, I explored the politics of space and contestation in what Annika Marlen Hinze has called "Turkish Berlin"—another historically divided city.[40]

Initially, the splits in secular space caused by the arrival of pious Muslims were the driving force of my curiosity. However, after I had spent a few months in the field, another unexpected finding shaped the course of my ethnography. I noted a process through which the inclusion of pious Muslims was transforming these disputed places in unforeseen ways. Often with incredulity, I observed, documented, and analyzed the rise of new and often unconventional alliances and spontaneous bonds that crosscut the previously taken-for-granted fault lines between devout and secular residents.[41] It is significant that these new bonds went beyond mere *deliberation* and were manifested in actual *practices* of smooth cohabitation and cooperation. Put differently, they were not akin to the "communicative action" that Jürgen Habermas so keenly relies on for the production of a miraculous agreement as the result of public debate. In contrast to deliberation or mere discussion, I observed these new affinities in urban daily practices and lifestyles.[42] Eventually, my findings on these new bonds and cooperation led to the overarching argument of the book. In the contested urban sites under scrutiny, the axis of conflict was shifting from Islamism versus secularism toward the defense of a deeper democracy versus authoritarianism. Accordingly, the exclusive focus on the bipolar clash between the devout and the secularist obscures the primacy of multiple conflicts between the defenders of democratization and authoritarianism.

After randomly perambulating numerous contested urban sites, I realized that the democratic alliances across ancient political divides were emerging at the most unexpected places in the city, namely, at the *cracks of the urban fault lines*. Subsequently, I picked the three sites, Teşvikiye, UF, and Kreuzberg in order to map the fault lines and to compare the patterns of divides and alliances generated by the deeply divided urban space. The intense negotiations over inclusion and accommodation of pious ways of life in these contested sites suggest a rethinking of the spatiality of rights and freedom. These places not only suggest strong affinities between urban space and freedom (and the lack thereof) but they also reveal how space and freedoms continuously interact—form, reform, or deform—each other. Hence, these divided sites provide a litmus test of democratic practices for both the urban residents and the pro-Islamic government. In these contested urban spaces, the limits and failures of the state in accommodating dissent and minorities are questioned, problematized, and challenged. The Kurdish ethnic minority, the Alawite religious minority, and LGBT sexual minorities in Turkey and the Turkish Muslim immigrants in Germany all qualify as discriminated against, excluded, or violated minorities.

Common wisdom sees urban disarray in divided cities as a threat to order, security, and political stability. Deep political fault lines in cities are often regarded as potentially capable of dividing and dragging societies into violence or civil war. In contested urban sites across the world, the most visible struggles seem to be over identitarian issues, such as ethnicity, nationality, religion, gender, and so on. Moreover, the increasing flow of immigrants across national borders further reinforces these urban divides and conflicts, particularly over issues of ethnicity and religion. But the contested urban spaces I examined in Istanbul and Berlin present important counterexamples. Urban space that is deeply divided by ideological and identitarian clashes generates new alliances over freedoms and rights. Put differently, out of urban space divided by ideology or identity politics comes a renewed interest in defending the more universal values of democracy.

By maintaining this counterintuitive argument about contestation and democracy, I do not wish to deny persistent tensions and discomforts created by the cohabitation of different lifestyles. The *dual entrance* of devout Muslims into secular urban space and the secular state in the new millennium was indicative of "deprivatization" of religion.[43] Once religion stepped out of the private sphere, it had unsettling and politicizing effects on the presumably secular public sphere. I also do not mean to romanticize the subsequent tensions and altercations as pleasant or desirable at the local level. In fact, these encounters are arduous, often exhausting, and do often take uncivilized forms. Moreover, provocative political leaders tend to capitalize on the dated Islamist-secularist polarization in order to empower themselves by dividing and ruling. But this ethnography juxtaposes these polarizing acts in the polity with the new democratic alliances—alliances that were obscured by exclusive attention to clashes and conflict.

In contrast to common wisdom that detests political fault lines and fears urban divides, the key to democratization is not the ultimate defeat and absence of conflict and cleavage. Democratization is rather the capacity of forming new and shifting coalitions out of bitter conflicts. The depth of a democracy depends largely on the quality of these shifting alliances. Donald Horowitz's study of ethnically divided societies evokes a similar line of thinking: "[C]oalitions do not follow from moderate conflict; instead, coalitions moderate the conflict."[44] Along these lines, I argue that in the aftermath of inclusion of pious Muslims into the city and polity, *highly contested urban space deflects deep conflict from the state.* The contested sites of the city assume the conflict that debilitates the governing branches of the state. This is why there is no reason to underestimate street, neighborhood, or campus politics in comparison to more formal channels of politics. Contested urban space and its residents and their lifestyles become pivotal for democracy under conditions of weakening democracy or increasing political supremacy.

DISRUPTIVE PLACES?

Cemal Kafadar, a prominent Ottoman historian at Harvard University, objected strongly to the depiction of famous historic sites in Istanbul such as Hagia Sofia, the Topkapı Palace, and the Grand Bazaar in Ben Affleck's Oscar-winning film *Argo* (since for political reasons, it could not be shot in Tehran). Kafadar was infuriated about the disrespect to these precious places of thousand-year-old-world civilizations, which were treated "as wallpaper" in the film, as if they were anonymous mundane places. He criticized Turkish politicians harshly for taking pride in these snapshots of Istanbul's historic sites in a Hollywood production:[45]

> Istanbul is not a film set that serves as a substitute for another place. It cannot be reduced to an object of tourism and a few scenes and souvenirs. It is not a source of ambiance stripped of its historical identity. This is a problem of

cultural identity. I am an admirer of Iranian culture, but can Istanbul be the double of Tehran? If you give credit to an approach which sees no distinction between "This Islamic society or the other," "Istanbul or Tehran," you would turn Istanbul to a "noplace" . . . devoid of any character and reduced to a few postcard images.[46]

Clearly, Istanbul's historic urban sites evolved through long-term, multi-layered historical, social, political, and economic processes. Like other historical cities with striking geopolitical significance, Istanbul stands out largely in terms of how its sites convey meaning and (re)generate power and change. This process endows urban space with an agency, a capacity to shape social reality and to act upon it.[47] However, like people or groups, places that have identities and meanings vary in their capacity to handle deep conflict and to bring about change.[48] Places become *agentic* under certain conditions.[49] Are contestation and deep fault lines enough to make a place pivotal in shaping power dynamics? The highly contested urban sites analyzed in this book—neighborhoods, campuses, squares, department stores, and so on—are agentic places, not only because they are remarkably capable of absorbing and coping with conflict but also because they attract controversy as they generate *safe spaces* for contestation and negotiation. Because these urban sites take on the conflict that is so divisive of the state, it is important that they provide a safe space and that they secure a "free zone" for struggle and negotiation.[50]

Why and in which ways are urban spaces such as Teşvikiye, the UF, and Kreuzberg different from any other contested place? The capacity of a social actor or a place to act upon, transform, or change social and political reality can only be understood in relation to wider social structures and political institutions.[51] More specifically, the capacity to generate power and change is ultimately tied to the constraints imposed on social actors by existing institutional webs of social structure, such as states, governments, judiciary, and religious organizations. Hence, the continuum of places ranges from the strongly agentic and transformative to "noplaces," to use Kafadar's term, that are sucked in by the dominant structures.[52] Like people, most places are located in-between these extreme ends.[53] Urban politics is an ongoing negotiation between urban residents, the city, and political institutions.[54]

As in every analysis of an interaction, there are competing approaches that explore the relations between the city and the government. While one school emphasized the structural aspects and institutions,[55] others problematized the decreasing power of *citizens* in the face of the neoliberal turn of national and international politics.[56] From this perspective, the global expansion of neoliberal regimes renders conventional forms of "democratic citizenship" irrelevant, undermined or suppressed, if not futile.[57] That leads to a romanticization of the local forms of democracy at the expense of democratic institutions at the national scale.[58] Motivated by an interest in the ongoing negotiation between urban space and the state,[59] this book parts ways with the apparent dichotomy between agency and structure.[60] It also refuses to privilege top-down versus bottom-up perspectives in examining space-state interaction. Urban politics is informed and shaped by both.

But under what conditions do certain urban sites turn into loci of democratic contestation and democratization? My findings show that urban space becomes pivotal in power politics when conflict accumulates in and divides the state, and when the government and opposition cannot effectively disagree, negotiate, and/or cooperate in the parliament. Subsequently, the failure of democratic contestation in political institutions is likely to lead to a weakening or violation of freedoms and rights and/or discrimination against minorities and dissenters. Urban space takes on the role of generating power and change and demanding liberties when democracies weaken in relation to the freedoms and rights of minorities, the discontents, oppositional political forces.

It is important to note that the contested sites under scrutiny here are not the sites of protest, such as Gezi Park and Tahrir Square, at which police and/or army attack with the excuse of restoring security and order. To the contrary, the contested sites examined in this book are the mundane urban spaces of neighborhoods, campuses, and streets. The responses and interventions by the government range from close monitoring and disapproval to various forms of prohibitions, condemnation, encroachment, bans, and punishment. A good example comes from the public address in Izmir by Minister of Transport, Maritime Affairs, and Communications Binali Yıldırım of AKP at a dinner reception for his alma mater, Istanbul Technical University. Yıldırım explained why he had opted for the Technical University instead of Bosphorus University, renowned for its liberal political culture and very competitive education:

> I was going to enroll either in Bosphorus University or Istanbul Technical University. First, I paid a visit to Bosphorus University. I looked around: it was *a different world*. Different buildings, a space surrounded by city walls [*surlar*]. Female and male students are sitting in its courtyard next to each other. I was

very surprised. I thought I would lose direction in this place. I had to study. Then I chose Technical University. I got married in the second year of my college education. In the third year, I had a baby, and the fourth year another one.[61]

Yıldırım's comments received extensive satirical coverage in *Penguen*, one of Turkey's leading humor magazines. On the cover, he was portrayed chatting with three Bosphorus University students in the campus courtyard. He asks the female student: "What is a nice girl like you doing in a place like this?" (Buraya nasıl düştün kızım? Literal translation: How has a nice girl like you *fallen* to this place?). She responds: "I studied for years and got the highest scores" (Yıllarca çalıştım. Sınavda en yüksek puanı aldım, girdim). The minister reassures her: "I will rescue you."[62]

The minister's strikingly spatial description of the campus showcases the discomfort and disapproval of the conservative government of the "liberal" campus territory. He deems the campus a clearly demarcated area of *conquest*— hence, it is surrounded by city walls. The buildings and the so-called city walls seem to embody a certain lifestyle and gender politics that is disturbing, not suitable and acceptable. He also refers to it as a "different world," which is clearly disruptive of his worldview and ways of life. But why was Yıldırım disturbed and intimidated by this campus?

Conventional wisdom suggests that the contested secular sites draw reactions from authoritarian pro-Islamic government for violating religious and moral norms and promoting un-Islamic codes of conduct. According to the secularist locals of Teşvikiye, the condemned secular conducts and lifestyles range from nonreligious and secularist to agnostic, atheist, hedonistic, and/or libertarian. Practices such as consumption of alcohol, display of eroticism and sexuality in public, wearing revealing outfits, and mixed gender socialization have recently received negative and punitive reactions from the pro-Islamic government.

Indeed, the incidents of government intrusion in Istanbul's "unruly" places are numerous. The banning of outdoor drinking and cleansing of the outdoor seating in Asmalı Mescit, a neighborhood renowned for its nightlife, stands out as an obvious case of government prohibition. The closing of the Atatürk Kültür Merkezi (Atatürk Cultural Center; henceforth AKM) is a striking case of the government's interference in cultural life. Since it opened in 1969, the AKM had been Istanbulites' main venue for art and culture, hosting classical music performances, ballet, modern dance, and theater. Its low, state-subsidized ticket prices attracted students, artists and intellectuals, connecting a very diverse body of Istanbul's art lovers with the world. By bringing people from all walks of life together, it also challenged the prevalent opinion that art is cherished mainly by upper- and upper-middle-class secularists. When the old building, with its exquisite concert halls, required major repairs during the AKP's second term in office, it was closed,[63] and since 2008, the AKP and local governments have consigned it to demolition.[64] This is perceived by many Istanbulites as a government attack, not only on Western forms of art, but on a focus of non-Islamic traditions.[65]

In general, when the AKP encroaches on urban space, it is widely perceived in the context of the Islamist-secularist divide. Similarly, when European democracies pick on Muslim neighborhoods and/or ghettos, it is assumed that they are reacting against the Islamic cultures or Muslim religiosity of a place that is surrounded by secular Judeo-Christian territory. My findings differ from this predominant view. My ethnography suggests that Teşvikiye and UF in Turkey and Kreuzberg in Germany drew reaction from conservative right-wing governments (Erdoğan's AKP and Merkel's Christian Democratic Union) specifically because they *unsettle* conventional ideological divides and *free* people from ancient fault lines. These sites upset the comfort zones of the polarized camps by creating divides within these camps and facilitating new alliances across them.

Contrary to the predominant assumption that segregated or exclusionary places, such as ethnic neighborhoods, intimidate governments, I argue that the particular *inclusion and mixing process* in contested urban space confuses and disturbs conservative governments. These mixed contested sites are not only disruptive of the governments, but also disturb some urban residents.[66] They emerge as unusually pro-democratic islands in divided cities and polarized polities. They owe this characteristic, not to their religiosity or secularity, but mainly to their disruption of the established categories of "us versus others." Not only conservative governments but also their urban supporters who aim to maintain a conventional "traditional order" are confused by these newly inclusive places—urban sites, where previously divided or antagonistic groups of people join ranks and unite against the political regime or dominant culture. The new alliances across old divides include, but not are limited to, the affinities and bonds between pious Muslims and secular groups in Turkey, as well as between those of Turkish descent and ethnic German residents in Germany. These contested places are the political learning ground for experimenting with disagreement/dissent, as well as consent and collaboration. Hence, although they may appear as "troublesome," stigmatized, or targeted, they are indeed the major outlets for political transformation.

Clearly, not all conservative governments are allergic to mixing and aim at segregating, dividing, and controlling urban space and their countries' populations. It largely depends on the historical trajectory of the state and the socioeconomic and political characteristics of the government in action at a particular time. However, many conservative governments find comfort in preserving the status quo rather than welcoming new political openings, alliances, and affinities that are likely to undermine their power or hegemony. As in the case of French Republic's treatment of ethnic banlieues, spatial exclusion may even be promoted by the state for the sake of containment of immigrant populations.[67] From this perspective, it is unsurprising that the former immigrant ghetto of Kreuzberg in Berlin, now increasingly mixed and contested, today attracts more attention and intrusion from urban planners and the German government, compared to the state's neglect of it in the 1970s and 1980s.

Contrary to conventional thinking, it is *not* because of secular nonreligious ways of life that exclude the devout or violate Islamic ways of life and practices that mixed and highly contested urban spaces such as Beyoğlu, Taksim, and Bosphorus University have been a focus of attention for the government. In fact, the campuses and neighborhoods that the AKP government targeted stood out in attracting and integrating striking numbers of pious Muslims. Rather, it is the liberal inclusive political culture of these mixed urban spaces that puzzles conservative governments and infuriates authoritarians.

Following violent police attacks on the peaceful "Gezi village" during the protests, the columnist Danzikyan Yetvart wrote: "During the camping of the protestors, [Gezi-Taksim] was safer and more full of life than it has probably ever been. Were you [the government] disturbed by people cohabiting freely and standing together, despite their differences?"[68] Similarly, Beyoğlu and the AKM concert hall constitute polar opposites of segregated and sterile urban space, which often remains uncontested and undivided, and is thus left alone by the government. Consistently Islamic neighborhoods, such as Fatih in Istanbul, and uncompromisingly secularist neighborhoods, such as Kordonboyu in Izmir,[69] are generally of less interest or concern to the government than inclusive contested places, such as the UF, Taksim, and Kreuzberg.[70] Homogeneous, exclusive venues such as bars, which pious Muslims refuse to enter in Turkey, private nude beaches, and the nightclubs where the LGBT community explores free sex in Kreuzberg constitute less of a problem for right-wing governments than mixed venues do.

Finally, among various responses, governments also react punitively to highly contested places regarded as disruptive by the ruling elite. In the aftermath of the Gezi protests, the AKP government enforced the construction of a road that passed through the campus of the insurgent ODTÜ (Middle East Technical University) campus. Not surprisingly, Erdoğan encountered ODTÜ protesters, who tried to save trees on their campus and protested against this new construction. Soon after these contestations in Ankara, Erdoğan also responded to the objections to the construction of the third bridge across the Bosphorus. His statement is telling about how unconditionally aggressive his encroachments on urban space became: "One would sacrifice anything to build new roads, because new roads are civilization. New roads know no obstacle. Even if there were a mosque on the way of the construction plans, we would knock down even the mosque."[71]

THE NEW URBANITES

Both the divides and the alliances generated by urban space inform the emergence of a new kind of urban inhabitant.[72] The new urbanite successfully prioritizes the negotiation of the terms of a deeper democracy over other divisive ideological matters, such as commitment to laicism, (anti)Islamism, (anti)Kemalism, (anti)capitalism, (anti)Marxism, and (anti)nationalism. By "deeper democracy," I mean a democratic regime in which freedoms and rights take precedence over identitarian or ideological confrontation. Hence, the rights and freedoms of all (rather than just of the self and the alike) are the main reference point and goal of this new urbanite. Because s/he is liberated from the ancient cages of ideological conflict, s/he is the key to achievement of freedoms and the attainment of a deeper democracy. Ironically, although (or because) s/he emerges out of deep fault lines in the city, s/he is highly capable of consistently standing above ideological political divides that debilitate formal political institutions. In her/his endeavor of gaining freedoms, s/he operates most efficiently in an intimate urban environment.

The new urbanite is first and foremost an ordinary city dweller, most often a non-activist, whose politics is intricately entwined with the city and urban life. S/he brings the existing discussions on the "right to the city" to center stage. Broadly speaking, the "right to the city," a term originally coined by Henri Lefebvre, refers to the right to utilize urban space, the related services and resources of the city. Originally, this right was articulated around the right of entering and participating in urban space and politics at the local level.[73] The right to the city is the right of access into urban space regardless of ownership of property or other contractual and ideological preconditions. Building up on Lefebvre's concept, David Harvey (2003) added that the issue at hand was not just the right of access, but also the right to make a change, rearrange, and participate in decision-making over the city and its subparts:

> The right to the city is . . . far more than a right of individual or group access to the resources that the city embodies: it is a right to change and *reinvent* the city after our own heart's desire. It is, moreover, a collective, rather than an individual right, since reinventing the city inevitably depends upon the exercise of a collective power over the process of urbanization.[74]

The new urbanite is highly skilled in and sensitively committed to spatial and political inclusion. This is exemplified by the newcomers to Teşvikiye and their objection to longtime residents' exclusionary attitudes to devout Muslim visitors.[75] Similarly, when the secular male students of the UF cooperated with pious Muslim students by putting on head scarves to protest the head-scarf ban on campus, they allied with the devout to support equal right of access to the campus and equality in higher education. In both cases, the inclusionary freedom seekers took a clear position against sociopolitical discrimination by primarily struggling with existing patterns of spatial exclusion. The new urbanites aim to share their neighborhoods and campuses with others who may not have similar lifestyles or agree with them on social and political issues.[76]

Accordingly, this new urbanite is also the reason why this book differs from the bulk of the debates on the right of the city. Violations of rights and freedoms by right-wing conservative or authoritarian governments are the main target of the new city dwellers. Although their objection often encompasses distaste for socioeconomic inequalities and injustices of neoliberalism, their ultimate goal in urban politics is a deeper democracy that grows with the institutionalization of liberties and rights. This goal can be tied, but not reduced, to the defeat of global capitalism. The youth, who take the leading role in the transformations in the city and politics, cherish their iPods, iPads, laptops, and Converse shoes. This is exactly why the backbone of urban contestation in Turkey, particularly the youth, has been misperceived and mislabeled as apolitical even though in truth the new urbanite is very political.[77] Wide open to cooperation across all classes, the new city dweller is mainly a middle-class citizen who enjoys bourgeois lifestyles, while defending freedoms and rights for all.

Max Weber's masterpiece *The City* established a strong and direct connection between urban space and the emancipation and empowerment of bourgeois citizens.[78] Weber's burghers are empowered against the king and the church, as well as other despotic figures, such as feudal lords, by virtue of "owning and protecting property rights."[79] In contrast to the actors of this historically specific European context,[80] the current urban actors are distinguished by their production of presence,[81] politics of lifestyle,[82] power of showing up,[83] and claims to enter and shape the city, referred as "right to the city."[84]

No doubt, the new city dweller is central to new forms of urbanism that are politically transformative. The deeper democracy that the new urbanite calls for is *no*t a local form of governance, referred to as urban or radical democracy—terms that decenter the concepts of citizenship and the nation-state. On the contrary, the new urbanite speaks to and negotiates explicitly with the government at the national level, as well as on an international scale. Rather than merely idealizing local urban space, s/he is in tune with and sometimes cooperates with the Turkish diaspora, the international community, and Western media for support. Moreover, the new urbanite is ultimately in favor of strengthening the institutional base of a rather fragile democracy, because s/he has come to distrust the government. This distrust materializes in any or all of the following institutions: an overempowered and/or unfair government, a politicized judiciary and law enforcement apparatus, police brutality, an impotent opposition in parliament, and silenced media. Paradoxically, rather than causing the new urbanites to despair of democratic institutions, distrust of government leads them to yearn for and demand political reform and a deeper democracy.

THE DEPTH OF DEMOCRACY: MUNDANE URBANITY VERSUS SENSATIONAL PROTESTS

The problem with Erdoğan's third term is "creeping political authoritarianism," in the words of Ziya Öniş, a prominent political scientist. To the secular democrats who previously supported his political reforms and trusted his commitment to the secular state during his first term, this shift has been difficult to grasp and swallow. Helpful guidance in the analysis of the weakening aspects of democracy comes from Tocqueville, particularly his letters written between 1852 and 1859.[85] As a self-defined "half Yankee,"[86] Tocqueville had to revisit and begin questioning his earlier admiration for the strengths of American democracy.[87] For democracy in America was subjected to a litmus test in the second half of the nineteenth century, leading Tocqueville to see it as a never-ending project, but rather *constantly in becoming*.[88] Put differently, democracy is a seamless trajectory that is maintained only by ongoing political contestation and negotiation.

Rather than being a constant or fixed entity, the majoritarian democracy has ups and downs that emerge from new challenges of inclusion and accommodation. During these demanding times, when freedoms and rights are at risk, democracy is better accommodated by multisited urban contestation. In this context, the new urbanite is advantaged by having the city at his or her service, since urban space becomes *a force* of political learning and experimenting. When representative democracy falls short of representing and responding to the needs of large masses of discontented citizens, the city turns into a hub for urban contestation and democratic alliances. It becomes better suited to political negotiation and inclusion than the ballot box, which often is in the service of the majority. Elections in majoritarian democracies reflect the choices of the majority often at the cost of the liberties and rights of minorities. Urban politics enables the new city dweller to reach beyond the ballot box and legislative bodies when these prove weak, unaccountable, or exclusionary. More important, urban politics generates new alliances across divided urban space and groups toward the formation of a unified opposition.

Rethinking Richard Sennett's (2012) diagnosis that "cities need more places that the public can call its own," this book asks and explores the questions, *Where* does the actual, arduous work of democratic contestation take place? *How far* do democratic contestations expand and echo from the local to the national and international realms? And *how deeply* are freedoms and/or violations of freedom rooted? These questions, which are as much spatial as they are political, presuppose both geopolitical and scalar interrogation. Instead of defending or promoting the priority of one scale over the others, I explore the continuity, links, and interplay between different scales of contestation. I use scale as both a political and a spatial indicator to explore the reach of the contestation (hence fault lines) and the depth of freedoms (or the lack thereof).[89]

With freedoms under attack by an increasingly paternalist pro-Islamic government in Turkey, the locus of my inquiry was originally Istanbul. When I moved my fieldwork to highly contested Kreuzberg, the largest Turkish neighborhood in Germany and Europe, I was wondering *how far* the fault lines and alliances stretched from a local urban site? Situated in a different web of discriminations against Muslims, I found out that the fault lines from the homeland and host land intersected in Kreuzberg. While the Turkish homeland was being shaken up by the increasing authoritarianism of the pro-Islamic government, the host country was embedded in an increasing Islamophobic Europe, where the freedoms and rights of ethno-religious Muslim minorities were at risk.

Locating political contestation spatially in contested urban space contributes a new understanding of the depth of democracy. Previous research on democracies has failed to pay attention to the spatiality of contestation over freedoms and rights. On the one hand, the bulk of conventional political science perfunctorily locates power struggles almost exclusively in political institutions, the state, and political society.[90] On the other hand, many political sociologists have focused their analysis of power dynamics on the intersections of state and society by exploring civil society, civility in everyday life, and the quality of social life.[91] However, urban politics in the city cannot be reduced to either the state or civil society. Most recently, the increasing frequency of urban struggles has raised new concerns and questions for social scientists. The new global politics requires us to rethink and extend the loci of democratic contestation and political transformation from the state and civil and political society to urban space. The zeitgeist has brought to our attention the so-called global street, which has turned into a widely shared outlet for political contestation and transformation across the world.[92] Political scientists and urbanists, who for a long time have talked past one another, therefore need to read and engage one another across these disciplines.[93]

Finally, there still remains the question of why we should care about these contested places. Concretely, how generalizable is the experience of contested places such as Teşvikiye, UF, and Kreuzberg in the larger context of geopolitics? How representative are these highly contested sites in the larger geography of Turkey, Germany, and Europe? What is their role and place in these geographies known as "democracies," but that prove weak, albeit in different degrees and ways, when it comes to inclusion of and power/space sharing with dissenters and/or minorities? If the inclusive contested places are the exception rather than the rule in divided cities, why should we take them seriously in regard to larger political transformations? These sites are important because practices and voices at micro-level locality do trigger and push for a macro-level political learning, engagement, and negotiation.

This book maintains that there is no correlation between the political *impact* of contested urban space and its spatial *size* measured by the square meter. In other words, the reach of political impact cannot be quantified by the size of a contested place—a small exceptional place compared to the size of the entire country. We have witnessed this by the global echoing and/or regional transformations triggered by recent urban protests in relatively small, unusual places, such as Tahrir Square and Gezi Park.

However, unlike the protest sites, we know much less about the multiscalar effects of nonstrategic contestation by mundane living in campuses, neighborhoods, and streets. Typically, most of the current attention to urban space and democracy has been paid almost exclusively to flashy protests rather than politics of urban everyday life. Urban protest is typically not a lifestyle, and cannot be maintained beyond a relatively short period of intense upheaval.[94] Protestors are also usually the main target of law enforcement. So then, what renders "bodies on the streets," squares, and in neighborhoods pivotal political actors? Under what conditions do urban places matter in forming a "democratically assembled . . . coherent opposition"?[95] The depth of democracy does not simply depend on the protests, which are destined to fade away. Unlike the short-lived protests, cross-ideological alliances originate, flourish and persist in mundane everyday life. Hence, a broader understanding of urban contestation that centers on the mundane politics of urban space and lifestyle is imperative for a broader grasp of democracy. The power of inclusive contested places originates from the multiscalar quality of the new forms of urbanism practiced by the new city dweller—that is, the extent to which it echoes in and shakes up a much wider geography.

Inviting a rethinking of the interplay between contested places and larger power structures, the present ethnography emphasizes two aspects of democracy: the *spatial reach* of democratic contestation (namely, *how far* do political divides and alliances travel across urban, national and international scales?) and the *spatiality* of freedoms (specifically, *where* are the quality, gravity, and depth of liberties negotiated and practiced?). I argue that the links between these two spatialities—reach of urban contestation and depth of freedoms—play major roles in shaping the quality of a democracy.

1 BETWEEN STATE SPACES AND AUTONOMOUS PLACES

IN AN INTERVIEW published in the daily newspaper *Taraf* on January 9, 2013, Cemal Kafadar, Vehbi Koç professor of Turkish Studies at Harvard University, expressed deep concern about transformations of the built environment in Istanbul:

> The construction of the Golden Horn Metro Bridge is always on my mind. I have lost sleep over this issue for two years. I invite the officials dealing with these issues to take a more serious and professional approach. They seem to suggest things like: "We'll reduce the height by three meters here; we'll change the lighting and color; we'll change a detail in the upper corner." Do these ease or solve our concerns? They [the planners] say the objections are ideological. Be reasonable; show mercy [*El insaf*]! It's no exaggeration to say that if there are a few places on earth favored above all others, this is one of them.[1]

Dismayed by political leaders' lack of cultural sensitivity, Kafadar called for public debate about urban construction projects, policies, and decisions affecting the exquisite city of Istanbul and its historic sites. He argued that decisions about places that belong to the public must be made by and with the public. Emphasizing the meeting points between the state officials and urban residents, Kafadar's words underlined the importance of local participation under an unresponsive state that ignores and disrespects urban residents' demands, interests, and needs.

A lot has been said about how states penetrate societies by dividing them,[2] permeating the city on an everyday basis,[3] and controlling, intervening in, and encroaching on urban space.[4] Going briefly over the Ottoman and Republican periods into the recent period under the AKP rule, this chapter explores major shifts in the interaction between political rule and urban space in Istanbul. Turkey is not an exception in regard to the formation of state spaces—a process that occurred at different historical periods before and after the consolidation of the Turkish Republic in 1923. In this respect, particular attention needs to be paid to the AKP's encroachment on Istanbul's historic sites. In which ways do political and urban contestations happen concurrently? Why are political and urban fault lines mapped onto each other? How is the government's infringement on city life countered by new alliances and the defense of freedoms and rights in urban space?[5]

SCALING STATE POWER: FORMATION OF STATE SPACES

Istanbul has historically been a showcase for several empires and states. After the Ottomans conquered Constantinople in 1453, the following decades witnessed thorough spatial reconstructions in order to transform the capital of the Christian Eastern Roman Empire into that of the Islamic Ottoman Empire. Not only was the conquest of the city pivotal for the empire but the making of the empire was tightly intertwined with rebuilding the city.[6] In every historical era, the grandiose refashioning of Istanbul has been the most visible expression of political dominance, enabling political rulers to take pride in their territorial sovereignty. Even Max Weber, who construed his "Occidental city" in opposition to the "Islamic city,"[7] differentiated the Ottoman city from his typology of the "Islamic city."[8] Istanbul was a misfit in Weber's theory. Unlike some of the previously colonized cities of the Muslim world, it cannot be easily made to conform to Weber's ideal-type of the Islamic city. It was the capital city of the Byzantine and Ottoman empires for almost sixteen centuries (between 330 CE and 1924) and has always displayed an amalgam of various cultural artifacts and religious architectures. In the nineteenth century, it was subject to both Islamic and European influences.[9]

Like the "imperialization" period, the making of the nation and its state after the fall of the Ottoman Empire in 1923 was characterized by the reconstruction of Turkey's cities. Typically, modernist city planning and architecture gained particular momentum during the nation-building period.[10] This relationship plays a crucial role in the state's assertiveness in the national project. "If nation is the constructed consensus of a collective memory, . . . and an assembled sense of belonging to a set of values, norms, historical memories and narratives, then architectural landscapes indeed are the most visibly powerful ways in which it is created."[11] In the decades following the consolidation of the secular Turkish Republic in 1923, the state initiated a massive de-Ottomanization of cities, followed by cultural defamiliarization and new forms of familiarizations in urban space. The mushrooming of statues of Kemal Atatürk across the urban landscape and the building of Atatürk's monumental mausoleum (*Anıtkabir*) in Ankara were signs of the rapid state production of Republican space. By forming new state spaces, the state scaled up its political authority and power, aiming to shape social life and control political dynamics in national territory. Christopher Houston observes in this respect that "urban planners/architects alike invoke the efficacy of the planned environment and the politics of design to constrain and guide social conduct."[12]

Similarly, when mosques are turned into churches (or vice versa) and/or into public museums, as in the case of Hagia Sofia, we are witnessing the refashioning of the built environment by the state. These changes in the built environment reflect the state's penetration of urban space with the goal of controlling, containing, and/or taming institutions, groups, people, and their behavior.[13] Pointing to the political alliance between state officials and architects through the 1950s, Sibel Bozdoğan refers to architecture as a field of visual politics. Indeed, more recently, the field of city planning and architecture has turned into a visual battlefield in Turkey.[14]

The manifestation of tension and rivalry between Islamists and secularists over the use and control of urban landscapes is not a new phenomenon—particularly because while the urges of secularist elite were manifested most visibly in cities, Islamist movements also blossomed and flourished in urban space.[15] From the late Ottoman period into the Republican era, Istanbul remained a locus of both secular and religious nostalgia for different people, reminding them of the different aspects of urbanity and various ways of life in the cosmopolitan city.[16] The different imageries of the city evolved in competition with each other, making Istanbul an even more precious cultural and political landscape.[17] From the mid-1980s on, Istanbul, like many cities in the Middle East, increasingly attracted Muslim groups and Islamist movements. This migration was largely propelled by the Turkish state's increasing tolerance for Islam as part of its battle against leftists in the aftermath of the military coup in 1980.

The Secular State Divides and Rules Urban Space

Actual contestations by Islamists for urban space, particularly over Istanbul, were fuelled in the mid-1990s, when "Islam" came to be seen as a major player in urban politics and a concern for urban policy manifested itself in both Tur-key and Europe.[18] When the Welfare Party (Refah Partisi; henceforth RP) won municipal elections in many Istanbul districts in 1994, the electoral victory was referred to by the RP as the "second conquest" by Islam after Fatih Sultan Mehmet's conquest in 1453,[19] implying that the city was being rescued from Westernization and decadent modernity. The party made efforts to Islamize the city by building new mosques, attempting to impose new restrictions on alcohol consumption, policing the red-light district in Beyoğlu more strictly, and so on. At the same time, Istanbul witnessed the expansion of efficient mu-nicipal services under the then mayor, Tayyip Erdoğan, later prime minister of Turkey (2002–present). While becoming increasingly afraid of the rise of political Islam, most Istanbulites appreciated the good local services provided by the RP.[20]

The victory of the RP in the national parliamentary elections in 1996 fuelled the fears and reactions of secular Istanbulites. However, when the RP came to power in a coalition government, neither the secularists' complaints nor the contested entrance of head-scarved women into the city landscape dramati-cally changed everyday life. The semi-military coup in 1997 served as a catalyst, because the state confronted the rapid rise of Islamic movements by invading their associations and intimidating them with several repressive measures. The RP was closed down while still in power, and political leaders, including Tayyip Erdoğan, were jailed. For a few years, successive Islamist parties (Fazilet and Saadet) remained marginal and weak. State intervention strategically repressed Islamists in the short run. Islamist activities in devout neighborhoods went un-derground. As Istanbul was already segregated into devout and secular neigh-borhoods, the state's ban on the head scarf in universities and public offices bolstered the city's segregation into mutually exclusive neighborhoods.

In the late 1990s, the majority of Istanbulites took care not to cross the in-visible fences between devout and secular urban space. The scale of physical separation along urban fault lines was remarkable. Fear arising out of the unfa-miliarity of the newcomers and elitism among old residents alienated the pious in the slums. Segregation was facilitated by the fact that these fault lines were not brand-new formations, but emerged originally from former patterns of set-tlement by the pious migrants. These boundaries existed between old and new neighborhoods within Istanbul before the revival of Islamism,[21] since the di-vides between poor and well-off parts of the city were reinforced by neoliberal policies and globalization.[22]

In the 1990s, Istanbul remained spatially segregated. When I invited some pious Muslim friends to a Euro-cafe in my neighborhood, Teşvikiye, on a cold winter day in 1998, the segregation of the city hit me in the face. I picked up three head-scarved women from the shuttle stop in Teşvikiye, and walked with them for less than five minutes to a café on the next block. During this short walk, every person on the street stared at us. The head-scarved women became increasingly self-conscious and embarrassed. When we entered the café, everybody in the small, cozy coffee shop looked at my guests with curious eyes, wondering what they were doing there, and what I was doing with them. Not having seen a veiled woman in the neighborhood café before, they turned us into spectacle.

I experienced the symptoms of a segregated city through another incident on a hot summer day in 1998, several months after the military intervention. During a city tour organized for a group of secular urban intellectuals and scholars, the bus stopped at Çamlıca Hill, a place revitalized as a public park by the Islamic municipality, where we took a break in a teahouse administered by the local government. Soon after we arrived, we realized we were the only group of people who did not look "modestly dressed." Some in our group were wearing shorts, short tops, or tight jeans. The locals, who gave disapproving looks, stared at the entire group. Some people in our group asked for beer, while many in our group stared at devout brides who had come to Çamlıca Park to take bridal pictures. The conservative bridal gowns covering the entire body and the head especially interested most people in our group. This bridal fashion was simply new and unfamiliar to the visitors, who had not seen it before. Made to feel uncomfortable by the visitors, several groups of people sitting around our large table left soon after we arrived. Back on the bus, people expressed disappointment about stopping in "neighborhoods invaded by the devout [dinci]." The tour guide apologized for the inconvenience.

Both of these events attest to the neat fences that demarcated Islamic and secular urban space in Istanbul in the late 1990s. Both the secular group's stop at Çamlıca and the devout women's visit to Teşvikiye illustrate exceptional instances of "transgression" of the fault lines. They illuminate social exclusion and segregation in public spaces, which were open to everyone *in principle* but were not preferred and utilized collectively *in practice*. While the entrance of devout or secular groups into the others' "unfamiliar territory" was unpleasant and involuntary, there seemed to be an undeclared comfort in segregation and conserving the status quo, which kept everything in place. More bluntly, social exclusion was embraced bilaterally and seemed to create mutual relief from uncomfortable contact with "the unwanted." In both cases, the most obvious reminder of transgression was the female body.

Although state intervention in 1998 divided the landscape and segregated urban residents of Istanbul in the short run, Islamism in Turkey soon started to transform itself in unforeseen directions. Abandoning the party's initial principle of siding with poor urban migrants, RP municipalities started to work on "rescuing Istanbul from barbarian provincials."[23] This clearly showed that "Istanbul [was] the key to [the Islamist RP's] *bargain* with the established structures of power."[24] Although the state's divide-and-rule policy intended to suppress and segregate Islamists by dividing urban space, it ended up indirectly facilitating their integration into the free market, the secular state, and secular urban space in the new millennium.[25]

Unintended by the State: From Segregated into Mixed City

Just ten years later, in 2007, when the pro-Islamic party was elected by free and fair elections for the second time in the secular Turkish Republic, the spatial organization of the city revealed a totally different story. As Muslim actors and head-scarved women have permeated the entire city landscape, as well as bourgeois lifestyles, Istanbul has changed from being a "divided" city into a more "integrated" mixed geography. Given the earlier segregation of Istanbul along religious lines, existing works distinguished between "Islamic" and "secular" spaces.[26] This was perceived as one of the main principles of urban inequality, exclusion, and discrimination.[27] Yet the new millennium was marked by a gradual shift from mutually exclusive Islamic and secular neighborhoods into a contested proximity and integration between these groups.

Paradoxically, instead of erasing the divides, this integration simply meant that the nature of the fault lines has gradually changed. As the unspoken fences between "Islamic and secular spaces" were casually transgressed in central Istanbul, the neat lines of segregation in the city have lent themselves to vocal microlevel urban contestations. More concretely, urban conflict deepened in one's immediate life sphere, as the ways of life and education levels of pious and secular urban residents have become more similar. The spatial proximity and leveling off of differences have forced the old secularist elite to share not only political power but also urban space with the new rising Muslim bourgeoisie. My findings suggest that urban space has become the locus of contestation triggered by uncomfortable proximity between pious and secular ways of life. Paradoxically, these discomforts trigger spatial processes of negotiation over rights and freedom.

The schemes and strategies of states do not always follow smoothly as planned. More concretely, states' overarching projects rooted in the nation-building period encounter a series of challenges and attacks from oppositional political forces. These contestations reshape the original agendas of founding fathers, and may mold them into new trajectories.[28] "[P]eople subvert, lucidly or practically, the intentions of states and their planners, and cities are partially constituted through the very resistance their built environments provoke," Houston notes.[29] The entrance and gradual integration of pious Muslims into urban spaces that were previously designated as secular sites interrupted and unsettled the environmental determinism of the previous secularist elite. Throughout the first decade of the new millennium, pious Muslims filtered into Istanbul's most secular "fortresses," which would not have considered allowing access to head-scarved women until a decade ago. During the first two terms of AKP rule (2002–11), this new mixing in the city was definitely an unintended outcome of state's divide-and-rule policy.

AKP Government Encroaching on Urban Space and Ways of Life

The successive political victories of the AKP (2002, 2007, 2011) gradually disrupted and obliterated the old alliance between the secularist Kemalist political elite and urban city planners. However, instead of terminating the convention of controlling social life through urban restructuring, the new Islamist political elite of Turkey reproduced it based on its own worldview by utilizing city planning. The authoritarianism of the Republic vis-à-vis urban space did not end, but simply changed hands, intensity, and direction. As the old secularist elite was replaced by the new Islamist one, social engineering took a dramatic spatial tone, not only to regulate social conduct but also to "own" urban space through semi-legitimate contracts (*ihaleler*) and large-scale corruption. Put differently, because of the AKP's unruly capitalist ambitions, the political targeting of urban space as a means for controlling social conduct was reincarnated in a new neoliberal and pious garb. Under the guise of promoting economic growth, Erdoğan's uncontainable political ambitions took aggressive forms.

Eight decades of secularist Republican rule left its marks in every corner of the urban life in Turkey's major cities, particularly Istanbul, Izmir, and Ankara. In order to transform Republican urban space and secular and liberal lifestyles, the AKP began targeting and attacking sites laden with historical, cultural, and/or social meaning for the residents.

In August 2011, just before the Ramadan fast began, Prime Minister Erdoğan paid an unexpected visit to the narrow streets of Asmalı Mescit near Taksim Square in the heart of downtown Istanbul. Over the past few years, Asmalı Mescit proliferated as a neighborhood of open-air, alcohol-serving taverns called *meyhane*. As locals tell it, on the way from the local government's building in Şişhane, the prime minister's large car got stuck in one of the tight streets partially blocked by outdoor tables and drinking people. Although the accounts by local business people are not entirely consistent, many indicate that Erdoğan became agitated by people raising glasses in the presence of his wife, and large-scale consumption of alcohol. In the wake of his excursion, the local AKP-run government curbed these establishments by ordering them to keep all their tables indoors and out of public throughways.

The Asmalı Mescit event is very telling in terms of the unintentionality and abrupt nature of state-space interaction. First, the incident shows that the intimate relationship between urban space and the state cannot be explained solely by urban policy and planning, and must be explored in the context of the spontaneity of everyday life. As David Harvey rightly puts it: "[S]omething different does *not* necessarily arise out of a conscious plan, but more simply out of what people feel, sense, and come to articulate as they seek meaning in their daily lives."[30] Hence, given the increasing importance of everyday politics for ordinary, often nonactivist, residents, strategic urban planning and planners are not the sole key actors in urban politics.

Second, the impact of the Asmalı Mescit case has unintentionally reverberated far beyond the borders of the neighborhood into the city and the nation, as many Istanbulites, particularly on the secular Left, became alarmed, irritated, and increasingly distrustful of the government's attitude toward already established rights and liberties. "We have a prime minister, who thinks he can organize Turkey as though he were organizing his home . . . a prime minister who [has] stretched the dated notion that 'I am accountable for the morality and honor of the neighborhood' to cover the morality and honor of the state," Ahmet Hakan complained in *Hürriyet*.[31]

The curious spectacle of a national head of government concerning himself with such local detail as the placement of sidewalk-café tables is a strong sign of the weight of neighborhood politics in current power politics. Rather than as a direct attack on the drinking culture of Asmalı Mescit, the officials framed this as a matter of public safety. They justified it as the protection of public space against the illegal use of streets by the local small businesses. But from the perspective of the residents, local business, and customers, this was seen as an encroachment on "their" urban space and individual freedom by the government. Many in the neighborhood complained bitterly by pointing out that some taverns had permits for open-air tables. They accused the prime minister of attacking the individual liberties to consume alcohol in order to impress his pious Muslim supporters.

As the AKP has grown increasingly more authoritarian and less accountable and responsible to society in its third term (2011–present), it has displayed increasingly authoritarian attitudes. However, unlike the state production of urban space during and soon after the creation of the Republic, the AKP was performing in a rather different political milieu and at a different time and place than the founding fathers. The AKP came to power thanks to established democratic institutions of majoritarian democracy, a strong civil society, and a free and fair electoral system that has been intact for six decades. Most important, AKP's inclusion in the polity was facilitated by major disagreements and splits among the secular about the accommodation of Muslim piety.

It is no secret that governments constitute, consolidate, and exercise their power through the "orchestration of urban space."³² Regimes, including democratic ones, do deconstruct, rearrange, and rebuild urban space. However, if a regime claims to be a democracy, there should be institutional limits to how much it can disregard the needs, demands, and discontent of the residents. Democracies curb and prevent corruption through judicial and political procedures. Instead, the urban discontent in Turkey's major cities, particularly in Istanbul, has become more and more of an encumbrance for the increasingly hegemonic AKP.

Istanbulites felt increasingly irritated, frustrated, and threatened by a series of aggressive urban transformations by the government and the minister of environment and urban planning, Erdoğan Bayraktar. He was the director of TOKİ (Toplu Konut İdaresi, the Public Housing Administration) and had supervised massive housing development projects prior to becoming a government minister, and then resigned in December 2013 due to a corruption scandal. As one of my informants said sarcastically, "Entrusting the city to the [former] director of TOKİ is entrusting the sheep to the wolf [*kuzuyu kurda teslim etmek*]." Unsurprisingly, the local government of Istanbul displayed ambivalent attitudes toward the city. While acquiring a strong reputation for turning parks and green zones into gray chunks of high-rises and shopping centers, the municipality also took good care of certain public space by planting flowers and expanding green scenes.

However, the government has been rather consistent in attacking sociocul-turally and historically meaningful sites. Residents became increasingly agitated by street-level aggression of officials, such as the rough treatment of shopkeep-ers by police forces during the evacuation of İnci Pastanesi, a pastry shop adored by Istanbulites that had lost its lease on the first floor of the historic Cercle d'Orient building on pedestrian İstiklal Street. This popular store was famous not only for its chocolate-covered cream puffs (profiteroles), a much-loved pas-try, which it had served for seventy years, but also as a place evoking nostalgia for old Istanbul. Significantly, it was also a major meeting point for non-Muslim minorities and secular Istanbulites.[33] As the result of the demolition of many other iconic places, such as the Emek movie theater, was numerous malls in the middle of downtown Istanbul, the residents felt that the AKP was taking their city away from them.

Equally important is the concern of ordinary residents, as well as artists, intellectuals, and scholars, that a historically rich civilization and art is under attack by the increasingly authoritarian AKP. Many Istanbulites have come to identify the party with ignorant vandalism because of its hasty authorization of projects that negatively impact the city's historically cosmopolitan cultural her-itage, such as the Golden Horn Metro Bridge.

Clearly in contrast to the nation-building period of the Turkish Republic, the AKP is not in a revolutionary phase of building new political institutions from scratch along with a large-scale production of Republican urban space. Unlike the goal of building a nation out of a multi-ethnic empire, the most widely shared demand of residents during the rise and rule of AKP has been political reform and democratization. Hence, Istanbulites during this period were reform-oriented rather than revolutionary. Particularly, the secular votes for the AKP came from a pro-democratic yearning for political pluralism and not for new forms of authoritarianism. Although the AKP came to power with the promise of political reform, it undermined and disapproved of urban space associated with progressive politics, such as liberal university campuses, di-verse neighborhoods, critical progressive art scenes, and so on. Unsurprisingly, the residents, who identify strongly with and cherish these urban spaces, have become increasingly defensive and protective of them.

The degree of the AKP's encroachments on urban space and lifestyles has called the legitimacy of the government into question. Along with corruption scandals, the government's intervention in the city has gradually made residents feel less trustful of it, particularly in terms of their rights, privacy, and freedom.

Most important, the government's avoidance of public discussion and its un-responsiveness to locals' demands and needs have contradicted what the party preached in order to come to power—a deeper and more inclusive democracy. Istanbulites are constantly reminded by AKP's spatial politics that democracy is not yet "the only game in town."[34]

CONTESTED ZONES OF FREEDOM: AUTONOMY FROM THE STATE?

Urban space is transformed into a chaotic territory of contestation by "both the mechanisms by which public space is claimed and the conflicts triggered by those claims," David Trouille suggests.[35] Although the deep fault lines and the disarray in Teşvikiye, Kreuzberg, and the UF were my initial interest, emerging alliances against freedom violations were my major finding there. Accordingly, I refer to these urban spaces as "zones of and for freedom." They are demarcated by clear physical boundaries, whether explicitly realized or not by insiders or outsiders. Their material borders as well as sociopolitical boundaries demarcate and distinguish them from other urban spaces. But, what makes these highly contested free zones different from others—whether disputed or undisputed—with regard to democracy? The key that differentiates these sites from other parts of the city is their relative "autonomy" from, or leverage with, the government. Let me be more specific in terms of the differences between the zones of freedom and other urban space.

Zones of and for freedom in Turkey are dramatically different from uncontested sites that are mute (or silenced) by authoritarian rule or regulations. For example, mute campuses with repressive political cultures tend not to be autonomous enough from the state. Most often, either their presidents and/or their campus community are not at liberty to question, disagree with, or stand up to the state-linked Higher Education Council, YÖK (Yüksek Öğretim Kurulu). Previously evacuated protest sites that are under rigid police surveillance also lose their contestational characteristics and stop being zones of freedom. Similarly, the free zones are remarkably different from uncontested places that do not open up to newcomers, whether they are pious, secular, or of some other nature. Gated (sub)urban communities, Islamist neighborhoods in Turkish cities such as Fatih, and segregated Muslim ghettos in Europe qualify as uncontested places that are exclusive and therefore not liberated from ideological divides. Neighborhoods that segregate either certain classes or ethnic and/or other minority groups qualify in this category. This was the case during the 1990s, when the state divided and ruled Istanbul by segregating pious migrants from the secular locals.

Just to complicate the issue a bit further, zones of and for freedom also differ from many other contested sites. There is no perfunctory correlation between contestation and democracy, since contested places may not necessarily be free places. Many contested places divide abruptly, but do not necessarily provide the needed *safe space* to disagree freely and form new political alliances. This was seen in the case of university campuses in Turkey throughout the 1970s, among other violent spaces.[36] In this period, many university campuses in Istanbul were unable to maintain safety and security because of the polarization and violent clashes between the left- and right-wing insurgents. The failure to maintain safety and security on campus was met with brutal police intervention until political violence ended with the military coup in 1980. Similarly, democratic practices do not blossom and flourish in contested places that marginalize and force out minorities and newcomers, as in the case of exclusive or conservative neighborhoods. A good example is Avcılar, where the locals allied with police in shaming, intimidating, and forcing out transgender residents, although there was no legal basis for this.[37]

None of the above urban sites qualify as zones of and for freedom, whether they are contested or not. What do these contested and uncontested places with no freedom aspirations (or freedom violations) tell us about "free places"? As the aforementioned places show, the presence or absence of contestation does not make a place free. In each case, the positioning and/or the leverage of the place toward an authoritarian or discriminating government is pivotal. This autonomy is a determining factor of whether it can attract freedom-seekers and generate democratic practices and alliances over freedoms. The capability of preventing intrusion by the state, particularly the police, is higher when a place maintains a nonviolent and safe environment in the aftermath of inclusion. Although the decision of letting the police on campus is given to all presidents of universities in Turkey, only free and contested campuses keep them out. This is particularly important for contemporary world politics, where states, including strong democracies, have heightened their security measures under the rubric of counterterrorism. Ironically, the disproportional use of security measures, as employed by Erdoğan in his visits to nonviolent campuses, end up harming the students by undermining their rights and freedoms.

The concept of "free space" was coined previously by a group of social movement theorists. Ironically, however, their interest in analyzing and theorizing these spaces was marginal, because the main focus was on exploring collective action and mobilization. Some examples of free spaces in these discussions were book clubs, tenant associations, bars, union halls, student lounges and hangouts, families, women's consciousness-raising groups, and lesbian feminist communities.[38] Not only the political but also the material aspects of space were largely undiscussed in this literature,[39] which merely treated the so-called free spaces as the *background* or *context* of social mobilization.[40]

These previous debates on free space raise a question: is there really social or political action that is devoid of a space/place? Unsurprisingly, there is no "space-less" social action or practice, whether local, national, or global, particularly after web sites and digital technologies are included as new globalized spaces.[41] As every social act—not just insurgency—happens in a place, space becomes the generic "wallpaper" of both social life and politics.[42] But of course, the recognition of some sort of shadowy space/place in the backdrop of social life or power dynamics does not do justice to the centrality of place in political processes.

In line with a prevalent tendency in conventional political science and political sociology, space as a variable is rarely treated as equal in importance to other sociological factors, such as class, ethnicity, race, or gender, in shaping social reality and change. This is not to say that space is more important than other social variables, but its consistent marginalization undermines in-depth understanding of political processes and a comprehensive grasp of democracy, particularly in contemporary world politics.

As in the use of other sociological variables such as gender, space/place adds a new lens to our vision and a layer to analysis. What can we detect and understand when we take space/place seriously? What are we missing out on when we cannot *emplace* social reality? Seeing space/place as a container or a contextual background is not sufficient: "'Context' is at best a shadowy presence," Robert Zussman says. "[It] is too weak a term."[43] Against the background of previous work that has marginalized space, cities and power dynamics *co-constitute* political struggles for freedom and rights. They generate an opposition to power structures at the national and international scale when formal institutional channels of opposition fail to do so efficiently. Furthermore, the ethnographies presented in this book differ from the aforementioned writings on free spaces, which have focused on strategic collective action. In contrast, zones of and for freedom are driven by nondeliberate aspects of everyday politics and mostly unintended urban transformations.

Part 1

Who speaks for place?

Arturo Escobar, "Culture Sits in Places"

There is something called "neighborhood pressure" in Turkey. This
was one of the biggest fears of Young Turks. This is an unexplored
and very difficult "mood" to be explained by social scientists.

Şerif Mardin cited in Ruşen Çakır, *Mahalle baskısı*

The apartment is rental but the neighborhood is ours.

Slogan spray-painted on a wall during the Gezi protests

ON NEIGHBORHOOD POLITICS

IN THE MUSLIM WORLD, Turkey has long been singled out as a staunchly secular land of "moderate" Islam. Religious politics did not transform the secular Republic into a Sharia-law-based state. However, the turn of the millennium also witnessed a shift in power politics after the pro-Islamic AKP attained power. As the AKP managed to stay in power in three successive elections, the victim role that the Muslims had previously assumed has changed gradually. Among the many triggers of the shifting balance of powers between pious Muslims and secularists was the rapid upward mobilization of pious Muslims. Along with political victories of the AKP, pious Muslims became richer and more educated, which led to the burgeoning of new pious bourgeois lifestyles. The "victims" of yesterday became today's newly empowered.

In its third term (2011–), AKP's increasing authoritarianism raised doubts about Erdoğan's commitment to secularism, as he began to take informal advice from ulema (religious scholars). However, the Turkish political crisis was not caused by Islamization of the state but by the violation of game rules by the Muslim elite. Because "becoming like Iran" was not really a threat to most Turkish citizens, secularists began to wonder if Turkey was perhaps becoming like Egypt, Islamizing *from the bottom up*.[1] As usual, the bottom was urban space, specifically the neighborhood. Were pious Muslims taking over the cities and imposing their way of life through close-knit neighborhood communities? Was the urban neighborhood becoming a more dangerous mediator of political transformation than the state itself? About half a decade into the new millennium, this fear instigated a nationwide public debate referred to as the *mahalle baskısı*. The literal translation of this term is "neighborhood pressure," but originally it was broadly perceived as "social pressure"[2] imposed on people who did not conform to the norms and ways of life of the dominant group.[3] Although the debate was opened up in very academic tones by Şerif Mardin,[4] it rapidly turned into a pretext for political polarization and social exclusion between secularists and devout Muslims. These fears have been mediated and reinforced by headlines in newspapers and television programs and detailed in insightful reports.[5]

Intense debates on *mahalle baskısı* did indeed reflect a *spatial quality* of contestation other than the literal translation of the term "social pressure" could capture. As deep fault lines and unrest divided Istanbul's neighborhoods, streets, and other public sites, the urban space of major cities has attached a whole new spatial meaning to politics. Whether the "pressure by the dominant group" was initially associated with urban space or not, it soon rendered the link between political contestation and urban space explicit.[6] The spatiality of power at urban sites became endemic as neighborhoods, squares, streets, and so on were utilized, claimed, or contested for political ends.

In 2013, Erdoğan's attack on mixed-gender student housing in urban neighborhoods was followed by haphazard raids on student houses in Istanbul by the police with no official authorization. Upon these acts of moral condemnation of mixed-gender education, Ruşen Çakır revisited the debate by emphasizing the links between government and the concept of neighborhood pressure.[7] The recurring debates about neighborhood pressure inform us about the *spatiality* of government's encroachment on individual liberties, lifestyles, and personal spheres. Put differently, AKP's infringements were spatial more often than not and frequently exploded in campuses and neighborhoods.[8]

Depending on the conditions, urban space allures, and is used by, governments and other political forces, both conservative and progressive. Different kinds of regimes, particularly authoritarian governments, have used and collaborated with local neighborhood networks to achieve their agendas,[9] for example, the Basij volunteer service in Iran to maintain control of the public and monitor locals' ways of life.[10] Using everyday sites has always been convenient for undemocratic governments, since it provides for easy concealment. On the other hand, neighborhood studies show how neighborhood politics became a transformative force, either empowering or emancipating the locals.[11] Accordingly, spatiality of freedom is neither a Muslim strategy to pressure or stifle the secular nor a secularist tool to manipulate or control devout Muslims. I use the concept of the spatiality of freedom as an analytical tool to explicate multilayered shifting power dynamics through which urbanites and governments contest and bargain over liberties, privacy, and rights.

ARE NEIGHBORHOOD POLITICS
OVERSHADOWED BY GLOBAL CAPITALISM?

Teşvikiye's recent transformations testify to one of the venues through which pious Muslims became empowered in Turkey—capitalist consumption and bourgeois lifestyles. Since haute-couture boutiques, high-end malls, restaurants, and cafés proliferated rapidly in the 1990s, the neighborhood increasingly attracted bourgeois Muslim consumers, particularly fashion-conscious head-scarved high-spenders. Very much like their secular counterparts, head-scarved fashionistas were keenly interested in displaying the symbols of upward social mobility.[12] It is important to note, however, that while these recent socioeconomic developments were certainly among the triggers of spatial and political change in the neighborhood, the globalization of capitalism is neither the sole nor a sufficient explanation of the depth and reach of urban politics in Teşvikiye and beyond. Escobar writes:

> [Y]es, capitalism operates at *all levels of scale*; yes, capitalism is always present in the production of place; moreover, capitalism has to operate on the basis of its incorporation of places, and there are probably as many varieties of this incorporation as there are places, despite capital's best efforts at normalizing its conditions of operation. Yet this also means that capitalism is at least to some degree transformed by places.[13]

Critics of the spatial expansion of capitalism into the Muslim world fail to recognize that this serves to single out "Islam" yet again among every other religion and civilization vulnerable to capitalism. Instead, we need to ask how the local shapes this global expansion of capitalism by molding it into its own specificities. Specifically, what happens to a staunchly secular neighborhood once pious Muslims become attracted to it because of their newly adopted lifestyles and patterns of high consumption?

Undoubtedly, the rise of Islamism has conventionally been understood mostly as a countermovement or rebellion against Western modernity, if not an attack on it. Islam has been juxtaposed particularly with the morality and ways of life associated with Western capitalism. Hence, the story of Teşvikiye may at first seem oxymoronic. Critics of global neoliberalism may not even regard Muslim high-spenders as worthy of analysis, since they cross fault lines in a segregated city to gratify their capitalist drives. However, it is problematic to single out Muslim people for their capitalist desires and endeavors, since no part of the world and no society has remained immune to global patterns of capitalist consumption. There is no reason to make yet another "exception" out of "Islam" or head-scarved women, who have already been singled out in many other ways. First and foremost, the urban mingling of Muslim residents was not occasioned only by their bourgeois needs, but also by their educational and international ambitions. Second, we have not sufficiently explored yet how these new pious urbanites transform global capitalist trends into new forms of urbanisms. How do the pious Muslim Istanbulites refashion their own consumerist drives into different ways of life and thereby trigger new political processes—intentionally or not?[14]

Although one of the triggers in urban restructuring was indeed the bourgeoisification of pious lifestyles in a neoliberal economy, the larger-scale neighborhood debates cannot be reduced to either a class struggle or the predicaments of neoliberalism. The literature is rich in critiques of the material aspects of urbanization and the economic and political implications of gentrification. However, neighborhood politics in Teşvikiye and Kreuzberg cannot be explained primarily by a critique of neoliberalism or an exclusively class-based analysis. Such an exclusive focus creates two major problems. First, by prioritizing economic processes and structures, it tends to obscure the "agentic" powers of quotidian urban sites and ordinary people, including but not limited to the middle class.[15] Agentic places and urban residents play integral, albeit abrupt and interruptive, roles in resisting and negotiating power dynamics and structures. More important, the preoccupation with global capitalism overshadows the emancipating and empowering effects of cities, which enable or facilitate residents' bargains over democratic liberties and rights.

In contrast to the most prevalent tendency in the literature to explain the politics of urban space almost exclusively in terms of socioeconomic factors and global neoliberal forces, I focus on the place-specific political processes.[16] While the global effects of capitalism on cities are undeniable, I take issue with the deprioritization of urban democratic contestation and neglect of the liberating and democratizing effects of urban space.[17] Without disagreeing with the critiques of gentrification, class-based politics, and global capitalism that dominate urban studies,[18] I suggest a shift of focus to the intersection of space, religion, and gender.[19] Concretely, in which spatial and political ways has the previously secularist and exclusive neighborhood of Teşvikiye been transformed into a new entity? What has become of it, as it first turned into a high-consumption locality after the 1980s, and then into a high-conflict urban space in the new millennium, and finally into a place that generates contestation for freedoms and rights? Places that (re)produce, fuel, and even "jump start" power require a more "assertive" spatial analysis to use Edward Soja's term.[20] This is why and how neighborhood as a contested political site comes under the microscope.

2 A NEIGHBORHOOD DIVIDED BY LIFESTYLES

FROM THE SECOND HALF of the nineteenth into the first decade of the twentieth century, the physical boundaries of Istanbul expanded remarkably. Construction on the hills facing the Bosphorus on the European side of the channel began in the 1870s and "reached a peak at the turn of the century, when the neighborhoods of Teşvikiye and Nişantasi acquired their definite structure."[1]

In Istanbul, as in other cosmopolitan cities, many people no longer know their next-door neighbors, given the high turnover of residents and the sense of detachment in hectic city life. Nevertheless, notwithstanding that Teşvikiye is a relatively new part of the city, neighborly ties, familiarities, and friendships there go back longer than in many other neighborhoods.

Neighborhoods identified as "Islamist" have often been regarded as relatively resistant to this "passing" of neighborhood feeling, mainly because of their strong commitment to the Muslim community, solidarity, and grassroots mobilization.[2] However, Teşvikiye and a few other secular neighborhoods challenge the predominant assumption that the neighborhood is held together mainly by the Muslim community and pious ways of life. Teşvikiye stands out among the secular parts of Istanbul, not only because of shared codes of conduct, lifestyles, and status symbols, but owing to a sense of belonging and interfamilial and intergenerational mutual familiarity over decades.

Born into a multigenerational Teşvikiye family, I was raised in and lived in this neighborhood until I graduated from college. Since then, this place has remained my "home," and my base during ongoing fieldwork in Turkey. Hence, my ties with longtime locals go way back, whereas my familiarization with newcomers to the neighborhood mostly occurred during this project. During the first fieldtrip conducted for this project in early May 2007, I met with four new-comers to Teşvikiye who later became my key informants. One was a longtime friend from high school who had moved to Teşvikiye after her divorce. I met the second one, a journalist, when he interviewed me about my previous book. I came to know the other two newcomer families after they became new neigh-bors and friends of my extended family in Teşvikiye and our long-term neigh-bors. The rest of the newcomers were introduced to me over the following six years through deliberate initiatives or the ongoing efforts and cooperation of established Teşvikiye residents and their neighborly and familial connections.

Many of Teşvikiye's current residents who were born, raised, and have lived all of their lives in the neighborhood feel and identify as locals from Teşvikiye (called "Teşvikiyeli"). Some proudly stated in my interviews that they had shopped at the same local market and butcher's all their lives. Most have fam-ily and friends (*eş dost*) living there and greet people, shopkeepers, and ac-quaintances on every corner as they walk through the narrow back streets of the neighborhood. Teşvikiye not only accommodates a considerable secularist majority but also a relatively large and influential Jewish minority, which is a close-knit community.

However, in the new millennium, this apparently "closed" and "privatized" territory has gradually been broken up in several ways. Under a rapidly grow-ing free market that has incorporated the pious Muslims, Teşvikiye's non-negotiable secular homogeneity has been challenged in unforeseen ways. In the past decade, outsiders and visitors have gradually lost the historical distinc-tion between Teşvikiye and the next-door Nişantaşı quarter, which commer-cialized much earlier than Teşvikiye. Some took it as the expansion of Nişantaşı at the expense of Teşvikiye. Teşvikiye was not erased from the map, however, but transformed by the politics of consumption in unforeseen ways. The "new geographies of Muslim consumption"[3] expanded the boundaries of shopping, fun, and leisure.[4]

In my conversations about this transition, local residents used the term "pri-vate sphere" (*özel alan*) in a very specific way to refer to a "collectively shared neighborhood space" that kept strangers out, rather than an individual or do-mestic space. Against the backdrop of this exclusionary discourse, Teşvikiye had gradually been invaded by an explosion of consumers and window shop-pers in the post-1980 period. These people were coming from "outside," as the locals put it. Soon, with the proliferation of high-end boutiques, a new mall, expensive cafes, top-notch restaurants, and a two-floor entertainment complex named the Reasürans Pasajı (Arcade), Teşvikiye became a major attraction for head-scarved women. This entire transformation, propelled by the rise of neo-liberalism,[5] happened in a tiny downtown neighborhood with heavy traffic at any time during the day or night. The people who came to Teşvikiye to relax and be seen on the terraces of Euro-cafes and restaurants there were willing to pay dollars in double figures for a fancy coffee or lemonade. With the rise of Islamic capital, head-scarved women gradually became fixtures at these neoliberal sites of leisure during or in between their shopping.

PIOUS OUTSIDERS THREATEN LOCALS' PRIVACY AND FREEDOM

When Teşvikiye began to host street festivals for New Year's Eve at the turn of millennium, the neighborhood began to attract people from all over the city. The crowds crossed the lines of class, religion, and political orientation, including people from slums (varoşlar). Derin, a thirty-eight-year-old nonreligious divorced woman who had head-scarved colleagues at her workplace but was among many residents unwilling to share "their" streets with devout outsiders, told me:

> On the night of the New Year's Eve celebration, I just stepped out of my apartment building. The street was packed and noisy. I took only a few steps and said to my boyfriend quietly, "What a mess! Where do all these people come from?" Immediately, I received an unexpected and unfriendly answer from the woman next to me: "What is it? You don't want us here?" I turned and saw a face in a head scarf and smoky makeup in disturbing proximity to mine. Why do I have to confront a "total stranger" at New Year on my doorsteps? I need peace and quiet where I live.

Why were the sidewalks of Teşvikiye, which were even difficult to walk on in some tight streets, becoming so hard to share? Urbanites "claiming public space as their own, and often at the expense or displeasure of others" are not a new phenomenon. As David Trouille writes, "[W]hile public and private spaces are customarily distinguished according to legal access, the line between the two is often fluid and contextual."[6] This fluidity becomes more explicit the closer the contested public sites are to the contester's residence and doorstep. Derin's reactions were simply protective of a certain neighborhood territory that the residents saw as belonging to their nonreligious lifestyles and liberties. Derin did it by blurring the lines between her private sphere—home—and the sidewalk that was supposed to be a public space.[7] This territorial behavior is explicitly political. The locals of Teşvikiye displayed more and more impulsive and defensive reactions against actual or potential judgments and encroachment by pious visitors.

Gözde, a thirty-three-year-old, nonreligious single woman whose extended family was Teşvikiyeli, told me that she had started feeling like a stranger in her own neighborhood. Gözde changed partners often, and, as she was very relaxed about saying, she took her share in the one-night-stand culture that flourished in her favorite Teşvikiye bars. This kind of lifestyle did not stand out in Teşvikiye, since it was neither monitored nor stigmatized by the residents. In fact, with the growing number of open-air nightclubs in the Reasürans, Teşvikiye produced its own micro "swinger culture." This nightlife was strongly associated with people from certain professions, primarily advertising and the art world.

Gözde emphasized that this was an accepted lifestyle for a single young woman in her neighborhood circle; "Living in Teşvikiye provides a comfort zone for us, who want to be free," she said. When I asked what she meant by *free*, she replied, "Free from tradition, religion, and the other mechanisms of control." She added: "Recently, I have noticed people in Teşvikiye who, I know, would object to, judge, and condemn my lifestyle. I am not sure what exactly makes this place attractive for them, since they don't drink, dress, or party like we do. I feel as though I am losing my nest to them, my privacy, my domain, and the center of my life."

Henri Lefebvre argued that social practices in urban space have a dual character, pulling in two opposite directions, such as integration and segregation or attraction and repulsion: "The integration and participation obsess the non-participants, the non-integrated, those who survive among the fragments of a possible society and the ruins of the past; excluded from the city, at the gates of the urban."[8] The dual character of urban life underlies the tension between co-habitation and contestation. This can clearly be observed in Teşvikiye, with its close-knit community feeling arising from a collectively shared lifestyle with distinct boundaries.

Teşvikiye is bordered by a relatively large public park, a green area that includes a playground. The head-scarved women in this park seemed more diverse across the lines of class and social status than the high-spending Muslim women in consumption-oriented sites in the neighborhood. Most were mothers watching their children alone or in small groups. The dynamics of interaction between residents and visitors were much different in the park, since the locals did not make territorial claims over its use. This is important in many ways. It shows the intricate link between consumption, urban space, and politics.[9] It also suggests the fragmented nature of urban space, in which "distinctions . . . between 'regulars' and 'newcomers,' are not fixed." Hence, "power relations are made and enforced" differently at various sites of the same neighborhood.[10] As the majority of the local residents did not use the park,[11] dog walkers were the main locals to be seen there. In this largely upper-middle class residential downtown area, pious mothers comfortably used the park without notable intervention or competition from the locals.[12]

In the new millennium, many other urban places in Istanbul previously regarded as secular or non-Muslim, such as Beyoğlu and Şişli, attract the devout, but without really undoing their marginality. As increasingly visible actors in urban life, head-scarved women take advantage of the Istanbul metropolitan area by overstepping the implicit lines of segregation. But are they becoming recognized as citizens of Istanbul and gaining the "right to the city"?[13]

As long as the AKP, in its first term in power (2002–7), continued to maintain good relations with the secular state and pushed Turkey's membership of the European Union, the secularists remained as puzzled, albeit uncomfortable, residents. They complained but did not engage in direct confrontation with the pious visitors. A highly controversial move by the AKP government in 2007, the nomination of Abdullah Gül from within the AKP for the presidency, put an end to this uneasy coexistence. The presidential crisis divided state departments while also upsetting everyday life in Istanbul in unprecedented ways.

THE CONTESTED NEIGHBORHOOD IN A DIVIDED STATE: CULTURAL FAULT LINES OR POLITICAL CONTESTATION?

Reacting to the news that Istanbul had been selected as the European Capital of Culture in 2010, an Istanbul-based photographer complained to me:

> I live in the capital of culture, Istanbul, with so many "cultured" people on the street [sarcastic smile]. I was out taking photos, and an idiot yelled at me, "Hey, whose photo are you taking?" He was furious that I was taking his wife's picture. I responded, "Why would someone take a photo of your wife who is hiding under her turban [i.e., head scarf], especially when even you don't look at her, since you walk two meters ahead of her?"

The photographer's friends told him that he was lucky that this pious man had not beaten him up. Indeed, the incidence of violent confrontations in neighborhoods increased in Istanbul during the second half of the first decade of the new millennium. When I dug into the details of the incident, the photographer told me that the couple were carrying shopping bags, and that "this would be the reason why they came to [*his*] neighborhood." What else could have brought these "uncultured" people there? Although neighborhood-based battles may initially look merely like cultural wars between clashing lifestyles, they are, in fact, primarily politically driven.

The year 2007 marked the rupture of smooth engagement and cooperation between Muslim actors and the secular state. It announced the beginning of concomitant contestations within the state and in urban daily life. Since 2007, both the city and the state were increasingly divided from within by deep fault lines.[14] Upon the military's warning to the AKP on May 1, 2007, the government promptly created a cleavage within the state in the aftermath of the presidential crisis. The Constitutional Court backed up the military by cancelling the first round of the presidential election with the excuse that the quorum rule in parliament had been violated.

The synchrony of contestation in the state and the city is difficult to dismiss. The conflict between the state's branches was immediately accompanied by massive vocal street protest, the Republican Marches (Cumhuriyet Mitingleri) against the AKP in the country's largest cities. Cities remained the locus of major political conflicts, which were often wrongly assumed to be merely cultural clashes. As with the rise of Islamist movements in the cities in the post-1980 period, a secularist backlash was experienced in the big cities of Turkey in the first decade of the millennium.[15] Soja contends that the current financial crisis (2008–present) is primarily a crisis of urbanization.[16] Akin to this observation, the increasing centrality of religious–secular conflict in world politics is also a primarily spatial and urban-generated predicament.

The late spring and summer of 2007 raised a whole new set of questions for me as an ethnographer of everyday life. When I arrived a few days after the military's warning to the AKP, I found myself in the middle of ongoing conflict and harassment on the streets, in restaurants, cafes, hair salons, supermarkets, boutiques, malls, public parks, shuttles, and so on. Almost every public site was divided indiscriminately. Whether one was in a cab trying to have a conversation with the driver or trying to have a quiet smoke outside a mall or office, it was difficult to avoid the clash of political opinions. Perhaps more important than the ideational quarrels were the power struggles manifested in the clash of lifestyles between ordinary people in and beyond Teşvikiye.

Just after the secularist Republican Marches in April and May 2007, I interviewed Gözde again—this time with her small group of Teşvikiyeli female friends in a focus group. A group of young women in expensive brand jeans, designer sunglasses, manicured nails, and fashionable hairdos came to meet with me at one of the Euro cafes in the neighborhood. I immediately noted a dramatic change in their attitudes from the discomfort and intimidation they had expressed a few years before in the midst of an aggressive secularist backlash. They no longer felt like alienated strangers in their neighborhood, but like the "designated rescuers" of their place, their city, and their Republic from the invasion of the devout. In our long discussion, they expressed anger and solidarity against these invaders, whom they associated with the *varoş* (slums). They complained in unison that these head-scarved women were now not only entering "their" streets, but also turning their neighborhood into a place of chronic tension and confrontation.

The secularist residents of Teşvikiye I interviewed in the aftermath of the Republican Marches expressed resentment of the impact of the devout visitors on this place. Their territorial defensiveness was coupled with their anger about the "Islamist government's transformation of [their] Republic." That summer, I heard a lot of stories of hurt feelings, anger, and frustration from the residents of Teşvikiye; they felt as though their most intimate sentiments of belonging to their neighborhood and the state were being jeopardized by the new pious invaders. As democratically elected Muslim leaders secured their position and power in the AKP government, the most immediate reflex of these residents was to get rid of the pious visitors in the neighborhood. For secularist residents, the neighborhood was an easier target to rescue than the state seemed to be.

The secularist backlash was erupting everywhere around me in the neighborhood. A head-scarved woman who was shopping in a high-end store in the neighborhood was yelled at by another customer: "If you are going to cover the fashion you pay so much for with a giant head scarf, what is the point of shopping here? And also, what the hell are you doing in this neighborhood? Did you lose your way?" The head-scarved woman retaliated even more aggressively: "Do you know who I am?" she snapped. "I can buy you, your fashion, and your fashionable friends." The incident got out of control, and the staff and management had to get involved to calm both sides down. Over a cup of coffee with the then CEO of this large brand-name company and director of the department store, I was told that these kinds of confrontations were becoming the rule rather than the exception in Teşvikiye.

Lefebvre argues that the right to the city is neither a contractual nor a natural one: "In the most 'positive' terms, [the right to the city] signifies the right of the citizens and city dwellers and of groups . . . to appear on all networks and circuits of communication, information and exchange. This depends neither upon an urbanistic ideology nor upon an architectural intervention, but upon an essential quality or property of urban space: centrality."[17]

People have the right to urban space because they reside in the city, where they are entitled to participate in urban life regardless of their lifestyles, ideology, contractual ownership (of housing, etc.), or religious orientation. But most Teşvikiyeli residents whom I talked to in the aftermath of the Republican Marches neither recognized nor agreed with this right.

In addition to high-end stores, cafes, and restaurants, Teşvikiye also provides the most exquisite spa-like hairdressing salons for women who wander the fashion-ridden streets of the neighborhood. In the summer of 2008, a highly educated, pious twenty-nine-year-old woman, Meral, told me that she had been slighted and ostracized in one of the women's high-end brand-name hair salons in Teşvikiye. Female customers sitting next to her said loudly: "If you're going to cover your hair, why spend your money on these expensive styles? Why don't you use this money for charity as your religion is supposed to teach you?"

"I'd never go back there but for the fact that I like the hair stylist," Meral told me. But she was going to go back, because she was continually drawn to the fashions that she was ready to fight for. She asked me: "Why do Istanbulites think that believing in God must make you blind to pleasures and devoid of taste and fashion? How did this dichotomy between Muslim piety and pleasure emerge, which bans us, the devout, from enjoying life? God does not ban me, but the women in the hairdresser's try to do so."[18]

Meral's objection must not be taken lightly as yet another trivial neighborhood catfight between Muslim and secular women. As Mike Featherstone predicted, "[W]e are moving toward a society without fixed status groups in which . . . styles of life (manifest in choice of clothes, leisure activities, consumer goods, bodily dispositions) which are fixed to specific groups have been surpassed." Featherstone's discussion on lifestyle and consumer culture has implications for individual liberties and spatiality of freedom. Being a pious Muslim, secular, socialist, or capitalist does not prevent people from questioning and/or violating "long-held fashion codes." The secular residents of Teşvikiye have long been aware of and assertive about "the war against uniformity."[19]

However, they seem to refuse to concede a similar kind of freedom to pious Muslim women who are implicitly resisting fixed status roles and lifestyles that were prescribed to them. If the secularists of Teşvikiye were genuine believers in freedom of lifestyle, as they seem to claim, would they not be in full support to Meral and the other head-scarved women carving out their own individual freedoms in Teşvikiye? Were these occasions missed opportunities for emerging alliances for emancipation, with both the local and pious visitor women failing to see beyond the Islamist–secular antagonism?

"The neighborhood must be cleansed of people who are not like 'us,'" Ayça, another longtime Teşvikiyeli, said after the Republican Marches. Educated abroad in interior design, she had founded her own business when she returned to Istanbul. When I asked her what she meant by "people like us," she explained: "You know . . . educated secular people who follow their leader, Atatürk, . . . 'us' . . . you know what I mean. I was so happy to see *people like us* in the Republican street protest in April."[20]

Ayça's dissociation of "us" from the "pious Muslims" cannot be understood merely on the basis of clashing cultures, class, education, or urban lifestyle. Most of the head-scarved women shopping at expensive boutiques or eating at upscale restaurants in Teşvikiye were neither of lower socioeconomic status nor uneducated. In the absence of spatial boundaries of segregation, the cultural, economic, and educational distinctions were no longer sufficient to differentiate Ayça's elite status from that of the new devout bourgeoisie. Hence, she was adopting another strong qualifier of group distinction, "followers of Kemal Atatürk." Although I have known Ayça for many years, and followed up with her in interviews from the late 1990s up to 2011, I had never heard her talking so politically. I also do not remember her emphasizing loyalties to Atatürk so strongly before the street protests in 2007. In fact, this was most probably the first time I had heard anything so distinctly ideological from her mouth.

Would these "new" young Atatürkists of Teşvikiye be so committed to this spatial and political battle if so many other distinctions between them and the new Islamic high-spenders had not declined so rapidly? The intersectionality of class, gender, and religion is evident in the sites of political confrontation. Although Teşvikiye leisure and entertainment facilities attracted well-off pious women, these places were not creating platforms of "shared culture," but rather mostly tension, disputes, and verbal assault. Cultural and spatial proximity was not solving but reinforcing political conflict,[21] and street-level confrontation peaked more than ever in neighborhood life. In the face of decreasing socioeconomic and cultural distinctions between the pious and the secularist, urban residents have increasingly leaned toward political contestation. The juxtaposition of the Turkish Republic's founding father Mustafa Kemal Atatürk with God on the streets of Teşvikiye is indicative of the overpoliticization of ordinary residents. The gradual mixing of Teşvikiye through the entrance of the pious highspenders has politicized the neighborhood. The fact that this is unintended politics, unplanned by urban planners or political leaders, does not make it less political and more cultural or economic. Hence, although the neighborhood conflicts originate from seemingly cultural discords of lifestyle and socioeconomic issues of consumption and social status, they end in sheer political confrontation. Unsurprisingly, the conflict in Teşvikiye is rooted in the fault lines that cross the boundaries of the neighborhood into the national territory and even the Turkish diaspora abroad.

WHAT LIES BEYOND THE ISLAMIST–SECULARIST CLASHES ON THE STREETS?

Clashes between longtime secularist Teşvikiyeli and devout newcomers were numerous. "While the relative accessibility and openness of public spaces provide the conditions for *inter-group* conflict to unfold, the degree and intensity of conflict over territory certainly varies," David Trouille observes. "[C]laiming space is best understood as a process whereby a group defines itself, and is recognized by others, as the *established proprietors* of that space."[22]

But, what happens when the locals themselves object to the legitimacy of the claims of the so-called established proprietors? Contestations crack the locals' claims for territoriality in public space. In this way, the above-discussed instances of urban unrest push for a reshaping of spatial configurations of right of usage—not only of the locals but also that of newcomers and of all potential users in general.

In a state where the new Muslim power elite replaced the old secular state elite, urban divides within neighborhoods must not be reduced to odd accidents that are exceptional, apolitical, or cultural. The street-level conflict must be situated in the larger context of power struggles within the polity, the governing institutions of the state, and beyond. The proprietors of both power and space are not fixed groups in democracies; they shift as the result of ongoing negotiations and power struggles. Most important, these neighborhood tensions must not be seen as local struggles. Rather, they are the manifestations of struggles for freedom at many levels: freedom of lifestyle, mobility, dissent, expression, and thought. Clearly, the contestations do not originate in the high-end mall or hair salon. Likewise, they do not end there. Even though the snapshots of neighborhood conflicts between the pious and the secularist may attract most attention, neighborhood conflicts are embedded within fault lines on a much larger scale caused by multiple conflicts. Ultimately, what is referred as "neighborhood pressure" is a local embodiment of disputes for political decency and civility. Clearly, these struggles are neither shaped nor solved solely by urban residents or planners.[23] This is what makes urban contestations and spatiality of freedom multiscalar. The next chapter ties the local and national scales of spatial politics to the global level through the international links, roots, and mobility of local Teşvikiyeli.

3 AFFINITIES IN THE ZONES OF FREEDOM

THERE HAS BEEN widespread consensus among scholars on the "creeping authoritarianism" apparent in Turkish democracy during the second and third terms of AKP rule.[1] As the government's tolerance for criticism and dissent decreased dramatically, pessimism about the recent direction of Turkish democracy has prevailed in both social life and scholarship. Leading social scientists have expressed despair about the possibility of a compromise or cooperation given the deep political and social cleavages.[2] Political leaders, particularly the political elite in government and opposition, have largely failed in coming to any kind of agreement or forming coalitions.

The AKP's attempts at institutional reform fell short of satisfying the yearnings for democratization. Constitutional reform in 2010 deserves attention in this respect. Turkey's current constitution is the most secular in the Muslim world, but it also carries an explicit legacy of authoritarian rule. A product of the 1980 military coup, the constitution is remarkably weak when it comes to protecting civil rights and individual liberties, but strong at protecting the state from having to account to its citizens and civil society. Despite this, the controversy between supporters and foes of the constitutional changes that the AKP submitted to a referendum on September 12, 2010, had little, if anything, to do with expanding freedoms. Rather than engaging with the AKP on constitutional agendas, its secularist opponents limited their disputes to whether that government was entitled to change the constitution. Concretely, the opposition was mostly concerned about "the change of balance of power in the judicial system,"[3] rather than the long-standing issue of individual liberties and civil rights. The constitution's most burning defects in the area of rights and freedoms were largely neglected because the opposition's main voices were motivated less by love of liberty than by fear of Erdoğan's growing power and domination of Turkish political life. Hence, instead of genuinely aiming at democratic institutional solutions, the debate leaned toward personalized power struggles—being for or against Erdoğan's individual cult and his party's increasing powers.[4] Despite Turkish city dwellers' increasing support for democratic practices, the nation's political elite was still entangled in ideological rivalry, rather than jointly committed to a deeper democracy.

Although, from this perspective, the outlook for a democratic recovery in this polarized world looks bleak, this dark picture is often the result of an exclusive focus on the level of political institutions and the political elite.[5] The regression of Turkish democracy under the AKP's electoral hegemony should not be allowed to obscure victories in urban politics. More specifically, the persisting polarization at the elite level should not be permitted to divert attention from democratic alliances and challenges to authoritarianism in many places and on many levels. We live in a historical period when urban contestations extend beyond the boundaries of formal political channels and shape political society. How does Teşvikiye translate its deep fault lines into new bonds, cooperation, and alliances? A close look reveals the contradiction between the dynamic neighborhood and a stagnant polity.

As Teşvikiye gradually evolved into a loud, chaotic, anonymous place, with noisy clubs, bars, and restaurants extending their tables onto the sidewalks and ceaseless traffic, many of its affluent longtime residents left for the expensive gated communities mushrooming on the outskirts of Istanbul.[6] They have been replaced by newcomers who don't mind the changes and contact with masses of visitors and strangers. In fact, unlike the longtime residents who moved out, many of the newcomers actually like having so many attractions drawing diverse people into their neighborhood. "Walking home and not needing a car after a couple of drinks is a luxury in a city with so much traffic, where having to take a breathalyzer test is the rule rather than the exception," one said. "Downtown is emancipating!"

Teşvikiye's transition led to a filtering process, or a litmus test, for retention of residents. Those who chose to remain in the neighborhood were a distinct, more diversity-friendly group of longtime residents. Some of these stayed for what the downtown neighborhood offers overall, *despite* some of the new inconveniences. Others stayed as a politically conscious choice, because they not only fit well into but also helped shape what Teşvikiye was becoming. Similarly, the newcomers were either diversity- or freedom-seekers who enjoyed how Teşvikiye was evolving and took pleasure in participating in the remaking of an old neighborhood. This group is probably best represented by some of the recent art produced in Teşvikiye—a remarkable synthesis arising from polarization. Teşvikiye in fact hosts some internationally renowned local artists whose work trespasses across boundaries thought to be impenetrable. But what kind of association can be drawn between the unruly nature of artistic synthesis and "transgression" and the new political mixing in the neighborhood triggered by the spatial inclusion of devout high-spenders?

BORDER CROSSING: FROM MUTUALLY EXCLUSIVE SEGREGATION TO INCLUSIVE MIXING

The internationally famous Turkish artist Berkan said of the polarized politics of art in Turkey:

> *Affedersiniz* [excuse my language]. If a *laikçi* (secularist) were to find a piece of paper with *çük* [dick] written on it in the old alphabet, he would condemn the old script as bigotry without knowing what it meant. If a pious calligrapher found the same piece of paper on the floor, he would kiss it and put it on his forehead (a gesture of respect in Turkish culture) out of reverence for the old script, regardless of what it says on it.

Such unthinking partisanship, Berkan lamented, was where things stood at present. Art was torn between two "fundamentalist" groups, the worshippers and haters of the old Turkish script. Clearly, the rift was shaped by politics rather than taste or appreciation for fine calligraphy. During our long conversation in his charming condo on one of the most vibrant streets in Teşvikiye, he used the term "fundamentalist" several times to refer to blind devotion to a belief, doctrine, or ideology. Prior to my interview with him, my interviews with leading calligraphers in Istanbul revealed deep-rooted frustration with the way the early Republic had banned the old script. The vandalized handwritten manuscripts in the early Republic haunted them. Not surprisingly, in the context of recent fault lines, the old script has become one of the objects of contestation between these two groups.

From Berkan's perspective, at the extreme level, blind devotion to Islamic tradition(alism) and secular West(ernism) were quite indistinguishable in form and content from one another. He emphasized that the similarity between them was manifest in their obsessive need to preserve sterile artistic forms by refusing and degrading, not only other forms, but also any synthesis of the two. Berkan saw this as a dead end for originality. This conflict between Westernist secularists and pious Islamists amounts to a war between two conservative groups, each claiming to be the gatekeepers in politics, not only in Turkey but also across the Middle East at different degrees. The agendas of both seem to be similar: blocking any new avenues for freedom of expression, criticism, contestation and creative ways of inclusion and blending. Berkan's work parted ways from this rigid exclusionism and polarization. He integrated the calligraphic forms and aesthetics of Islamic arts into modern art. Put differently, his art stood up for mixing and inclusion against the rigidity of ideological polarization. Our long chat made clear his passion for freedom of experimenting with artistic forms that were conventionally divided, segregated, and alienated from each other in Turkish culture.

In the middle of our conversation, he showed me one of his pieces saved on his computer and asked me to interpret what I was seeing. I looked at the mannequin on his screen dressed in a white wedding gown, in smoky makeup, standing at the very front edge of a ferry carrying passengers between the Asian and European sides of the Bosphorus. I said, "I see a sad-looking or perhaps tired bride." He smiled again and explained: "This is a hopeless [çaresiz] bride who keeps traveling between Asia and Europe. She is exhausted because she cannot decide whether she should marry the West or the East [he smiled]. I made her travel for weeks on that public ferry during the heated discussions on Turkey's EU membership."

Both the physical split between Europe and Asia constituted by the Bosphorus channel and the exhaustion evident in the "nomadic" bride's face were symptomatic of the politics of contestation in Turkey's divided urban space. Berkan's work linked the spatial divide of the Bosphorus as a physical fault line and the ongoing conflict generated by its sociopolitical counterparts. His art illustrated the unruly nature of the synthesis of artistic forms and political processes. Mixing was possible, but it called for an arduous commitment to questioning boundaries and the hard work of resistance to fault lines.

During the next couple of hours, Berkan took me on a pleasant tour of his art both on his computer and in his museumlike home. His place was full of pieces of art he had collected, which he displayed on every corner, wall, table, and even on the floor. His collection blended into his own work mixing forms that were "supposed" to remain separate, or rather pure, according to the groups he referred to as fundamentalist. My previous interviews with calligraphers who were critical or unaccepting of Berkan's work confirmed his claims: he was crossing boundaries and mixing forms that made him a "trespasser" in the eyes of the conventional calligraphers. His use of calligraphic images and old script in other modern forms of art was criticized by the calligraphers not only for artistic reasons but also for religious and political ones. Berkan's art was a blunt challenge to all sterile forms and exclusions framed by borders that were established to maintain segregation and turned into unforgiving fault lines. His home and workshop were the spatial embodiment of the new hybridity that Teşvikiye was breeding, but his art was regarded as "contamination" by both devout calligraphers and secular modernists alike, who felt intimidated by such by mixing.

In the middle of our conversations, I noted something that I did not expect. Although critical of both orthodox secularist and Islamist perspectives, Berkan's work embraced a highly provocative amalgamation of spiritual/mystic and profane aesthetics. As we walked toward another room full of exquisite art, I noticed in the hallway some framed black-and-white photographs of old wise-looking men with long white beards, who, Berkan told me, were Sufis. After listening to him for hours on his insurgent, provocative art, these pictures made me curious. I asked him curiously without giving any prior thought to the appropriateness of my question: "Do you believe in God?" The moment my question came out of my mouth, I realized that I was intruding on his privacy, not just spatially in his home but also spiritually. When he smiled wisely and warmly, I took a deep breath, because he was not offended. "Yes," he said. "You are surprised, aren't you?"

Why was I surprised, anyway? Over the past decade and a half of hands-on field research, I had met hundreds of practicing Muslims who believed in God and expressed it in their own distinct ways, both personally and collectively. My reaction was an amalgam of the spatial politics I was being introduced to. The fact that Berkan's art displayed in his private sphere challenged conventional categories, including the politics of sexuality and gender, made it difficult for me to see through the hybridity. I had difficulty recognizing that people, places, and art that straddled borders were not essentially a different kind, a new species, or unworldly, as they might be seen by conservative fans of boundaries. The hybrid was not entirely removed or disconnected from the elements it united. Rather, the synthesis was a cross section[7] *where* differences and conflicts met and interacted. From a spatially sensitive perspective, it was important that this meeting, mingling, and mixing was taking place in the heart of Teşvikiye, a place that was blending people from previously ideologically divided camps.

Berkan's condo was in the heart of Teşvikiye both symbolically and physically, where differences, discrepancies, and disagreements were to be reconciled.

As he explained to me piece by piece, Sufism rather than orthodox Islam inspired the mystic themes in his work. Typically, Sufism is known for the tolerance and ritual-oriented egalitarian culture associated with the folk and their "low culture," as opposed to the doctrinal, hierarchical rigidity of the "high culture."[8] In one of his pieces, Berkan printed symbols of identity politics, such as gay and lesbian, feminist, and Kurdish symbols from 1980s and 1990s in Turkey, on Fatima's hand, an apotropaic amulet named for the Prophet Muhammad's daughter Fatima, which is believed to ward off the evil eye, but also, referred to as *ehli beht*, represents "the people in the household" (*hane halkı*), specifically, the family who live together. Berkan said, "all of these repressed and marginalized 'Others' who have been suffering, are our *hane halkı*, our household" in Turkey. Berkan's appreciation of mysticism was probably the most surprising part of our conversation for me. The fusion of religious, sacred symbols with his liberal politics aroused harsh reactions not only in Turkey but also abroad. Islamist media, such as *Yeni Şafak Daily* and the Samanyolu television station (of the Gülen Movement), were infuriated by the representation of gay culture on a sacred symbol, Fatima's hand. In Denmark, there has been a request to remove his piece from the exhibit. There were petitions against it. Briefly, Berkan's art on the inclusion of "the excluded" in the intimate place symbolized by the "household" led to furious contestation internationally. This is because it crossed borders that were not supposed to be trespassed. But according to whom? These gatekeepers and power holders in art were representative of political authoritarianism that benefits from maintaining the fault lines.

Political decency and tolerance become central assets of everyday politics in these inclusive places. First and foremost, the trespassers and the places that integrate the border crossers have to be polite and accepting of one another, and they need to be sheltered in a safe place. Moreover, "the importance of being civil"[9] matters most in these mixed places, because they need to establish, and rely heavily on, methods of contestation and (dis)agreement, which make the mixing possible.

Polarized camps, such as the pious Islamic calligraphers and Westernist secular artists, often find trespassers difficult to understand. They are therefore often regarded as simply strange and "out of place." That is why a secular/impious bigot or a religious/pious progressive seems to perplex people most. Pious and progressive are often regarded as conflicting categories. But upon careful consideration, piety and impiety are qualifiers on a religious axis, while bigotry and progressiveness are political positions. There are numerous possible combinations that crosscut religious and political orientations. There are democracies that respect and accommodate religion (such as the United States) and dictatorships that ban or restrict religion (such as the former USSR). However, the most usual milieu for creating new bonds and/or alliances across presumably antagonistic groups is an inclusive and safe space that is capable of containing and accommodating conflict. These places are most often obscured or left unnoticed by social science, because they are regarded as simply marginal, exceptional, or, at best, unrepresentative. The selective neglect of these places must be problematized, since it has political implications. The question to be asked is: of what are these inclusive places "unrepresentative"? Are they unrepresentative of a world divided by civilizational fault lines, as Samuel Huntington contends? This could be true if segregation, voluntary or not, were an inherent quality of social or civic life. But it is not. Then, why have these inclusive places been understudied in urban or political studies, although they play a central role in diffusing conflict and/or undoing divides? One reason is that they disturb people's comfort zones by puncturing and gradually opening up established boundaries, whether sociopolitical, religious, or spatial.[10]

In 2010 and 2011, I interviewed six of the most prominent calligraphers in Istanbul, most of whom were based in religiously oriented neighborhoods such as Üsküdar and Ümraniye. The only two exceptions to this geographical trend were Mahmut, a calligrapher who was an architect by education, and Berkan, who included calligraphic forms in his art. Both Mahmut and Berkan worked and lived in Teşvikiye. They were both crossing boundaries between Islamic and modern art by mixing forms of each in their work.

Uğur Derman, the main Islamic art critic and teacher, who is referred to as the father of Islamic arts in Turkey,[11] told me in my interview with him: "I do not respect 'modern art' because I don't like the strange, arbitrary combination of things [çelik çomak]. But look [showing me a piece on his wall at his home], I have this tulip-shaped calligraphy by Mahmut. . . . It says God [Allah]. Now, this is a different thing. It is unique. It is precious."

The religiously oriented calligraphers that I interviewed were highly critical of Mahmut's art, which was "a modern product carved out of classical calligraphy."[12] None of them acknowledged Berkan's work either, which they regarded as an unacceptable patchwork of arbitrary insertions of calligraphic forms into modern art.

Although Mahmut shared the moral and religious universe of other pious calligraphers in Istanbul, the location of his workshop and his home was atypical. When I asked him why, unlike other calligraphers, he was based in Teşvikiye, he responded that his clientele was in Teşvikiye. The people who enjoyed, cherished, and purchased his art lived or at least shopped there. Despite his religious personality and lifestyle, Mahmut and his art thus belonged to this neighborhood. There was an elective affinity between art and politics that crossed fault lines. Diverging pathways merged in Teşvikiye.

THE EMERGENCE OF THE NEW URBAN RESIDENT IN TEŞVİKİYE?

The temptations of Teşvikiye included, but were not limited to, encountering opposing political views and incongruent lifestyles. The cultural capital that the neighborhood provides through the numerous bookstores, art galleries, and theaters is a major attraction for diversity seekers. It goes without saying that university students, intellectuals, writers, and artists were at the top of the list of these highly educated newcomers. Some have moved into small studios and one-bedroom apartments on the more affordable outskirts of Teşvikiye that border socioeconomically lower quarters, particularly Beşiktaş, Fulya, and Akaretler.[13] While the economic class of most of these newcomers was lower than that of the longtime upper-middle-class residents of Teşvikiye, the newcomers' social status, in the Weberian sense, and their cultural capital, in Bourdieu's terms, were a good fit for this neighborhood.

Unlike head-scarved women, these secular newcomers were easily accepted and integrated into the unspoken but highly cherished lifestyles and codes of conduct of the neighborhood. Partly because, unlike the devout, these newcomers happily adapted to the neighborhood-specific consumption patterns banned by Islam, such as drinking alcohol, dressing in unconventional and sometimes revealing ways, buying pork from the neighborhood charcuterie, and so on. These secular newcomers carved out their own realm of freedom in this highly contested space, where most longtime residents felt stifled by the invasion of devout outsiders.

Unlike the old elite of Teşvikiye, who frequently had several expensive cars and needed a lot of parking spaces that Teşvikiye could no longer offer, these newcomers preferred walking or public transportation, especially by the shuttles that line up on small Teşvikiye streets. More important, they did not mind sharing public transport vehicles with head-scarved consumers or other visitors from various class backgrounds. In my daily use of public transportation,

I noted that the old shuttle cars that ran between Teşvikiye and other neighborhoods were filled increasingly by these newcomers and the devout visitors. Their coexistence in close proximity did not create any tension between them. On the contrary, this was a desired habitat for the diversity-seeking newcomers.

In my interviews, these secular newcomers were clearly cognizant of their differences, tensions, and splits with the majority of longtime secular residents of Teşvikiye. Ahmet, a thirty-eight-year-old journalist who had moved to Teşvikiye almost a year before, observed to me:

> The entire building is occupied by people who have known each other all their lives. . . . [and] they agree strikingly on political issues. They all dislike seeing the symbols of Islam in the neighborhood, on television, or hearing about them in a conversation. I have a hard time talking to them about anything that relates to Islam. . . . I find it easier to connect with their children, who are more or less of my generation. Some of these younger Teşvikiyeli are happy to see a more mixed neighborhood. Some of this generation have married and/or moved out. A few have stayed in Teşvikiye and moved into other, often smaller, places. I was introduced to a couple of these relatively younger Teşvikiyeli by their parents, my neighbors. . . . We chat about the neighborhood, to which most of them feel a strong sense of belonging. Except for the nostalgia for their childhood, they say, they like it better this way—a more complicated but also more diverse and exciting place to live.

Ahmet introduced me to Merve, the daughter of his new landlord. Merve, who was thirty-six, had spent all her life in Teşvikiye, except for her graduate education in the United States. After returning to Turkey a few years earlier, she had moved in with her boyfriend in a smaller condo in Teşvikiye. My frequent chats with Ahmet, Merve, and their peers revealed an apparent generational shift in the politics of space among longtime Teşvikiyeli:

> It is not just the new faces of piety that disturb the Teşvikiyeli old-timers. My parents and their friends can't stop complaining about not knowing the people who walk on "their" streets and who move into "their" neighborhood anymore [she twice puts the word "their" in quotation marks with her hands]. They are upset about continual robberies and would rather keep the neighborhood as a "gated community" [she laughs]. They talk darkly about the new tenants at the Beşiktaş and Fulya borders [referred to as the "lower" streets, *aşağı sokaklar*]. I moved to those "lower" streets. My partner and I really enjoy the new anonymity in this place. People move in and move out quite often, as their work

contracts end or as they travel. It is much more fun than the sterile streets of old Teşvikiye, where you could not walk with a boyfriend without introducing him to many people on the street. There was no anonymity, because everyone would somehow be connected to one another though friends and family.

Teşvikiye's new divides extend beyond the splits between secular newcomers and old-timers into more complicated splits *within* the longtime resident community itself. While some of these disagreements were the effect of generational differences within longtime resident families, some political dissent I encountered was independent of age and generation. These new urban residents of Teşvikiye, newcomers or not, have become "committed participants" who take sides in the contestations over the inclusion of pious Muslims. In my interviews, several expressed discontent with the secularist backlash in the neighborhood, sharing their experiences of witnessing the verbal harassment and insulting of head-scarved women and disapproving of all exclusionary and offensive behavior. Unlike some of their longtime Teşvikiyeli counterparts, the new secular residents cheerfully accommodated pious Muslims in everyday settings. By successfully distinguishing their dislike for the Islamic government from their feelings about ordinary Muslim visitors, they interacted with the latter as equal citizens. Instead of being threatened by the lifestyles of either the pious visitors or the longtime secularists, these new democratic voices complained in my interviews about the violation of the codes of civility through shaming or harassment in their neighborhood.

AN EMERGING COMMUNITY OF ACTIVISTS, OR THE POLITICS OF LIFESTYLE?

In his discussion of radical democracy, Mark Purcell uses the term "agonism," as distinct from "antagonism," to explain the political dynamics of local democratic contestations. According to Purcell, unlike antagonism, agonism "refers to groups consciously struggling *against each other to gain hegemony*, but each recognizes the other's right to exist."[14] The new democratic residents of Teşvikiye are good illustrations of the shift from antagonism to agonism described by Purcell, since they condemn exclusionary political hegemony by the secularists in the neighborhood, as they simultaneously condemn the hegemony of Islamic AKP in the government. The ethnographic evidence on Teşvikiye supports Purcell's argument that conflict and political pluralism are two sides of the same coin. Both are imperative for democracy.[15]

In my multiple visits to Teşvikiye in 2011 and 2012, most of my conversations with the freedom-seeking newcomers revealed that they were quite content to share their most immediate neighborhood with pious Muslim visitors. At the same time, our discussions often revolved around violations of freedom such as suspicious arrests and unsubstantiated long-term detentions under the AKP government. Upon hearing these shared sentiments, I started searching for democratic activism and some deliberate advocacy of "urban democracy" in the neighborhood.[16] However, I soon found out that none of the freedom-seeking residents I interviewed were either organizing or involved in neighborhood networks or any form of local community activism. The influence of these new secular residents is simply in their accepting, accommodating presence and lifestyle.[17] Their ways of life include respect for others' freedoms and right to the city. They change the sociopolitical dynamics in the neighborhood simply by being and residing there and participating in urban life. Their presence mitigates hardedged confrontation in an unintended, rather than collectively mobilized way.

In this respect, it is important to note that it is the *loose ties* of the least embedded newcomers to the neighborhood that make the spatial politics of the new Teşvikiyeli remarkable, not the close-knit community. Put differently, a certain urban individuality, rather than communalism, rules the new politics of Teşvikiye. The newcomers ignite new dynamics and shifting loyalties in the neighborhood without really being part of the older ones. Hence, the key is not the shared histories of residential community, but the inclusion and merging of new residents with various pasts and future. Neither is the emerging consensus and accommodation generated by local activists' mobilization. The emergent bonds and alliances for the freedoms and rights *of all* do not originate in associational life or active networking. On the contrary, loose quotidian and sporadic relations predominate among neighbors and friends in the neighborhood. In this sense, politics of space, neighborhood, and lifestyle are different from political engagements of civil society, grassroots organizations, and community activism. Many urbanites may not be participating in civic life and organizations.[18] However, the so-called "declining social capital" does not undo the fact that many urbanites are politically influential, since they may express, practice, and influence power dynamics by simply living, rather than through organized collective action or memberships in associations.[19]

Most important, the new inhabitant discussed above becomes more effective in inclusion to the extent that s/he lets go other ideological, identitarian, and/or communitarian commitments. Many of my interviewees were engaged in similar critiques of both the pro-Islamic government and its weak secularist opposition. They accused both the government and its opposition of violating civil liberties and rights. As the emerging alliances of the newcomers that come out of this politics of presence are neither strategic nor mobilizational, they have little or no reflection in political society or party politics yet. Hence, it should not be surprising that we do not see a clear reflection of this political position in the secularist opposition party, the Republican People's Party (Cumhuriyet Halk Partisi; CHP), or in party politics in general in Turkey.[20]

The shared critique of the regression of democracy did not emerge out of gatherings or community organizations. In the larger national context in Turkey, where political authoritarianism has crept in, Teşvikiye and other highly contested sites attracted the diversity- and freedom-seeking residents. At the larger national scale of politics, these democratic urbanites may exist as a scattered minority group that is at best *loosely connected*, if at all. But their recent concentration in certain neighborhoods and other urban places makes a bigger difference. For example, in Teşvikiye, they are no longer a trivial minority but a middle class with transformative influence and powers. This kind of resistance to political authoritarianism does not always require an organized countermovement, but simply a spatial turn in political advocacy of rights and freedoms.

The new inhabitant may not be too deeply embedded in the local community, but s/he is a cornerstone in larger spatial and political processes that bridge nationwide fault lines. More concretely, the new resident is a microcosm of a new urbanism that consciously refuses to take sides on the Islamist-secularist divides in the city. Ironically, this refusal strengthens his/her cause and potential to resist the authoritarian government. His/her attitude is underlined by a distance from each end of the continuum. His/her democratic priorities cut across this binary. The politics of the new democratic inhabitant confuses not only the secularist old-timers, but also the pious Muslim visitors. Many people in both groups could not make sense of this relatively new progressive urban politics. The new secular residents of Teşvikiye readily accept the pious visitors or others spontaneously "on the spot." This is an "attitudinal response," to use Linz and Stepan's terminology, or a political stance that does not need prior preparation, contemplation, or mobilization. These nondeliberate linkages between newcomers and devout visitors work to the extent that their political trajectories and spatial locations merge with others in defense of more freedoms and rights. According to them, these liberties and rights apply *indiscriminately* for all citizens—not just for themselves or for one group. For example, their advocacy for the freedom to wear the head scarf or have faith-based ways of life goes consistently together with their advocacy of recognition for other marginalized groups, such as Kurds, women, or the LGBT.

Nevertheless, several of the newcomers I interviewed mentioned that their love and passion for freedom and rights has been ridiculed as naïve. Their defense of democratic liberties for all has often been pejoratively labelled as *liboş* (slang term for flaky liberalism that is pretentious or without substance). A few also mentioned that their progressive politics was looked down upon as "'American liberalism" and was dismissed as "nice, but useless" (*hoş ama boş*). One informant complained: "It is easier to insist on and stick to Islam–secularist partisanship or defend class 'equality' rather than to fight for freedoms in this country, since freedom is the most 'underdeveloped' and misunderstood subject for the majority here."[21] The misperception of political liberalism also does not help in this context, along with implicit hostility toward the passion for individual freedoms in Turkey.[22] This can partly be explained by the confusion of individual freedoms with the ethics of self-interest promoted by neoliberal economics. The conflation of freedom with selfish forms of self-interest[23] goes hand in hand with neglect, misunderstanding, and denial of the political liberalism that originated with Enlightenment thinking.[24]

LOCALS THAT BELONG ACROSS NATIONAL BORDERS

Today, Teşvikiye is a neighborhood that includes and shelters an internationally connected community situated in a global political economy. In addition to the foreigners, who came to Turkey to teach languages or work as expatriates, the neighborhood attracts a noticeable section of resident citizens of Turkey, who either travel internationally on a regular basis or reside simultaneously in different parts of the world. The multiple residencies enable these Teşvikiyeli to participate in the social and political life of other democracies. It is not too unusual for the new generation of Teşvikiyeli to hold permanent residency status or citizenship in Western countries. Some have married across national boundaries, raised children between (or beyond) religious and ethnic groups, earned degrees abroad, and/or bought property abroad. Others have lived through long commutes between work abroad and family obligations in Teşvikiye. Yet these international Teşvikiyelis have not lost their feelings of belonging. Nor is their social presence in the life of Teşvikiye diminished. The Nobel Prize winner Orhan Pamuk, for example, comes from a longtime Teşvikiyeli family. However, since receiving the Nobel Prize, he has been challenged politically for his writings and has been criticized harshly and harassed for his personal political views expressed in his books. Between these violations of freedom of expression and the international invitations he receives, he spends a lot of time out of the country. Recently, he taught in New York City. However, in the eyes of the public, this has not weakened his personal ties to the neighborhood about which he has written extensively. For his readers and the residents of Teşvikiye, Pamuk perhaps remains more Teşvikiyeli than Teşvikiye's permanent residents who have never moved out.

Arturo Escobar's concern that "with globalization place often drops out of sight" is mitigated by Teşvikiye's famous global residents. Escobar rightly makes the point that the local has a "place-specific (even if not place-bound or place-determined) way of endowing the world with meaning."[25] At the same time, master works of globally connected and internationally renowned intellectuals emerge out of their place-specific sensitivities, as in Pamuk's brilliant novel *The Black Book*, about his neighborhood, Teşvikiye. From this perspective, place becomes an integral part of world politics and global political economy.

In addition to international artists and intellectuals who reside there, such as the journalist Ahmet Hakan, the neighborhood is highly connected to other parts of the world through residents from ethnic minority groups. The influential Jewish community is intimately linked to other world cities, and Turkish Armenian jewelers catering to Teşvikiyeli women and recent visitors regularly travel abroad to explore new trends and fashions or find Western partners. One of them, who has become a good friend of mine over a decade of intense conversations about life and politics in his small jeweler's shop in the center of Teşvikiye, told me about his increasingly heterogeneous clientele:

> I used to sell almost exclusively to the residents of Teşvikiye and Nişantaşı. Now, I rarely have any idea which customer is from where. Even you, do you consider yourself a resident of Teşvikiye? [We laugh]. Also, tastes have become more eclectic, and carry fewer class symbols. Initially, I was intimidated by the head-scarved consumers, and thought that they would object to my Armenian origins. But it turns out that they care about my jewels not my religion or ethnicity. I personally don't like the Islamic government, but through my chats with devout Muslims, I have learned, to my surprise, that some of the high-spending Muslim customers don't agree with the government's anti-democratic moves either. . . . I am happy to be able to interact and chat with these people, with whom I had no contact up until a decade ago.

He is not involved in any community activism or political decision-making about the restructuring of the neighborhood. But, along with his established and rapidly growing consumer networks across cities, countries, and continents, he not only serves as an agent of the economic integration of Istanbul into global markets,[26] but has also been an important player in neighborhood politics, since his store brings people from different religious and political orientations into close proximity with one another.

While there is a clear class element that has facilitated the global mobility of the children of longtime residents, the middle-class newcomers owe their international mobility largely to their careers and professional success. Most of the newcomers that I interviewed took strong positions against the pro-Islamic government's violation of rights and liberties. Many emphasized particularly the AKP's crackdown on Kurdish citizens (until the attempts for peace process) or unfair detentions and arrests of people from all walks of life and political standing, including the secularist opposition party. This clearly reveals that their conflict is not one of Islamism versus secularism, but on the continuum of authoritarianism versus liberal democracy.

Almost none of the newcomers with whom I talked voted for the AKP government or its secularist opposition, the CHP. Some stated that they voted for the Pro-Kurdish Peace and Democracy Party (Barış ve Demokrasi Partisi; BDP), and others indicated that they voted for independent candidates. Several told me that they refused to vote because party politics in Turkey was no longer a viable channel of democratic participation. This changed to a certain extent during the local elections in March 2014, when the democrats were forced to choose between the AKP and CHP owing to the absence of any other opposition. Although the AKP vote declined a bit, the government won in most cities. Hence, in the absence of meaningful electoral outcomes that defeat the AKP, the politics of space remains central for pro-democratic action.

Although these newcomer residents are not self-defined activists, their voices are heard through their intellectual and artistic production as journalists, writers, academics, professors, artists, and students. Hence, their discontents with authoritarianism are integral parts of the ongoing process of diversification among secular urbanites. Their discontents range over a large variety of political issues, including the limits and accommodation of various religious and ethnic groups, failed political and judicial reforms, violation of civil rights and liberties, police brutality, and so on. What we observe in Teşvikiye is not mere deliberation or deliberative democracy, but the actual practices and experience of democratic principles—such as inclusion, accommodation, respect for freedoms and rights, and so on—in everyday life.

More important, neighborhood politics must not be understood as cultural politics on the local level or a form of identity politics, because it ultimately ends up contesting the resources, freedoms, and rights *not* of one identity group or another, but of everybody. While local politics largely vary from neighborhood to neighborhood, I argue that spatially framed contestations in the urban sphere are born out of distrust in political institutions and the government. This distrust is often manifested in insecurity about losing freedoms and rights in everyday life. Subsequently, these contestations aim at negotiating the terms of democracy through a yearning for a more responsive and reliable state. This is particularly important, since the issue of violations of freedom constitutes a major block to the consolidation of democracy in Turkey.

What is most striking about this story is that these new bonds and alliances have emerged out of a place that has been shaken up first by the explosion of capitalist consumption and then by local political contestation. Ethnographic evidence collected for this study challenges the general view of "neighborhood wars" as a failure or bankruptcy of democratization. I argue that although contestations at the level of the neighborhood may be unpleasant and exhausting in the short run, they turn out to contribute to democratic negotiations in the long run.

A drive for the efficient transformation of urban and national politics has manifested itself in the *aftermath of the inclusion* of devout Muslims. Secular urban zones that open up to the latter facilitate interaction and collaboration between previously antagonistic camps. The strategic importance of these zones of and for freedom lies in their unusual and inventive inclusion of the previously excluded groups. Accordingly, I refer to this particular urban politics as *contestation within inclusion*. Highly contested mixed neighborhoods acquire a particularly important political role, especially when the government's respect and commitment for disagreement, dissent, and freedoms shrinks. In these contested sites, authoritarianism confronts new demands for liberal democracy and is weakened and gradually dispelled.

Under these conditions, these divided urban sites open up spaces for democratic contestation rather than denoting a shift to either a more religious or secularist politics. Whether backed by non-negotiable blind faith or aggressive forms of secularism, authoritarian conservatism resists social and political change by excluding dissent, both spatially and politically. Unlike the uncontested or voluntarily segregated parts of the city, such as the newer gated communities, the contested neighborhoods become the places where most of the arduous work of democracy takes place.

CONCLUSION

The ethnography of Teşvikiye illustrates transformation from a neighborhood of social exclusion to a place of contestation in the aftermath of inclusion. Political splits in the aftermath of inclusion protect democracy by opening the way for emerging alliances in urban space. On the basis of ethnographic evidence, I discuss what becomes of a deeply divided secular neighborhood, which, unlike the increasingly authoritarian government, is capable of containing conflict and accommodating contestation. As illustrated in the case of the hybrid art, inclusive lifestyles and shifting dynamics of power in the neighborhood, "contestation within inclusion" facilitates the achievement of democratic pluralism in everyday practices.

Çağlar Keyder rightly observes that "conflict arises when public space cannot be privatized, where interaction is unavoidable."[27] By the same token, affinities, shared goals, and political alliances also originate from contested urban space. No doubt, interaction is preferable to segregation, although it may take the form of deep contestation propelled by uncomfortable proximities. Typically, Teşvikiye's transformation reveals the ways in which power struggles are entwined closely with urban space—a space that is never "neutral" or innocent. I argue that, when political institutions fail to accommodate political dissent and the freedom of minorities, political power and urban space become more intimately mapped onto each other.

Part 1 revealed and analyzed the emergence of new political bonds between the children of secularist longtime residents, the new high-spending devout visitors, and non-religious middle class newcomers in Teşvikiye, and how these new affinities grew out of a deeply divided neighborhood.

In revealing a generational shift and the accord between the politics of devout newcomers and the children of longtime secularist Teşvikiyeli, this book challenges an established bias. I argued that what seems to be a bipolar clash between secularism and public piety, is in fact a multifaceted political contestation between diverse groups. The neighborhood, very much like the state, is an inconsistent and multilayered space where persistent authoritarian conservatism meets the new demands of liberal democracy.

The study of secular urban space problematizes the charge that devout Muslims stifle secularists in urban life, a predominant theme of "neighborhood pressure" debates in Turkey. On the contrary, this book suggests that piety is not inherently the source of authoritarianism in Turkey or elsewhere. Moreover, ethnography suggests that neither religious nor secular politics has an automatic link with the defense of authoritarianism or liberal democracy. Urban space and political power come together in both authoritarian forms of exclusion and liberal forms of inclusion in everyday life. Urban unrest in the neighborhoods is *not* simply reinforced by the cultural clash of lifestyles—devout versus secular—as many observers and scholars previously assumed. The more the lifestyles and social status of devout visitors to and secular residents of Teşvikiye have become similar, and they have come into close proximity, the more political conflict and harassment in daily life have increased. Hence, instead of blaming culture and clashing lifestyles, I maintain that contestations in urban space are symptomatic of the failure of political institutions to protect and secure freedoms and rights.[28]

Leading political scientists of democratization often tend to look exclusively at political institutions, narrowly defined electoral democracy, or political society. Political reform is indeed a strong signifier of democratization. But the Turkish case illustrates that it can go hand in hand with major violations of freedoms and rights. Hence, an exclusive focus on political institutions is unlikely to be helpful in revealing and analyzing the larger picture. Accordingly, without dismissing the state as a major site of contestations for power, I have explored the urban neighborhood as a coexisting and alternative place of power- and space-sharing. As Henri Lefebvre states, "[T]here is no urban reality without a centre, without a gathering of all that can be born in space and can be produced in it. . . ."[29] Contestation within inclusion finds refuge in these highly divided "zones of and for freedom." I argue that these contested places stand out in Turkey as an embodiment (or a microcosm) of nationwide negotiations over liberties and rights.

Part 1 also portrayed a new urban inhabitant, who becomes the cornerstone in these highly contested sites and the key for democratic contestation in Turkey. Whether s/he is a Muslim devout or non-religious, s/he thrives in seeing, talking, and acting beyond the increasingly irrelevant and inefficient Islamist–secularist binary. S/he plays a key role in forming new bonds out of these highly contested sites that advance the attainment of freedom and rights indiscriminately for all citizens. Subsequently, the Islamist–secularist axis is becoming less and less relevant, as the politics of contestation within inclusion first deeply divides and then "reshuffles" and realigns a wide range of groups across the political spectrum for the defense of a deeper liberal democracy.

The story makes two points about the aftermath of inclusion: First, there is nothing inherently detrimental and threatening about political contestation and urban divides. Splits don't harm democracies as long as they are curbed by political decency and include a safe place for contesters. To the contrary, cleavage that is "properly accommodated" in urban space punctures political hegemony that creeps into democratic rule. Second, by dividing political authoritarianism, splits that are properly accommodated clear space for emerging alliances for freedoms and rights.

Part 2

If we are going to have a progressive place, there has got to be an explicit debate about the nature of that place.

Ken Livingstone

Place-based activists, intellectuals, and common citizens . . . do not act as detached contributors to public debate . . . but are able to articulate the concerns of their constituencies in such a way that the relevant background practices are changed.

Arturo Escobar, "Culture Sits in Places"

Place is security, space is freedom: we are attached to the one and long for the other.

Yi-Fu Tuan, *Space and Place*

ON CAMPUS POLITICS

IN MY INFORMAL CHATS with faculty from several universities across Turkey, I was given numerous accounts of how rectors (presidents) rule their universities as one-man-shows. A colleague from a large, politicized state university in Istanbul observed to me:

> You enter the office of the rector, which is almost the size of a public square in a mid-sized town. . . . You walk for a couple of minutes to reach his huge desk at the other end of his office, as he watches you walking toward him. Even before reaching the president in person, you are already intimidated by the grandiosity of the place.[1]

Clearly, this spatial arrangement is very telling of the rector's unquestionable "supremacy," which sets the parameters of the interaction between the "ordinary" members of the campus and the "ruler." These authoritarian rectors are also infamous for repressing any form of student activism. In a university based at a city not too far from Istanbul, a professor even whispered to me during our quiet chats in his office for fear of being wiretapped by the rector. For a country that claims to be the leading democratizing force in the Middle East, daily life on Turkish university campuses was rather suffocating and despairing in the first decade of the new millennium.

In contrast to the illiberal campus culture found in many universities, some campuses have either resisted or to some extent avoided this authoritarianism. The locus of my analysis is what I shall call the University of Freedom (henceforth UF),[2] which has earned a historical reputation for its academic competitiveness and liberal democratic political culture. I have been criticized for choosing UF for my research, because there is a unanimous agreement in Turkey that it is not representative of the country's other universities. Of course, being considered one of the top universities of Turkey and having an established international reputation have earned UF the leeway to negotiate its autonomy from the state, and it has successfully claimed freedoms and rights. This is exactly why I chose UF. Contrary to general expectations in social research, my goal is not overall generalizability, but rather to focus on a place that is capable of contesting, challenging, and puncturing holes in the seemingly indestructible supremacy of political rule. UF's image as a safe haven for freedom of expression and dissent was not damaged or undermined during the second and third terms of AKP rule, although fault lines on its campus peaked particularly between 2008 and 2009. Along with a few other campuses, UF has become one of the important islands that have struggled for freedom during major violations of it since 2011.

RETHINKING CAMPUS POLITICS AND THE STATE

Although universities have historically been notorious for attracting not only student/youth movements but also a wide-range of political conflict, the campus as *a political place* is understudied in previous literature. This is particularly so in the context of the Middle East.[3] The misleading demarcation between the university and the political realm is the main reason why campuses were largely neglected as major sites of political contestation. As discussed in Max Weber's lecture "Science as a Vocation," the university is perceived mainly as a place for the production and dissemination of science and knowledge.[4] The recent Occupy protests on university campuses raise questions about the plausibility of this view.

Despite the obvious role of the campus during the 1960s student movement and more recent Occupy movement, we know very little about the links between the power struggle at multisited universities and an incoherent state. Most often, the campus is brought to the attention of observers *only* if and when a demonstration breaks out in its publicly most visible territory. But recent political processes brought campus space to the forefront of democratic contestation. What makes the university campus a political place—with or without the protests?

Betrween the University and the State: Autonomy Versus Patronage

From a mainstream policy perspective, the "good terms" between the university and the government are constructive for political stability and development.[5] While not problematizing good terms between the two, sociological traditions have often been critical and cautious about particularly strong links between the university and the state. More specifically, there are wide-ranging sociological concerns about state patronage, favoritism, or political control over critical thinking in academia.

Max Weber harshly criticized the eager submission of German academia to state authority.[6] Weber viewed German professors' inclination to endorse the prestige and power of the empire as both a moral and a political problem. Although "in the University of Berlin, as elsewhere, there are not a few men of strong character who continue the proud tradition of academic solidarity and independence vis-à-vis the higher authorities," he writes, "this group is not increasing."[7]

The establishment of the Council of Higher Education (Yüksek Öğretim Kurulu; hereafter referred to as YÖK) following the military coup in Turkey in 1980 makes the linkage between the state and universities not only direct and explicit, but also deeply problematic. According to the YÖK regime of higher education, universities are governed by rectors appointed by Turkey's president. Although faculty vote on appointments, the president makes the final choice from among the elected candidates. Paradoxically, as Turkey has claimed to liberalize and democratize through political reform, authoritarian rule over campuses has worsened indiscriminately. Before and shortly after coming to power, the AKP raised numerous issues with YÖK complaining that YÖK hinders academic freedom. During its electoral campaign, the AKP promised political educational reform if it was elected. When President Abdullah Gül came to power, he initially disparaged his task of appointing rectors, but the government has since mostly reinforced YÖK's top-down rule rather than curbing it.

What Is an "Engaged" Campus? Civic Virtue Versus Freedom of Dissent

A few educationalists have paid special attention to urban campuses in politically contested cities, discussing both the links and disconnects between the campus, the city, and urban politics.[8] The idea of an "engaged" campus was developed as an alternative to the disengaged ivory tower and the corporatized universities "dominated" by market forces in the United States and across the globe. Benjamin Barber suggests the "breaking down of the artificial walls that divide classroom from the street, and library from the playground" to counter these neoliberal trends.[9] Here, he specifically refers to the involvement of students as "citizens-to-be" and citizens as "permanent students." Accordingly, the engaged university is a politically significant place mainly because of its *civic commitment* to the urban community. What made UF politically significant, beyond the strategic commitment to urban community or civic virtue?

The Politics of Space on Campus Versus Revolutionary Spirit

Campuses have come under the radar of journalists and researchers mostly when there has been a long-lasting and/or large-scale social movement. Hence, the main exception to the dearth of research on the campus as a political site are studies of student movements.[10] Unsurprisingly, most work on student movements is focused on Western campuses in the 1960s.[11] This work was done mainly by educators and occasionally by historians. Rather than revealing a particular social movement or large-scale, long-lasting collective action, quotidian politics at UF consists of a series of place-based, mundane interactions, debates, and practices, along with abrupt events and infrequent short-lived protests. Hence, instead of studying a social movement associated with the university, I explore the campus as a place that generates, contains, and fuels contestations over freedoms in daily life.

Although the UF campus has several political activists from faculty and the student body involved in larger social movements, my main focus is on how the spatiality of freedom and political divides map onto each other in everyday life on campus. In this respect, I borrow from Asef Bayat's notion of "street politics," in which "conflict originates from the *active use* of public space" by people who are allowed to use it only *passively*. Bayat notes that any active use of public space would present a challenge to officials, "who see themselves as the sole authority to establish and control public order."[12] In this study, the passive use of the urban campus would refer to taking or teaching classes, doing research, and being exclusively involved in knowledge production and/or dissemination. Beyond this passive use of the campus space, however, Part 2 of this book focuses on the active and/or strategic use of urban space through heated faculty debates, resistance to the government's violations of freedom, demonstrations against state policies at the university's main gates, the occupation of certain sites on campus by students, and so on. Clearly, these forms of active use of urban space in daily life are often disparaged by the state, the police, and often the media. In close connection with the political culture on campus that the student body of the university attracts, the leading academic interests of the university (whether they be in the social sciences or the hard sciences) determine the nature of the university's engagement with society and politics.

The University as an Apolitical Space?

In the aftermath of harsh police treatment of student protesters against Prime Minister Erdoğan's campus visit to the Middle East Technical University (METU) in Ankara in 2012, the head of YÖK, Professor Dr. Gökhan Çetinkaya, reiterated that the most important functions of universities were "education-teaching, research and community service."[13]

According to Max Weber, in an overpoliticized university, professors may substitute "preaching their personal political views" for doing their job of giving students the benefit of their "knowledge and scientific exposure." Weber cautions us that "the prophet and the demagogue do not belong on the academic platform."[14] Weber's argument is convincing, but needs to be further "spatialized." Excluding political preaching from the classroom makes a lot of sense, especially when we consider the power dynamics between professors and students. However, spatially speaking, the campus as a political space cannot be reduced to the classroom. It is more multifaceted, with multiple venues of sociability, including dormitories for students, campus housing for faculty, cafeterias, cafes, leisure outlets, libraries, and restaurants. The campus embraces a large portion of the life world of students and some faculty. The public life of the academy cannot be detached from the larger political dynamics that exist alongside classrooms and laboratories. As Craig Calhoun observes: "[T]he productivity of academe depends on the extent to which *it is internally organized as a public sphere*—with a set of *nested* and sometimes overlapping public discussions providing for the continual *critique and correction* of new arguments and tentatively stabilized truths."[15]

From this perspective, a sharp division between the campus as a workplace and as a political site becomes rather arbitrary. It makes more sense to acknowledge the multifaceted, multisited nature of campus space, marked by its spatial identifiers, borders, buildings, gates, and so on. On some campuses, faculty and students share a substantial social life outside the classroom. They hang out, eat, drink, chat, debate, mobilize, and even party together both on and around the campus. Hence, a radical disconnect between the university and urban life is both artificial and unproductive.[16]

More important, campus politics often makes its agendas heard through multiple contestations, ranging from protests in the city to forums and international conferences aboard. This aspect of campus politics became very clear when the Gezi resistance received a lot of support from university students and faculty. My findings on contestations at UF between 2008 and 2013 suggest that the liberal campus provided a rehearsal space for freedom-seekers.

Safety on a Free Campus

Scholars of social movements perhaps use the term "free space" too generously.[17] It has been employed in a wide variety of contexts, ranging from associational life and groups to the mobilization sites of social movements. Some have referred to specific *safe spaces* or *protected places*.[18] Free spaces are often characterized by the absence of state control or domination by a political authority. They are thus often depicted as sites of opposition to the dominant power. However, the question of how they are kept safe for dissent, opposition, and contestation is not sufficiently explored. This is partly because the centrality of space and place is not developed in the analysis of "free spaces."[19] Accordingly, the next two chapters address the question of what makes these zones of freedom safe and protected. To what extent and under what conditions do these zones of freedom include, contain, and accommodate oppositional groups?

Finally, the scholarly literature is rather weak in developing a broader framework or theory of "campus politics" useful for comparative analysis. Within the United States, for example, owing to the focus on violence and security, campus politics is often narrowly associated with campus crime and campus police.[20] Since there has been scant comparative work on campus politics, a broader analysis of campuses at an international level is largely missing. For example, in Turkey and several other Middle Eastern countries, the presence of police on campuses is often viewed as an impediment to students' individual freedom and civil liberties, rather than contributing to their safety. The METU demonstrations in December 2012 and the Gezi resistance in May 2013, both of which sparked protests on the national level, showed a positive correlation between police presence and violence at sites of nonviolent demonstrations for freedoms and rights.

THE "REIGN" OF THE RECTORS:
RULING THE STATE AND THE UNIVERSITY

YÖK undermined the autonomy of higher education at a time when Turkish society was making dynamic moves toward a stronger civil society in the post-1980 period.[21] Although YÖK's original mission was the creation of "apolitical campuses," its top-down control and appointment procedures have politicized universities in the long run. Most important, it has rendered campuses vulnerable to political shifts, particularly to changes in the government and presidency. It is responsible, not only for centralization in university affairs, but also for the formal banning of head scarves ban at universities.

Both the 1982 Turkish Constitution and YÖK are the products of the 1980 military coup. Modern Turkey has experienced periodic military coups, which, although purportedly aimed at crushing insurgencies, have ended up diminishing civil liberties and hurting civil society. University campuses were especially affected by these coups, and students have demonstrated against them. During the 1971 state intervention, when the police came onto the campus to arrest students for political action, many of the UF faculty protected students by lying to the police about the students' whereabouts. The military coup in 1980 put an end to violent clashes between Left and Right on campuses at the cost of violating civil rights by arresting political activists and leaders, including students and academics. The 1982 Constitution aimed at depolitization by distancing people and places, society and cities, from politics.[22]

The 1982 Constitution expanded the executive authority and powers of the president and the prime minister. Parallel to this, university rectors were given sweeping powers on their campuses. The rule of the university rectors thus came to resemble that of the president of the country, each giving rise to similar patterns of authoritarianism. Haldun Gülalp explains the pitfalls in the YÖK-framed hierarchical politics of higher education:

> The military government of September 12 [1980] passed law no. 2547, which nobody could agree to remove later. Law no. 2547 imposes a system of top-down negative power. The administrative powers on the highly hierarchical ladder are authorized to block the demands and suggestions of the people under them but cannot perform positive functions on their own initiative.[23]

Owing to a political culture of top-down authoritarianism, Turkey's secularist ruling elite, which dominated state departments for decades, did not hesitate to sweepingly empower the presidents both of the state and of the university. It failed to foresee the emergence of a new political rival in the form of a pious Islamic elite. As long as government departments and the universities were ruled by like-minded secularists under their monopoly of power, the secularist elite showed no intention to reform this undemocratic institutional structure. Clearly, the architects of the 1982 Constitution lacked the foresight to envision having to share these power structures with devout Muslims—or losing control of them to the latter entirely.

Many university rectors followed the public request of the National Security Council (Milli Güvenlik Konseyi; MGK) that "harmful" books should be taken out of university libraries, so that students are educated with books and publications that tie them to the state.[24] As my interviews with faculty from various universities showed, university rectors controlled and curbed many campus activities, ranging from student clubs and artistic productions to book purchases for the libraries and even the private lives of faculty members. Unfortunately, the reign of the rector undermined the most dynamic two groups in society, the youth and the academics, who are often best equipped for critical thinking.

When the pro-Islamic AKP elected the devout Abdullah Gül as president of the secular Turkish Republic in the summer of 2008, after ten successive secularist-minded presidents, the power to appoint university rectors (and high court judges as well) shifted to a pious president. This turned both the presidency of the state and the rectorships of universities, which previously had been taken for granted to be secular, into sites of deep contestation. It came as a shock to the secular Kemalists when they lost both of these positions of authority. Only then did the secularists object to the undemocratic process that led to the "reign of the president." The secularist backlash in the aftermath of Republican Marches in 2007 was mostly about losing power and authority, rather than calling for a deeper democracy and more freedom.[25]

Although there was no clause that directly talked about the head scarf in the Turkish Constitution,[26] the AKP's proposed lifting of the head-scarf ban was objected to, contested, and denied by secularists, and finally rejected by the Constitutional Court. This confused not only laypeople and students but also legal experts, who disagreed among themselves. As a temporary solution to the much-contested lifting of the ban, rectors were given leeway to decide how to apply the head-scarf policy during the spring semester of 2008. Clearly, this decision only reinforced the reign of the rectors. In this context of judicial chaos, university rectors were turned into agents of law enforcement and policy-making, while paradoxically politicians, lawyers, and the judiciary continued their futile disagreement about how to interpret and apply the law. Whether the much-empowered rectors were tolerant or intolerant of the head scarf, they were put in a position of serving as boundary markers or gatekeepers, just as campuses turned into highly contested territory.

4 FAULT LINES ON CAMPUS

MANY URBAN SITES were divided in the aftermath of the Republican Marches in 2007. But the campuses turned into highly contested places mainly after the AKP's feeble attempt to lift the much contested head-scarf ban at universities on February 9, 2008. Campus manners worsened when the Constitutional Court overruled the government's decision to lift the ban on June 5. Ironically, both the lifting and the reinstating of the ban had the similar effect of dividing university campuses. A few months after this to-ing and fro-ing between the branches of the state, a UF faculty member observed to me: "When I run into Professors X, Y, and Z on campus, I feel morally obliged to walk away. I can't greet some of the faculty after hearing their advocacy for the head-scarf ban and other policies imposed by state institutions, such as YÖK, that are the by-products of the military coup in 1980."

UF has been famous for its highly developed liberal culture and autonomy. Turkish academics like to say that it has "proved its maturity and competence" (*rüştünü ispatladı*).[1] In the past, while most of the other well-respected universities in Istanbul had followed the head-scarf ban and marginalized or excluded head-scarved students since the early 1990s, UF had continued attracting and accommodating an increasingly high number of pious Muslim students. Most recently, the transnational Gülen Movement, the largest Islamic movement in Turkey, has managed to place a rising number of pious students into this prestigious university mostly owing to the competitive scientific education provided by Gülen's schools. These recent developments put the campus on the radar of most of the secularist newspapers. Making flashy news of UF as a new hotbed for Islamists, the secularist media accused the campus of bending the state's head-scarf policy for decades.

Undoubtedly, UF was not alone in being deeply divided over the rapidly changing head-scarf issues and policies. The zigzags in the government's head-scarf policies arose from deep conflicts between the branches of the state. The polarization between the AKP government and the presidency versus the military and the Constitutional Court peaked between February and June 2008, turning UF into a highly contested space. In the aftermath of these splits in the state, the campus slid into verbal abuse and incivility. The everyday tensions and disputes created fault lines across the faculty, the students, and the administration.

Paradoxically, the contestation took place not because of UF's alignment with the divided state but mainly because the campus has conventionally maintained its autonomy from the state. Because of this autonomy, its faculty and students were accustomed to expressing their political discontent freely. In the past, UF's internal autonomy had been reinforced by its image in the government's eyes, which was earned mostly by its distinguished faculty and student body. In addition, UF's cultural capital gave its rector leeway in terms of negotiating its autonomy with the state. In the past, the campus had smoothly welcomed student protests, faculty opposition, and intellectual criticism of successive governments. But now Turkey's governing institutions themselves were split by deep fault lines. UF's commitment to maintaining academic freedom and autonomy was complicated when the state itself was divided in its commitments and policies. Sociopolitical hostilities bred multiple levels of discontent and disagreement within the UF community, turning this hitherto free-spirited campus into a controversial place.

On the surface, the contestation and splits seemed to be about rising Islamic piety and the accommodation of religious ways of life at urban sites previously designated as secular.[2] The university and the state are distinct examples of these places associated with nonnegotiable secularity. Hence, the increasing symbols and practices of piety (religious practices, fasting, head-scarf wearing, and so on) on a secular campus were seen as a dramatic shift in UF's "urban sociability." Campus actors displayed a wide range of reactions against this shift, ranging from support, accommodation, and concern to irritation, anger, and aggression. Because the state's head-scarf ban fueled and became the focal point of conflict at this particular time period, I identify two oppositional camps on the campus in the aftermath of presidential crisis: the pro-ban and anti-ban groups for the lack of a better term. Both groups comprised faculty members, administrative staff, and students.[3]

BETWEEN THE STATE AND THE INDIVIDUAL:
ZONES RESCUED BY LIBERAL EDUCATION

Soon after I started free-floating between several university campuses, I was introduced to a "legendary" figure in the history of UF's longtime tolerance of head-scarf wearing. When the Turkish state first banned the head scarf officially in 1998, the then rector of UF, President Aydın (1992–2000), agreed to cooperate with YÖK on many issues provided it left UF free to handle the head-scarf issue. With a strong sense of Turkish politics, Aydın landed a "good deal" with YÖK and its then chair, Kemal Gürüz. YÖK under Gürüz represented a larger political agenda, but he was often remembered as the "head-scarf persecutor." With a view to preserving UF's autonomy from the state, President Aydın took care to establish good relations with him and with YÖK.

During Aydın's administration, UF witnessed the first appearance of head-scarved students, but this new phenomenon was so marginal that it did not divide the campus as yet. In the mid- and late 1990s, head-scarved students mostly aroused intellectual curiosity in social science classes. Some students and faculty even found them exotic. During those days, Aydın truly governed *through* the campus by making himself available both as a friend and a mentor to students. In my interview with him, he told me that he even offered his cell phone number to students. Needless to say, this image of his presidency was entirely the opposite of a "reign of the president" that was aloof, authoritarian, and even intimidating, not only to students but also to faculty.

Clearly, Aydın's soft head-scarf policy did not arise from his personal piety or conciliatory stance toward Islam. On the contrary, he maneuvered campus politics rather strategically and carefully. He told me in our chat in 2008: "Islamist students were becoming increasingly interested in [the] Public Administration [Department] in the mid-1990s. When we changed the department's name to Political Science and International Relations, the interest of Islamist circles went down."

Aydın's approach to campus politics was pragmatic. He told me: "Although university presidents could not ignore or bend the government's rules, head-scarved students, who had earned the right to study in this prestigious institution, have had the right to study and graduate." Highlighting the fact that the university had to protect itself legally too, he had "indeed followed the rules, but at a much slower pace, and with much more tolerant staff members. The rules of attire were applied rigidly only for the graduation ceremony." UF's uncompromising liberal principles are likely to have helped the hardliners on the YÖK to moderate a little during Aydın's period in office. UF faculty took pride in this successful maneuver and united around major political issues. All of these "smooth operations" helped maintain the university as a "free place" (*özgür bir yer*). They did not trigger discontent on campus until a decade later, when the governing institutions of the state came into conflict with each other.

"YÖK's structure no longer reflects the realities," Aydın told me. He was not an advocate of either secularist or religious education; his genuine commitment was to *liberal education* and freedom of the youth, in which both the secularist elite and the Islamist grass roots have failed, albeit in different ways. "While the secularist elite has been busy trying to inject education from above, the pious have rapidly succeeded in reaching the youth from below," Aydın said. "But neither were trying to emancipate them or to give them enough space to experiment or voice to express themselves." The aim was to mold the youth, since they were young enough to be shaped. When in power, both secularists and Islamists participated in the "reign of the presidents," and imposed authoritarianism on campus life. Against the backdrop of their illiberal education projects, Aydın and like-minded colleagues built a solid tradition of liberal education, preserving zones of freedom and free critical thinking.

When I asked how he managed to contain disagreement on campus, he told me that he was working with different kinds of people on all fronts—in the government, the YÖK, and on campus. He added, "Political conditions have changed in Turkey." The pro-Islamic AKP came to power for the first time in 2002 during the presidency of Aydın's successor (2000–2004). When the YÖK authorized university rectors to "reign" over their own campuses, UF's next president banned head-scarf wearing for a limited time. This required Islamist students to wear hats instead of head scarves to cover their hair. In 2002, Professor Aydın, who was no longer rector, received a phone call from and met with three head-scarved students in a pastry shop close to the main gates of the campus.[4] The female students related their grievances and asked Aydın for advice. Advising pragmatic solutions and calling for peace on campus, Aydın told them: "Wear your hats. Don't blame your rector. It is all about climate change in Ankara." Although Aydın tried to reconcile the new rector and the head-scarved students, it was obvious that UF was becoming increasingly vulnerable to regime changes. Clearly, this was hurting pious female students more than any one else on campus.

BEFORE 2008: KEEPING THE POLICE OFF CAMPUS?

Professor Narin (2004–8) became rector of UF at a time when Turkey was going through rapid change. The successive victories of Islamists in the national elections led to a mounting secularist backlash both within the state and society.[5] With both a divided state and divided cities, the UF was also shaken by conflict. One specific campus protest deserves special attention as an illustration of how the UF gates kept the campus a safe haven for all students. Under the leadership of a liberal association referred to as the Genç Siviller (young civils), UF students marched to protest the assassination of the Turkish Armenian journalist and writer Hrant Dink, who was known as a liberal democrat and a peace promoter. As usual, the UF students demonstrated unhindered on campus, since the majority of the faculty and administration shared their anger. However, when the students stepped out of the main gates of the main campus and crossed the street that divided the campus into two parts, they encountered an unexpected problem. This was mainly a spatial problem, and like most spatial issues and crises, it was not obvious and thereby unexpected, because space is the easiest factor to ignore and omit from consideration, even for the intellectuals.

UF has several campuses adjacent to each other, divided by the street that the student protestors were crossing. Hence, the students did not expect to find themselves "outside" campus territory while crossing the street since it was simply a "passageway" for them between two sides of the campus. However, once they stepped out of the gates, the police had the right to arrest them, because the street was not the university's property. This was an unexpected crisis, since both students and faculty took the "undivided safe territory" of the campus for granted.

Being a police-free campus distinguished UF from many other campuses, which welcomed the police to maintain order.[6] During the Hrant Dink protest, first some UF faculty and then President Narin walked the ten-minute uphill road to the gates of the campus to support the students and protect them from the police. Narin stormed to the gates in her high heels and asked the students using a loudspeaker to step back in through the gates. At my interview with her,[7] I was told that the faculty had successfully called the students back into their safe zone, where they belonged. The police at the gates were left with no choice and had to leave. It is important to note the resistance of top administration and faculty against the police. In such spatially framed campus actions, pro-democratic students were learning the art of trust and cooperation with other freedom-seekers in building coalitions on campus.

The spatiality of campus and the sociopolitical significance of its gates took on a much clearer meaning and power in this crisis.[8] Both the sociopolitical centrality and material reality of boundaries were reaffirmed as they were crossed and as they demarcated a political space.[9] The campus community realized that the UF gates demarcated the different dynamics of power and freedom inside and outside the campus.[10] While the students were recognized and respected as dissident political actors inside the university gates, they were vulnerable to being criminalized for civic disobedience outside them.

SPLITS WITHIN THE SECULAR LEFT

In the divisive post-2007 period, UF has found itself with deep fault lines, not only among the faculty, but also within and between the faculty, top administration, and the students. How and why has the UF campus become a deeply divided space? Starting shortly before the election by faculty of the university's rector in June 2008, the campus had become a microcosm of the deep splits that divided the entire country and the state. In 2008, President Narin found herself under pressure from the backlash of a rising secularist group, who feared losing their rights and free campus. A considerable portion of the UF faculty joined the secularist backlash, and began attacking the university's presumably "loose and too tolerant" attitudes toward Islamism and the head scarf. President Narin became the target of this rising tide of pro-head-scarf-ban reaction. Other faculty, who found the demands of the pro-ban faculty contradictory to the UF's identity and liberal education, stood up for the head-scarved students in full support.

During the "constitutional zigzags"[11] in the spring semester of 2008, head-scarved students of UF complained: "We are taking very demanding classes without even knowing if we will be allowed to write the final exams at the end of the term." The faculty who were divided over this political and academic issue were all secular—and mostly left-wing. There were no pious Muslim or head-scarved professors at UF who participated in these contestations.[12]

In the aftermath of the Republican Marches, secularist backlashes became tumultuous across the nation. Many university senates in Istanbul were condemning the head scarf on campus and attacking the AKP's attempt to lift the ban. Ironically, while some campuses were concurrently silent because of authoritarian rectors,[13] the rapidly increasing bickering on the UF campus was accompanied by a "quiet" Senate. The UF senate persistently withheld political statements. President Narin insisted that in order to protect the freedoms of all groups on campus without privileging one over the other, the university senate should remain apolitical, and that the administration should not take sides.[14]

Faced with deep polarization between anti- and pro-scarf faculty, President Narin consulted with lawyers and prosecutors, and announced that the new constitutional rearrangements initiated by the AKP were falling short of bringing a policy change on campuses. Accordingly, the university was to maintain the head-scarf policy and tolerance that the former President Aydın had adopted, until the Constitutional Court finalized the decision. However, the concerns of the pro-ban faculty were much bigger, and could by no means be reduced to the head-scarf controversy. In some fifty interviews over the next two years, some complained to me about UF's "decaying" image. They were concerned that the UF, with its tolerance of piety on campus, "stood out" among other, competitive universities. Ashamed of the news about the UF on television and newspapers, Professor B told me: "I am worried that the liberal image of this campus is becoming a vehicle for Islamization. Our respect for freedoms is being used by these bigots for ends that we do not agree with."

Some pro-ban faculty expressed anxiety about UF's growing body of devout students and alumni, saying that an Islamist image ran counter to the university's enlightened agenda. Others feared that increasingly wealthy Islamic alumni were approaching UF students to proselytize among them and integrate them into their Islamic communities. Professor C snapped:

> The discourse of rights, individual rights, human rights, women's rights . . . Well, of course! In the Republic of Mars, I would defend the freedom to wear a head scarf on campuses. But unfortunately, UF is based on Earth, and more important, not very close to Scandinavia, but next to Iran, Iraq, and Syria in the Middle East. I call on our faculty to remember "the context," please!

The anti-ban faculty interpreted these statements as attacks and offenses against the UF's liberal tradition of individual rights and freedoms. On the one hand, the pro-ban faculty found the anti-ban camp apologetic. On the other hand, the anti-ban faculty accused the pro-ban camp of discriminating against pious female students for the sake of obeying the government's policies. A considerable section of the pro-ban faculty who were proactively involved in these heated debates had in the past confronted the state in their leftist or feminist politics. Paradoxically, in dealing with the head-scarf issue—the right of "other" women—they were changing their previous position and bonding with the secular state and laicism (state control of religion).

Beyond their justification of the state's head-scarf ban, some pro-ban faculty raised legitimate worries and questions in my interviews. Professor D, from the engineering faculty, raised practical issues of "how to live a decent life together on campus and beyond":

> The numbers of veiled students are very low in the engineering faculty, but high in (elementary and early child) education. . . . Female Muslim students chose to take on the responsibility of early child education. But what will these students do with their diplomas in a country where they cannot teach wearing a head scarf? Or do we want our kids to be educated by pious veiled teachers? Shouldn't we give our kids enough time until they can make their own decisions about God and faith?

Parallel to Professor D's question, Ayşe, a pious UF alum asked me "Why would every Turkish citizen have the right to 'protect' their child from religion in elementary education, while I don't have the right to educate my child religiously and teach him the love of God?"[15] The controversies that deeply divided the predominantly leftist secular faculty were numerous.[16] During my fieldwork, I found that the most striking divide was between the pro-ban engineering faculty and anti-ban social scientists, particularly from sociology and political science. For the majority of Turkish social scientists, the YÖK was a *darbe kurumu*—an institution created by the military coup and secularist authoritarianism—and anything associated with it was unacceptable, irrelevant, or even illegitimate. In contrast, the pro-ban engineers often defended laicism at any cost as one of the Republic's founding principles.

Professor H, a pro-scarf social scientist whom I interviewed several times, complained about declining civility and respect for expert authority. She was particularly upset about the silent treatment and sarcastic or critical responses of secularist faculty in other fields. In her message to the faculty as a whole, she criticized it for not showing respect and recognizing the expertise that social science deserved: "When we research these issues, we are told the results are not reliable. When we share our writings, we are told [that it's a] 'topsy-turvy world.' When we cite some scholarly literature to create a platform for discussion, nobody replies or somebody sends a clipping from *Milliyet* or *Hürriyet* [daily newspapers]."

Some pro-ban faculty accused Professor H of creating false distinctions between social and "other" scientists. Others underlined that these issues involved everybody's lives, choices, and political views. Hence, they could not be monopolized or territorialized by self-proclaimed "experts." There is no doubt that engineers and social scientists have different ways of looking at and understanding the world, and they also use different methods and tools for analysis. As President Narin emphasized, engineers enjoyed precision, solution, and clarity. They like models, while most social scientists are interested in the diversity and complexity of social phenomena, which cannot be easily modeled. In fact, sociologists often aim to "problematize" and "complicate" the issue at hand. Craig Calhoun puts these disciplinary fault lines in perspective, promoting interdisciplinary boundary-crossing: "[F]ields with no borders are apt to be overrun, like farms invaded by unsought plants. And so too the university system as a whole: if its walls are too strong, it risks becoming irrelevant or having those who control its resources decide externally on how it should change."[17]

Calhoun's point helps us think about academic borders in the context of spatial boundaries on campuses. Borders that separate academic disciplines are not much different from the walls that divide the campus and separate the university from the larger urban and political context. Crossing them makes contested issues more visible and inflammatory. Would there be so much contestation if social scientists and engineers stopped interacting entirely and restricted themselves to their separate academic fields and departments? It sounds unlikely. Mixing rather than segregation is an important trigger of academic debate and political dispute.

The intersection between disciplinary boundaries and class differences among the faculty also reinforced political divides on campus. Professor M argued that a considerable section of the social science faculty came from a relatively more advantaged class background, and that their understanding of the universe was shaped by their privilege. It is true that the social science faculty comprises some faculty who are relatively more privileged than others in terms of class, but this pattern has changed amongst the junior faculty, who are, on average, middle-class. In contrast, engineering faculty were often self-made people from middle- and lower-middle-class backgrounds. A considerable portion of the engineering faculty and students were originally from outside of Istanbul. Hence, Professor M added, engineers were more committed to class

politics and socioeconomic equality than the trendy identity politics among social scientists, which culminated in a defense of pious Muslims.

But the defense of Muslim students by many anti-ban faculty had almost
nothing to do with identity politics. They were taking these students' side
because of their commitment to individual rights and civil liberties. Put differently, rather than allying with the head-scarved students on the basis of
piety, they were forming coalitions across the ancient pious-secular divide
over the defense of rights and freedoms. Instead of identity politics, their
commitment was to a deeper democracy. Moreover, in my interviews, they
did not shy away from criticizing the authoritarian tendencies of Islamic politics, such as its widely accepted views on homosexuality, the AKP's problematic gender politics, and so on. For them, this was a democracy problem, not
a defense of religion.

In contrast, when an anti-ban social scientist argued that Islamists and Kemalists were alike in their political authoritarianism, the secularists responded: "Let's
fix one thing at a time. We can take on Kemalism another time, perhaps after we
deal with the imminent crisis of the Islamization of education." Another engineer said, "Just because we can't fix Kemalism, doesn't mean we have to defend
the greater evil of Islamism. It's apples and oranges."

The UF campus, like the Istanbul metropolitan area and the Turkish state,
may at first thus seem to be torn apart by and polarized between Islamism and
secularism. However, an in-depth look into each of these reveals that the head-
scarf controversy was not about this seeming dichotomy. The explosion of piety
on the most liberal secular Turkish campus did not pit the Islamists against the
secularists; rather, it split the secular Left. In fact, it has occasioned efficient
large-scale negotiations between defenders of democracy and authoritarianism
that cut across the Islamist–secularist binary.

BEYOND "DELIBERATION": DEMOCRATIC PRACTICES
AND COMMITMENT TO LIBERTIES

When social actors get to make a splash by (dis)agreeing freely over highly
contested issues, this is often picked up by the press and other national media.
This means that their voices and words may be heard beyond the local site;
but does it lead to any change in power politics? This question is the key
to explaining the link between local urban politics and macro-level power
politics. I argue that the relations and links between the campus and the state
challenge and unsettle power dynamics, whereas mere deliberation in many

forms of democratic participation may often fall short of changing power dynamics and structures. The university was a locus, not only of debate and deliberation, but of action arising out of large-scale fault lines and power struggles. It was this that shook up the entire country, rather than just the words of the campus actors.

Eventually, the strong backlash from the pro-ban engineers culminated in the nomination of a new candidate for rector, Professor Bilgin, an engineer and a former Marxist, in the 2008 presidential elections at the UF. Bilgin voiced the pro-ban engineers' concerns about a "political vacuum" associated with "the *excessive* culture of freedoms" on campus. When I interviewed him right before the campus elections in 2008, he told me:

> There are very few female students in our department. Only two of them used to cover their heads. I talked to them personally, explaining the rules and regulations. They cooperated with me, and willingly took off their head scarves. As I expected, they were wearing a head scarf because of family pressure. Hence, they benefited from my intervention, since it protected them against pressure from their families and religious authority.[18]

Surveys in Turkey neither deny nor rule out the possibility of family pressure obliging women to cover their heads, as Bilgin assumed. But even if we assume that the small gender and religious minority of two head-scarved students in an engineering department gave up their head scarves willingly, the unequal power dynamics between Bilgin and a head-scarved student make the professor's contention moot.[19] Promising the pro-ban faculty a solution to the head-scarf problem along with many other benefits such as campus housing, Bilgin was elected rector, replacing Narin.[20]

This secularist victory was a big frustration for the anti-ban faculty. Both the pious students and the faculty who defended their rights were intimidated by the new regime that represented the secularist backlash on campus. Bilgin backed his secularist slogans with a strong class politics, accusing the pro-ban faculty of being "apologists for Islam" and engaging in right-wing class politics.

Having only served for one term, President Narin stepped down willingly in compliance with the faculty's choice. Had she not freely stood down, however, she would likely have been appointed rector by Turkey's President Gül, who had the final say in the matter. Clearly, Gül would have preferred Narin's presidency, given her tolerance of Muslim students, to Bilgin's staunch secularism, although he was the first choice of the faculty. In an interview after losing in the UF elections, Narin explained to me that hanging on to the rectorship in this way would not have accorded with UF's democratic values and academic culture. Put differently, by immediately stepping down, she removed the possibility of being elected by the president of the Turkish Republic, upholding the tradition of democratic governance at UF.

Was the 2008 rectorship election a victory for the pro-ban camp at UF? What or whom did the victorious President Bilgin defeat in these elections? In this respect, President Narin's attitude is telling. Her behavior, which is considered very UF-like, is an important indicator of how UF resisted the authoritarian rule of the Turkish state and the country's president. She served as a rector who respected individual and academic freedoms, and transferred the presidency willingly by respecting the democratic procedures on campus.[21] In this way, she resisted the anti-democratic aspects of the 1982 constitution and thereby managed to finesse some of the major institutional barriers to a deeper democracy. She did not obey the authoritarian tendencies of this top-down management of the universities. Her politics was not shaped by the out-of-date fights between Islamism and secularism. On the contrary, she was able to ally with politically like-minded people across the lines of faculty, students, or political leaders in her commitment for a better democracy. In this sense, the electoral victory of Bilgin suggests the victory of a zone of freedom, the democratic campus, more than a victory against Islam or head-scarved students. More important, it was not a deliberative success but demonstrated through democratic practices and acts on campus.

After she stepped down, President Narin gave a speech at the graduation ceremony, where she handed over the rectorship to Professor Bilgin:

> In the Presidential Hall, the pictures of previous rectors of UF hang on the walls. After I "graduate" from presidency, my picture will hang there among the fifteen previous male presidents. I shall be the only woman in a century and half of institutional history. I extend an invitation to all the female students who are graduating at UF this year. Please do not leave me alone there. I am calling for a second female rector, a brave, hardworking UF alumna who shares UF's noble principles, academic values, and culture of freedom. Don't forget, I shall be waiting there [on the wall] for you . . .

Narin's inclusive politics must be understood in the context of feminism and respect for individual freedoms, including, but not limited to, sartorial choices. The UF campus typically accommodates a wide range of outfits, particularly for students, but also for faculty. It is not surprising to see men and women in swimming suits, shorts, or other swimming outwear on campus, because the campus has a swimming pool. Respect for individual choices, which is not limited to but includes attire, has been a cornerstone of the UF political culture.[22] Yet, the pro-ban faculty was intimidated by religion and its symbols as an enemy of feminism. Professor C, a left-wing, secularist engineer, offered a thought-provoking critical view, sharing an e-mail that she had sent to the entire faculty with me:

> A default, in computer science, refers to a setting or value automatically assigned to [a] software application, computer program or device, outside of user intervention. For example, in variables that help us count, this value is zero. You start counting from zero. YÖK's university handbook describes [the] default student as bareheaded. They are trying to change this default. [The] Diyanet İşleri [Directory of Religious Affairs] states that according to Islam, the default is a veiled woman. . . . Similarly, the prime minister explained on TV this weekend: "WE RECOGNIZE WOMEN'S RIGHT TO WEAR A HEAD SCARF. IF A WOMAN DOES NOT WISH TO USE THIS FREEDOM TO VEIL, WE SHALL NOT ASK HER WHY . . ." Nobody is asking what [this] means. . . . Here, the prime minister is redefining the default woman. She is veiled, and any other woman who chooses to step out of the default is "tolerated" by him. Well, I disagree. Default woman is equal to man. Muslim faith carries the risk of imposing gender inequality.[23]

Professor C was very keen on keeping her immediate environment, especially the campus, free of religious observance, since she was afraid of losing her privacy and freedom to be nonreligious. She was already feeling suffocated and pressured by increasing religious practices, such as fasting on campus during Ramadan. Professor C objects to Prime Minister Erdoğan's statements from a feminist standpoint. At the same time, however, this raises questions about how her feminism handles pious Muslim women's agency, rights, and freedoms. In this respect, she added: "I am against political Islam, and do not think the head scarf should be a component of campus life. However, I disagree with the proposed punishment, which is disproportionately harsh. One should not expel a student for wearing it."

Instead, she proposed milder warnings by the disciplinary committee, and perhaps a few days of grounding as fair penalties. Although she was highly vocal in her opposition to Islamism, she also felt strongly about female students' equal right to higher education. Unlike many pro-ban professors at other universities, she was cognizant of the anti-democratic nature of the head-scarf ban on campus. It is important to note the intersectionality between urban space, gender, and religion in this respect. Along these lines, Yeşim Arat is concerned that so much energy goes into debating head-scarf policies while more pressing gender-related issues are neglected: "[I]t is not the lifting of the much-publicized Islamist head-scarf ban in the universities that we should prioritize as a danger, but the propagation of patriarchal religious values sanctioning secondary roles for women through state bureaucracy, as well as through the educational system and civil society organizations."[24]

THE CAMPUS GATES AFTER 2008: POLICING TO KEEP THE STUDENTS OUT?

The secularist camp on campus focused on some misleading and accusatory headlines in newspapers, which compared UF with some privately owned Islamist universities. The secularist backlashers either failed to realize or consciously ignored the fact that the pious students were being admitted to UF because of their very competitive high school educations and their outstanding performance on the university entrance exam. As Calhoun states, "Universities are widely caught between populist calls for access . . . and self-interested pursuit of prestige, both as an end in itself and as a basis for privilege and profit. It is a serious question whether a way to balance excellence and access is available."[25] Facing similar dilemmas, UF's new secularist president assumed his office in 2008. His first action was immediately to announce a head scarf ban on campus.

During the first few days of the fall semester in 2008, crowds gathered at the main UF gates. They included not only head-scarved students, who were not permitted to go through the gates, but also police, the media, and activists— particularly feminist activists. When the head-scarved students were denied access to the campus, they received a considerable amount of support from other UF students. Their many supporters included members of the civil society association called the Young Civils, whose flexible and floating agendas permit them to support a wide-range of social groups whose freedoms and rights have been violated.[26] Motivated by the Young Civils and other student groups, male UF students put on head scarves in support of the head-scarved female students. Altogether, they pushed through the UF gates as a large anonymous mass of head-scarved men and women. This spontaneous alliance must not be underestimated since it crosses the lines of gender, religion, and definitely class.

Facing students' resistance, the new president asked the head-scarved students to sign a letter if they insisted upon entering the university with a head scarf. The document stated that these students admitted violation of the state's law by demanding access and forcing their way into the university. Coming from a Marxist tradition and having advocated an anti-state politics in his past, President Bilgin's way of documenting students' acts seemed paradoxical. His new head-scarf policy and punitive steps alarmed both activist faculty and feminist groups on and beyond the campus. First and foremost, it was not clear how the university would use these signatures. Many conscientious supporters warned the students that they should not give their signatures but should rather wait a couple of days to enter the campus. The president's action was not regarded highly among academic circles, mainly because the YÖK and the constantly shifting state-university links in Turkey were politicizing campuses precariously and making the students vulnerable to political tides.

In the following days, an ad hoc group of some twenty professors, led by feminists and other leftist activists became pioneering forces in fighting for and with the head-scarved students. In the face of increasing complaints and pressure from the pro-scarf faculty and students, President Bilgin met with a small representative body of the anti-ban group. He explained to them that the student signatures were to protect the university. He affirmed in several conversations that he was not collecting these signatures to harm the students or as an act of espionage for the state. Instead, he insisted that he was simply asking the students to take their own political responsibility. After those first few days, head-scarved students found their way onto the campus in one way or other, by wearing substitute clothing, such as baggy outfits with hoods or wigs that covered their hair.

Once they managed to pass through the gates, the head-scarved students were very inventive in adapting, maneuvering around, or coping with the rules of conduct in campus space. In my interviews, they told me that they knew every tunnel, underground passage, hidden corner, or side road on campus in order to hide their head scarves from the authorities. Most of these spatial negotiations are spontaneous and individually coordinated in daily life rather than long-planned collective actions. They succeeded to the extent that the actors knew the space intimately and were capable of using it "actively," in Asef Bayat's terms. A head-scarved student observed to me: "I come and go quickly, never spend time on campus. It is like we are allowed here in constant hiding . . . like we are made to feel chronically guilty of being somewhere we are not supposed to be. . . . I am here because of my high scores. But this situation is not very conducive to feelings of belonging and feeling appreciated, is it?"[27]

The resilience of head-scarved students was reflected in their spatial politics. Their politics of space created different degrees of discontent among the pro-ban faculty. They felt disappointed with the new developments and how the new president had failed to keep his promises. The conflict deepened further, when the education faculty raised objections to teaching in classrooms that had a majority of head-scarved students. They snapped: "Should our children be entrusted to these Islamist teachers, who seem to increasingly dominate the field of early childhood education, and who would brainwash small kids?"[28] Several engineering professors backed the education faculty up by telling stories about their own experiences. Being educated by pious teachers, the children of the secular faculty were asking their scientist parents religious or theological questions such as what heaven was. They were also questioning their parents' presumably ignorant, if not "sinful" behavior and existence. Not only the pro-ban faculty, but also some secular anti-ban professors were disturbed by and puzzled about how to answer and cope with such questions.

Another legitimate concern of the education faculty was the damage that these head-scarved students were doing to their off-campus contacts. Typically, professors of education help their students be placed in prestigious preschools and elementary schools to pursue their internships. They have successfully developed strong ties and trust relations with highly competitive private schools of early education in the well-off secular surrounding neighborhoods. When these schools accept the highly competitive UF students as interns, they do not expect the head scarf to be an issue. The faculty were in despair because they stated that in the event of recurring problems with the head scarf, some of these institutions are already inclined not to work with UF any longer.[29]

These issues raised by the education faculty are telling in terms of the universities' contested ties with society. These ties are marked by larger fault lines that extend beyond the campus. An urban campus is deeply embedded in the urban landscape through its controversial political role and delivery of its wider urban commitment. The Islamism–secularism controversy seemed, not just to divide the university community, but also to create conflict and a "disconnect between the university community and the communities [it] nominally serves."[30] The campus serves as a mediating site for Muslim female students to gain access to the surrounding neighborhoods. The conflict was fueled when head-scarved UF students crossed into the surrounding urban spaces, which were previously designated as secular. Although the head-scarf ban brings up mainly the issue of access and the right to the city, the city of Istanbul is no longer discussing the right of the pious to the city. The discussions are about ways to accommodate and integrate pious city dwellers while resisting religion's tendency to transform urban space in its own image.[31] Accordingly, this is not simply campus politics but must be understood in the context of larger fault lines and political dilemmas about how to share space and power.

The issue became explosive when the education faculty required students to take their head scarves off in the classroom, even though they were allowed to cover their heads on campus. Soon, the female bathrooms in the education building turned into back stages of costume design and stage-acting, where students were getting dressed, undressed, and redressed in a rush for classes. Chaos ruled the School of Education for months. In my interviews with the students, I was told that the professors were picking on the head-scarved students, punishing them with bad grades, or even failing them. Conversely, in my interviews with education professors, I was told that head-scarved students were failing because their head-scarves prevented them from completing their internship requirements. My interviews turned up many contradictory versions of the same stories, issues, and events. A few anti-ban faculty in the higher administration also confidentially admitted that the problem was not handled wisely in the School of Education because of lack of communication and a mutual understanding between faculty and pious students. The tension peaked during the fall term, as both students and faculty were feeling threatened, estranged, and intimidated by each other.

As the result of deepening tension, sixteen students were sent to the disciplinary committee by the education faculty, who asked for a punishment for these "unruly" students. This was followed by a silent protest. The head-scarved students were again supported by other male students. Some hundred students gathered in a corridor of the education faculty's building, standing still in silence in front of the office of one faculty member who had been rather harsh about the "head-scarf regime" in her classes. As the professor attempted to go to her office through this silent and immobile crowd, she felt threatened and intimidated by the number of students who collectively and mutely stared at her. According to the professors of education that I interviewed, the head-scarved students brought their male friends from Islamist circles outside the campus.

Typically, a contrasting story was told to me by several head-scarved students, who participated in the silence protest:

> This was a peaceful action. There were no outsiders in that protest. There was cooperation between UF's pious, conscientious students, who were sick and tired of this head-scarf controversy. The faculty or administration could have asked for our UF identity cards, and we would have happily showed our IDs, but no one even seemed to wonder who we were. They also did not care about what we wanted. Typically, we were treated as a bunch of Islamist bigots, a mass with no diversity, no name, no individuality, no rights, but just as Islamists.

As President Bilgin failed to satisfy the requests of the secularist faculty, both fault lines and frustrations have gone deeper. For example, the head-scarved students charged by a discipline violation were left hanging with their cases unresolved, as the committee continued deferring a decision for months and avoided finalizing the case eventually. Instead of making a punitive decision that would contradict the UF tradition, they left the case open to expire of its own accord.

During Bilgin's presidency, my interviews with UF faculty revealed a wide range of discontent about the degeneration of relations between the university and the YÖK. While UF had previously maintained a respectful leeway from the state under the former rectors, Bilgin's rectorship failed to continue this tradition. Furthermore, it sucked the campus into the ancient fault lines between Islamism and secularism, which UF had successfully stood above until then. The failed attempts at banning the head scarf, along with a vocal secularist backlash on campus, turned the AKP government against UF. Numerous faculty members told me that the university was punished by the YÖK and the government and has suffered severely during this period in several ways. For example, UF was denied new tenure lines (*kadro*). The situation became so bad that the administration was unable to offer a faculty post to a newly hired PhD from an Ivy League university in the United States and was forced to appoint that person as a teaching assistant. As a loyal UF alumnus, the faculty member patiently waited for an actual faculty post for several years.

The dire situation at UF was due to two systemic issues. First, previous rectors had remained loyal to the principle of freedom and antidiscrimination among students. They had worked toward democratic participation of the students and faculty in decision-making by keeping the state and the police out of the campus. In their commitments to democratic governance, they also prioritized the protection and safety of the students. Opposite this previous position, the pro-ban rector and his followers fell into the larger nationwide conflict along the axis of Islamism and secularism. This secularist backlash contradicted with and compromised some of the UF's nonnegotiable commitments to freedoms.

In the next two years, the AKP was reelected for the third time in 2011, re-placed the members of YÖK with like-minded and mostly pious people, and lifted the head-scarf ban from campuses. Professor Bilgin lost the next election in 2012. In the following years, the YÖK under the AKP legitimized the head scarf on all campuses, while violating freedoms in major ways in other aspects of everyday life. How did the ongoing contestations affect campus politics dur-ing the AKP's third term?

UF's relative autonomy facilitated solid resistance and opposition to the AKP government, particularly during its remarkably authoritarian third term (2011–). Similarly, UF and other similar zones of freedom that were built on the shoulders of strong liberal education and an internationally competitive cur-riculum supplied safe places where students practiced disagreement, opposi-tion, and contestation without being undermined. Put differently, these are the sites where the youth familiarized themselves with and became acclimatized to critical thinking and freedom of expression. The process through which they were sheltered by progressive friends, faculty, and administration provided a rehearsal for the Gezi protests simmering across urban space. Hence, these lib-eral campuses and the actors who played out these contestations were the key in explaining the new role of the youth in opposing arbitrary authoritarian rule. The political learning at these urban sites was imperative for the political transi-tion from divisive to unifying opposition to the AKP.

5 NEW COALITIONS IN SAFE ZONES

IN 2010, a group of students made a documentary about the head-scarf ban on the UF campus. Their broader goal was to illustrate and discuss the effects of the head-scarf controversies on head-scarved students' lives. The documentary voiced the head-scarf-related conflicts on campus that have been the key to the political fault lines during 2008–9. The students strategically avoided a focus on negative aspects and hurt feelings in order not to fuel an already deep conflict. Instead, the documentary aimed at building a platform of cooperation by calling for a deeper mutual understanding of and a solution for the problem. The producers of the documentary emphasized in interviews that they wished to create a common ground and room for compromise between head-scarved students and others who care about recognition and freedoms and rights of all. Accordingly, their documentary was not *about* the head-scarved students but rather a collaborative project *with* them. This main motivation of the project is more telling about UF's campus politics in many ways than the contents and the end result of the documentary. Put differently, the major agenda and intention that gave rise to this documentary was kindred in spirit with the UF political culture that prioritized cooperation over disputes and inclusivity over discrimination.

Although the campus was deeply divided in the aftermath of Republican Marches in 2007, UF generated strong alliances between previously antagonistic groups in the post-2011 period. The campus united indiscriminately and very promptly against the violation of academic freedoms, arbitrary detentions, and the government's crackdown on Kurds. Most important, campuswide protests bridged the fault lines between practicing Muslims and the secular, creating new alliances between them in the interests of a deeper democracy. This is yet another example of *contestation within inclusion*.

Some of the faculty and head-scarved students at UF are journalists and columnists in leading newspapers. Unsurprisingly, they were the first to object to the AKP's attempt to ban abortions and caesarean deliveries in Turkey. I had a four-hour interview with a head-scarved graduate student at UF, Fatma, who was a columnist in a major newspaper. Fatma told me that she rejected abortion for herself because of her religious beliefs, but she also rejected government interference in women's decisions over their own bodies. In her column, Fatma openly criticized the prime minister in her defense of women's rights and freedom.[1] This, I argue, is a very impressive case that undermines prevalent arguments on the incompatibility of Islam and democracy, or Muslim society and freedoms. Fatma's objection to the AKP's policy is extremely important, not only because her voice as an insider reached many constituents and voters of the AKP but also because it represents new divides and disagreement among pious Muslims on women's freedoms and rights. Although AKP coopted some of these democratic voices among liberal Muslims in time, UF maintains its distinctly unifying territory in which divided groups ally in defense of rights and freedoms.

The campus united most strongly during the 2011–12 period in producing vocal opposition to government's violation of freedoms and rights. At trials in 2010–11, a large number of military officials charged with being members of an alleged terrorist organization called Ergenekon were found guilty of planning a coup d'état. At the same time, hundreds of journalists, many leading academics, and some seven hundred students were arrested and imprisoned on false or unsubstantiated charges of being involved with anti-state and terrorist groups. In this period, the deeply divided UF campus showed an impressive capacity to speak with one unified voice in defense of academic and individual freedoms, as well as civil and political rights. It is neither surprising nor accidental that these dissenting voices are heard primarily at UF and other progressive universities where strong civil rights alliances have arisen.

When Nihan, an undergraduate at UF, was taken into custody in 2013 on the grounds that she had made a telephone call to a lawyer charged with alleged involvement in a terrorist operation, UF faculty and students stood up and demanded her release. The protestors gathered and walked to the main gates demanding freedom and shouting, "We want freedom for Nihan!" Very typically of UF political culture, the chair of the department walked with the rest of the protestors to the main gates and declared on behalf of the faculty that the university denied Nihan's involvement in illegal activity. She also announced that the university wanted Nihan to be released and to return to her classes. For months, UF stood together in defense of Nihan's rights. It is important to note that in the age of increasing campus protests across the globe, we do not very often witness this kind of unified and persistent support of student protestors from faculty and university against the officials even in strong democracies. Nihan was released after five months. Her story received wide coverage in major newspapers. Her case drew the attention of globally renowned human right activists, columnists, and bloggers.

The controversy about animal rights on the UF campus is also telling of the new bridges that cut across and overcame the old pious-secular dichotomy. UF has always famously sheltered street cats, because the faculty, students, and shopkeepers (of coffee shops, cafeterias, restaurants, etc.) on campus fed and protected these cats. In response, there has always been an anti-animal sentiment on campus, with people complaining about cats jumping on their lunch tables and into their classrooms, making noise, and creating a mess all around the campus. Unsurprisingly, in Turkey, even the animal rights issue has found its way into the archaic fault lines between piety and secularism. According to the stereotypes, the secular Westernist elite of Turkey is regarded as more pet-friendly. They are perceived as more inclined to have pets at home and in their immediate environments. Because one of the Prophet Mohammed's hadiths cautions against the dirt of certain animals, such as dogs and pigs, there has been an implicit understanding that animal rights would create yet another national divide between pious Muslims and secularists. In contrast to this perception, many head-scarved students at UF joined the culture of animal rights, while many secular faculty members objected to UF's becoming "an open-air zoo."

In the following years, resistance, protest, and alliances over animal rights at different city sites stood above ideological fault lines.[2] This is another clear indicator that the defense of rights and freedoms cannot be explained by a government's or person's religiosity or secularity, but by their commitment to democracy or authoritarianism.

The inclusion and participation of Muslim students in campuswide protests against the pro-Islamic government revealed the triviality and fragility of existing fault lines. Despite the fact that not all pious students have been actively involved in anti-government action and protests, the mixing across the

Islamist-secularist divide in daily life is a rather important political matter. Regardless of the ratio of devout students in anti-government actions on campus, their participation calls the association between religiosity and political authoritarianism into question. This shows that although contestations over urban inclusion/exclusion may often reflect power struggles in parliament and within the state, highly contested urban sites are more capable of readjusting their local politics to generate democratic practices, inclusion, and solidarity. UF had to cope with contestation in the aftermath of Muslim inclusion, and had to negotiate the terms and boundaries of democratic integration and the protection of other marginalized or minority groups.

The AKP's unfair and authoritarian treatment of the university overlapped with its nationwide violations of freedoms and rights in its third term. These injustices reinforced alliances over burning problems of democracy that overshadowed and gradually superseded campus conflicts over Muslim politics. When injustices and authoritarianism were committed by the AKP government, the UF campus unified behind support for freedoms, regardless of who was pious or not, or who was pro-head-scarf, anti-head-scarf, or head-scarved. Both faculty opposed to the head-scarf ban and those in favor of it subordinated their ideological demands to the need to form a more united opposition to the Erdoğan regime. While the proximity and attentiveness to students of UF faculty played a major role in leading these divided groups to enter into new alliances, the AKP's increasing authoritarianism gave the divided campus a shared mission of resistance.

On the basis of my fieldwork between 2007 and 2013, I argue that the campus went through a remarkable transition from a deeply divided space to a strongly allied place. This certainly does not mean that disagreement and discontent on campus entirely disappeared. However, with the formation of new alliances, the major axis of conflict has shifted from Islamism-secularism toward the conflict between authoritarianism and a deeper democracy.

Like social movements and protests, the dynamics of urban life evolve through interaction with the government and the state. The Turkish state has historically been appreciative of and responsive to UF, and past governments have cooperated with the university's leadership. Moreover, UF's liberal politics had always played a prominent role in shaping public opinion. When the ties between the university and the government deteriorated, the university's voice proved difficult to silence. Invading the safe, peaceful UF campus was not a free ride for law enforcement.

WHY PIT SECURITY AGAINST FREEDOM ON CAMPUS?

People versus armed gunmen in an open field are a different condition from people in a dense urban setting versus such gunmen.

Saskia Sassen, "The Global Street: *Making* the Political"

On December 18, 2012, Prime Minister Erdoğan visited the Ankara campus of the Middle East Technical University (ODTÜ), one of Turkey's top-ranking schools, known for its liberal educational policy and secular democratic politics. The prime minister's visit was to attend the launching of the Göktürk-2 satellite from the TÜBİTAK Space Technologies Research Institute at ODTÜ. However, he made his appearance escorted by eight water-cannon vehicles, twenty tanks, 105 bodyguards, and a large number of police (estimated at 2,000–3,500, depending on the source). Understandably, observers and columnists in Turkey questioned why a prime minister would enter one of the most liberal and prestigious campuses, which is also one of the top academic institutions in the country, with "this army."[3]

Erdoğan's tumultuous visits to liberal campuses were not an entirely new phenomenon. More than two years prior to the ODTÜ incident, there was a student protest at UF during Prime Minister Erdoğan's visit for an opening on campus. Contained by the campus, the UF protests remained on a much smaller scale and did not spread out beyond the UF campus. Very much like the ODTÜ solidarity, however, the UF protest was impromptu. It was a spontaneous reaction against Erdoğan's arrival, which brought the police to a typically police-free campus. Not surprisingly, neither Erdoğan nor the police were welcomed by the student body. His visit led to vocal protest against the AKP government: groups of students shouting "AKP get out! The universities are ours" and "We will not leave the university to the Bigot." Disrupting UF's peaceful political culture, police forces used tear gas. Some students got hurt, and faculty supported and allied with the students. The entire campus community condemned the violence introduced into this very safe haven on the pretext of restoring security.[4]

The ODTÜ incident was an alarming example of the emerging encounters between students and police. As similar encounters erupted on campuses across the world, the ODTÜ incident must be understood in the context of new global campus politics, including the most advanced countries. For example, the ODTÜ protest took place one year after students at McGill University in Montreal faced harsh treatment by police, including tear gas. Before this incident, these harsh methods had last been used on McGill's campus in 1969.

The McGill administration admitted having called the police in November 2011, when students were demonstrating peacefully against tuition increases. However, astonished by the heavy-handed methods used by the police, the university administration changed sides and opened an investigation against the police forces.[5] Similarly, the Occupy movement, led mainly by students and progressive activists, was silenced, repressed, and eliminated by the use of tear gas on several campuses in the United States. The past few years have witnessed shifting dynamics in the interactions between police and campuses at diverse locations, including universities in advanced democracies. Such disconnected campus incidents have become endemic across the world, illustrating the global rise of a "security" edge in the management of democratic nonviolent opposition, particularly youth protests.

Not surprisingly, Erdoğan's administration shared in this wave of "securing" urban space, particularly the campus territories. The ODTÜ campus displayed strong solidarity against police intrusion and violence and the undemocratic treatment of the students by the government. Student protestors received solid support from their professors, who cancelled their classes and joined the student protestors.[6] Major newspapers gave large coverage to news about the offenses of the police against an entirely nonviolent student group, backed up by observers, participants, and columnists.[7] The next day, several ODTÜ students were picked up from their houses and arrested.[8] Instead of civilians seeking an investigation of the police, the YÖK launched an investigation of the ODTÜ. YÖK, under the AKP regime, argued that the university was not a political space but a place of teaching, research, and knowledge production. The ODTÜ faculty and top administration stood in unity and did not shy away from public announcements defending the right of their students to civil disobedience.

In response, Prime Minister Erdoğan defended the use of force by the police, including tear gas fired even in ODTÜ's daycare area. He publicly condemned ODTÜ students and faculty for exercising their right to protest. Although Erdoğan had lived through an era of repressive secularist rule, he himself is no defender of democracy. He and his AKP government have in fact adopted the undemocratic tactics used against Islamists under the secular Republic. However, the universities took them by surprise. The campus dissenters had nothing in common with either the previous secularist elite or the current Erdoğan regime, and the university students' democratic demands puzzled the AKP, formed in a struggle with secularist authoritarians. Neither Erdoğan nor the police understood the motives, demands, and needs of this new opposition burgeoning on university campuses.

From the perspective of an outside observer, these campuses may appear to be hotbeds of polarization and chaos. But they have been the key factor in forming a meaningful democratic opposition across ideological lines to the AKP—a government that has ruled without an efficient opposition in the parliament for a decade.

On the Spatiality of Freedom

Ten days after Erdoğan's visit, the ODTÜ campus was still protesting in full force through an uncompromising alliance between faculty, administration, and students. The use of violence and other harsh, undemocratic methods by the police on the ODTÜ campus gave rise to a chain of campus protests against the government across the country. The ODTÜ protest received strong support from and participation by outsiders, even from some members of the opposition CHP party and the major music groups Gündoğarken and Bulutsuzluk Özlemi.[9] Why did members of parliament find the campus an alternative or more efficient site of dissent despite their parliamentary access? What made urban space preferable to the formal channels of party politics?

Campus politics were in some respects of the utmost importance in the nationwide protests against the government's violations of freedoms and civil rights, inasmuch as the protestors opted to stage their dissent entirely within the marked boundaries of university campuses. Whether this was a strategic choice or a spontaneous response to police actions on campus, the protests consistently remained within the borders of campuses. The diverse body of protestors insisted on going through the gates of the campuses and forced their way through the doors in order to undertake their protests. They ended up protesting successfully within rather than outside or in front of the campuses. This was partially due to the unanimous agreement, manifested in campus culture, to demarcate and keep the campus a safe place for the students. Put differently, the youthful protestors felt safer on campuses, where the entrance of police was blocked or could be disputed. They were committed to making a spatial statement by keeping it that way. This is much different from social movements or rebellions with revolutionary rather than spatially framed democratic goals.

The spatiality of expression of dissent is of utmost importance here. The campus crisis in Turkey was triggered by the spatiality of freedoms. It was born of and fueled by the campus space that has provided the youth with freedoms and safety. Moreover, it rapidly expanded through the campus spaces of similar universities across the nation. Erdoğan did not enter every public site or university accompanied by armed forces, tanks, and water cannon. He only entered the unspoken zones of freedom with large police escorts because of his expectation of and inability to deal with opposition. AKP's anti-democratic opposition-hostile behavior ignited zones of freedom, and the ODTÜ and UF campuses, with their liberal university traditions, were well equipped to respond. Moreover, such agentic spaces are embedded in and supported by a global political geography of freedom and dissent. Not all public spaces are capable of initiating and enabling democratic protests on the national level and prompting mobilization without any preplanning, intention, or strategy, but they were.

Even the weak CHP opposition party, which is incapable of generating constructive discussion and contestation in parliament, joined the ODTÜ protestors. Was the campus more tempting because it fuelled more opposition than the CHP could ever have dreamed of mobilizing since the rise of the AKP? One would have expected the leaders of the opposition party to have had "higher" ground on which to express resistance. Their participation in the ODTÜ protests on December 27, 2012, should be seen as a wake-up call: the spatial politics of the campus generated a larger-scale, more powerful opposition than that of the CHP in parliament. The main reason for this was that the campus, unlike parliament, hosted the politics of a new generation who were above and uninterested in the ancient power struggles between the secularists and the Islamists. Hence, unlike parliament, some campuses were pioneering and "free" enough to contest, condemn, and overcome the ancient fault lines between Islamists and secularists. Campuses that freed and secured their territory for students' experimentation with political contestation were pioneers in the making of new political patterns. Liberal universities that foster critical thinking and allow disagreement and opposition are the leading forces in the new urban politics, since they nurture the desire for freedom and rights for all, rather than the power to dominate.

The Epidemic: Contagious Freedom-Seeking on Campuses

The campus crisis worked as a litmus test to measure the extent to which individual campuses were able to accommodate democratic contestation and generate the advocacy of freedoms and rights. The immediate responses and participation of campuses in the protests varied widely depending on the political culture of each campus. Clearly, not every campus was as ready and equipped for democratic contestation and protest as ODTÜ was. And few campuses were capable of uniting the top administration, faculty, and students like ODTÜ.

The ODTÜ incident divided major universities in their reactions to the protestors and the police. The rectors of more than ten universities declared support for keeping the campus as an apolitical place. Associating being apolitical with nonpartisanship under authoritarian rule, they assumed that an apolitical campus was necessary for freedom of thought.[10] Other major universities criticized the police for using violence against students by defending students' rights of civic disobedience, protest, and disagreement. UF typically stood out in not hesitating a moment before uniting behind support for ODTÜ and condemning the police assault on it. The UF press release was soon followed by similar announcements from faculty of several other universities.

Considering the liberal democratic tradition at both ODTÜ and UF, it is not surprising that these universities united against the government's violation of freedom. Soon afterward, Bilgi University, a liberal private university, joined them. "In a place where opposition is not tolerated, one cannot talk about freedom of thought and expression. In a place where there is no freedom of thought and expression, one cannot speak of existence of universities," Bilgi's faculty declared.[11] It is significant that the universities that united over freedom and rights were divided and contested vocally on other issues.

Albeit incapable of a *prompt* alliance for freedoms, there was another category of campuses. They also fall into the scope of this study, since they displayed deep fault lines in the aftermath of the ODTÜ incident. The rectors of eleven campuses, including major universities in Istanbul, announced support for the government and expressed disapproval of the ODTÜ protestors.[12] These statements by the rectors came as a big surprise to the majority of faculty and students of these universities. Faculty objected to their rectors' public announcements, which had been made without consulting with them. The campus communities of these universities felt betrayed. As exemplified by Galatasaray University, the faculties of some of these campuses organized *despite* their rectors. They issued press releases and signed petitions criticizing the disproportionate use of police violence against nonviolent students. Galatasaray University's administration were split on the issue, however, unlike those of ODTÜ and UF, which, although deeply divided over political/ideological issues, united promptly on the issue of campus rights.

A few Galatasaray faculty members whom I talked to expressed deep frustration with the rector, who was an engineer. They complained that engineers in top-ranking positions failed to observe democratic norms and engage democratic governance and progressive conversations with faculty and students. The faculties of these progressive universities used the slogan "Don't Touch Our Students!" (Öğrencime dokunma!). While they organized press releases and petitions, their students organized campus protests. More than a week after the ODTÜ event, the Galatasaray students were still protesting on campus peacefully, demanding the resignation of their rector, who, according to the students, violated the principles of democratic representation and freedom of protest. The campus kept police forces out and the protests remained calm and nonviolent. Some faculty stated: "Our protest will remain nonviolent as long as the police are not let in." These nationwide campus protests provided laboratories for democratic contestation in a state that has increasingly used the excuse of security to suffocate freedom-seekers and eradicate zones of and for freedom.

UF and similarly contested universities rejected the government's security excuses. Ironically, safety and security at UF are achieved by keeping the police out of the campus, and not vice versa. These campus spaces clearly show that freedom and security are not mutually exclusive. On the contrary, UF's spatial politics suggest that there are elective affinities between freedom of expression and safety. Both are needed for political decency, civility, and democratic liberties to prevail.

Many urban campuses did not collectively participate in campus protests, however, and outside Turkey's major cities, most universities were silent on the issue. Those universities were not of direct interest for this study because of the lack of contestation on their campuses. Recep Tayyip Erdoğan University in Rize, a small city on the Black Sea coast, where Erdoğan's family is from, is a noteworthy example of a silent campus. The only public response from this university came from the rector, who merely expressed thanks and gratitude (şükran) to Prime Minister Tayyip Erdoğan (it was sarcastically suggested that this was because the university was named after the prime minister).[13] Meanwhile, Zaman, the newspaper of the Islamic Gülen Movement, accused the student protestors of turning the university campus into a place of confrontation and political disorder.[14]

The generalizability of urban space is not one of the goals of this study. Unlike the results of elections, the impact of spatial politics cannot and must not be measured by the number of places or the size or percentage of space involved. The scale of spatial politics and how far it reverberates are very often disproportionate to the size of the contested place. We do not need to measure how many square feet Tahrir Square comprises, for example, in order to analyze its impact. Similarly, the size of ODTÜ's campus had nothing to do with the impact of the protests there or at other Turkish universities, sending very strong, direct messages to the government and law enforcement.

CONCLUSION

The majority of research on youth/student movements pits campus politics against the government, the state, and/or the market economy.[15] However, the fault lines on campuses during the 2008–10 period reflected the divides within the governing institutions of the Turkish state. Although the campus divided deeply over the seemingly central question of Muslim inclusion, it united indiscriminately and promptly over rights and freedoms, including but not limited to academic freedom of expression.

As the book neared publication, the previously divided UF campus, so prone to fault lines, united (*kenetlenme*) once again in opposition to the AKP government's refusal to support Kurdish resistance to the forces of the so-called Islamic State of Iraq and Syria (ISIS) in Kobane, a city emblematic of independence for Syrian Kurds.

During the third term of AKP rule, liberal campuses with relative autonomy from the government united against the government's violation of freedoms. Broadly speaking, most of the alliances—and the following protests—on campuses revolved around the issue of authoritarianism versus a deeper democracy. The campus community in UF and a few other campuses succeeded in liberating itself from ideological fault lines and formed alliances for freedoms and civil rights. A politically liberal campus is a place that attracts and accommodates conflict and complication, while turning them into pro-active democratic contestation. This political and spatial process renders the UF campus an agentic place, which (re)generates sound, united resistance and opposition to authoritarian government.

When the government and official political channels became intolerant of and hostile toward opposition, the UF campus provided a free and safe platform for dissent. When the police abused their power in the aftermath of the Gezi protests, university campuses stood out with a distinct privilege: the rectors of universities decided whether the police were allowed or not onto campus territory. Keeping the police out, free campuses turned into safe islands negotiating the terms of democracy, particularly at a time when the government and its opposition were equally uninterested in and/or incapable of promoting civil liberties and rights. However, the resulting protests had an effect beyond the universities, because campus politics generated alliances across ideological, religious, ethnic, and class differences. Place-based contestation on urban campuses thus contributed to multisited negotiations in the wider society. University campuses are embedded in the larger urban politics and political culture of the country, and they also play a central role in transforming their surroundings and city life, while their intellectual community shapes political debates and public agendas.[16]

Finally, for security reasons, university campuses both in and outside of Turkey accommodate a strong police presence. Since they have a reputation for rapidly fueling political conflict, campuses all around the world are patrolled and monitored by heavy-handed law enforcement. The UF and some other liberal universities in Turkey counter this global trend by excluding police from their campuses and academic social and political life.

Part 3

The social is no longer seen as bound by "societies," but as caught up
in a complex array of twenty-first-century mobilities. . . . Mobility
as progress, as freedom, as opportunity, and as modernity, sit side by
side with mobility as shiftlessness, as deviance and as resistance.

Tim Cresswell, *On the Move*

ON "ETHNIC" NEIGHBORHOODS

BERLIN'S KREUZBERG is home to the largest Turkish immigrant community in the world. Among notable residents of Turkish descent are numerous renowned artists, filmmakers, actors, writers, and musicians, as well as many political leaders, policymakers, and activists. Two Bundestag members representing Germany's Green Party, Cem Özdemir (co-chair of the party) and Özcan Mutlu, have long resided in Kreuzberg. Considering that Kreuzberg is the hub of Turkish immigrant community in Germany, its strategic importance for the Turkish and German governments needs no further explanation.

Similarly, there are plenty of reasons why the Turkish diaspora matters to the Turkish government. National elections are among these reasons. Members of the Turkish diaspora abroad are allowed to vote in Turkish presidential elections, making Germany's two million Turkish immigrants pivotal. This explains Erdoğan's visit to Cologne in May 2014 to drum up support. However, his visit, which was right after the Soma mining disaster, in which many hundreds of miners died because of government's failure to enforce safety measures, led to a major controversy in Germany. Having been accused of using polarizing language and encouraging offensive attitudes toward Germany's chancellor, Angela Merkel, Erdoğan was not welcome in Germany. Engaging a polemic with Erdoğan in the following days, Cem Özdemir declared that the prime minister had lost the support of the Turkish immigrant community.[1] Having taken for granted the votes of an increasingly pious Turkish Muslim community in Germany, Erdoğan did not expect this backlash. Despite the large pious pro-AKP community in Germany, and in spite of a striking concentration of them in Cologne, he typically had presumed that the Turkish diaspora was unified and monolithic, underestimating its divided nature. States' "political interests in cultivating ties with 'their' transnational diaspora," is no secret to anyone.[2] However, in the case of urban diasporic space in Germany, the political patterns traversing local, national, and international levels are the fault lines—the divisive issues that lead to contestation. Highly contested urban spaces, including but not limited to diasporic space and university campuses, epitomize these fault lines and contestations. Although Erdoğan won the presidential elections, he remains dismissive of these divides and contestations in and out of Turkey.

The politics of immigration is a heavily spatial matter. Three specific spatialities are at work in this context. The first spatiality is the ongoing *mobility* between homeland and host land. As Erdoğan's controversial visit showcased, the movement of political leaders and activists points to power dynamics and conflicts that travel across the borders. The mobility of the business community indicates the interconnectedness of the market and the movement of capital, while the mobility of the artist community stands for the links and affinities of art. A second spatiality is the *multiscalar* nature of urban contestation that echoes and travels between local/urban, national, and international levels. Thirdly, the most contested immigration-related issues are political and *sociospatial inclusion*. This third spatiality renders politics of diasporic place central for issues of integration, inclusion, and mixing in the ethnic neighborhood.

From the perspectives of these three spatialities—mobility, scale, and inclusivity[3]—the ethnic neighborhood stands out with its specific location at the intersection of cracks both within and between the home- and host lands. Accordingly, since it is "ultra-affected" by local splits and political contestation in both countries, its impact on pro-democratic alliances calls for special attention. Then, the question is whether the immigrant neighborhood falls into one of these multilevel fault lines or propels pro-democratic practices and alliances in the home- and/or host lands. To what extent is the ethnic neighborhood affected by political turbulence in the homeland? In which ways is the ethnic Turkish neighborhood also affected by the disputes on immigration issues and policies in the host land at a time when Islamophobia is peaking? And most important, what comes out of the intersection of these multilevel fault lines in this contested place?

In the aftermath of 9/11, Islam has come to be seen as the "problem child" of the West and European democracies. Ethnic neighborhoods where immigrants from the Middle East/North Africa region are concentrated have since come to be referred as "Muslim neighborhoods" in Europe. Unsurprisingly, these neighborhoods have been increasingly associated with conflict and disorder.[4] Germany, with its large Turkish immigrant population, has been at the forefront of the debates on Islam in Europe.[5] Along with rising Islamophobia in the region, negative sentiments against Turkish immigrants have gradually escalated over the past decade. The backlash against immigrants is revealed at its best by the popularity of Thilo Sarrazin's book *Deutschland schafft sich ab* (Germany Abolishes Itself).[6] Meanwhile, the discovery in 2013 of the violence and murders committed by a racist, neo-Nazi "National Socialist Underground" (NSU) shook Germany's democratic image.[7]

Undoubtedly, German democracy is institutionally stable, safe, and sound. However, when it comes to the controversial issue of immigration, the polity does not seem to leave much room for efficient political contestation and democratic alliances. The right wing of Chancellor Merkel's Christian Democratic Union Party (CDU) continues to complain that Muslim immigrants have been poorly integrated, and in October 2010, Merkel herself alluded to the failure of multiculturalism in Germany. Her comments reinforced a political image of Germany that is neither Islam- nor immigration-friendly. Merkel may have hoped that "anti-immigration" rhetoric would win votes, but although conservative right-wing groups shared her standpoint, her speech aroused heated debates and deepened fault lines in the German political landscape. Opposition parties condemned it, and the deputy head of the Turkish community in Germany declared that "the government's immigration bashing is sending a signal to far-right parties and will only encourage extremism."[8] Moreover, there is disagreement within Merkel's CDU about these controversial issues.[9] Individual members can express their disagreement in the CDU, unlike in the top-down, hierarchical AKP, where opposing Erdoğan is very difficult.[10] Although a wide range of proposals for immigration reform have proven difficult to pursue further during Merkel's chancellorship,[11] the German political party system is entirely capable of addressing disagreements and discontents. Yet until the "Grand Coalition" was formed between the Social Democratic Party (Sozialdemocratische Partei Deutschlands; SPD) and the CDU in the 2013 elections,[12] Merkel's CDU continued to win sweeping victories, dominating the political realm.

INTEGRATION VERSUS ACCOMMODATION

German democracy, like many others in Europe, is deeply challenged by the "immigration problem." While competing explanations such as racism, fascism, and other ideological motivations exist in explaining anti-immigrant behavior and Islamophobia, most of the daily tensions are manifested in conflicting lifestyles in the cities. Conflicts range from clashing ways of life—such as practices of recycling, sartorial choices, and gender dynamics—to matters of religious observance. For example tensions surface in daily life between the environment-friendly Germans and observing immigrants of Turkish descent, whose religion requires them to sacrifice animals during the sacred month of Ramadan. These tensions often peak, and are manifested through various forms of incivility in everyday life.[13]

In this highly sensitive political context, residential segregation and concentration of immigrants remains a highly contested issue. Is ethnic segregation caused primarily by immigrants' voluntary choice of housing because they feel safer and more comfortable or cherish a strong sense of belonging through self-segregation? Or is segregation mainly shaped by the state's behavior, urban policies, and/or socioeconomic conditions that disadvantage and discriminate against immigrants? A nationwide backlash against immigrants blames them for failing to "integrate" into Germany's dominant culture (*Leitkultur*).[14] This leads to critical views or condemnation of ethnically concentrated urban spaces.[15] Previous studies have explored if residential segregation or concentration correlates with religious conservatism and/or other sociological factors, such as lower-class status and lower levels of education.[16] "The hegemonic explanation for ethnic residential segregation is that immigrants do not want to integrate into German society and to mingle with German people but rather prefer to build so-called 'parallel societies' with their own cultural norms and practices," Sabina Grüner writes.[17]

But clearly, ethnic segregation is also caused by structural and institutional factors. Hence, the immigrants' sensibilities and choices cannot be understood separately from the state's immigration policies and urban and institutional infrastructure. In both ethnic enclaves and minority ghettos,[18] for example, there is "a prevalence of cheap and densely populated housing stock . . . poverty, and other indicators of dependency. The difference is that the enclave is understood to be a temporary residential way-station, while the ghetto is thought to ensnare people in a system"[19] that prevents minorities from becoming immigrants. It is important to note here that the place (*Ort*) both as an analytical category and as an actual place plays a role in shaping the status attached to membership in the host land. Spatiality in this context is regarded as a pivotal factor shaping the future possibilities of inclusion in the host society. Along these lines, ethnically concentrated places are differentiated from each other,[20] since, unlike enclaves and ghettos, some ethnic neighborhoods are formed by *preference* and *taste* rather than economic obligation. In contrast to these nuanced categorizations, research by leading urbanists in Germany indicates that residential segregation in Germany cannot be explained by the voluntary residential choices of immigrants, because social and economic constraints are too strong to ignore.[21]

However, this debate overall remains fixated on the persisting topics of assimilation and integration and therefore overshadows the key issue in immigration: the German state's failure to accommodate immigrants. Does integration require "becoming" and "living like" residents of German descent and adopting their lifestyles and worldviews?[22] Or does integration refer to a *more inclusive* approach, as in Canada's thriving multiculturalism experiment, where multiple communities coexist and cohabit in cities?[23] This question brings the contested space and the state to the forefront of the immigration debates, which have mainly been driven by the parameters of integration.

No doubt, the state's attitude and government policies toward immigrants matter deeply.[24] As Turkey, the German state bears an infamous historical burden of ethnic nationalism and the atrocities that came out of it. Both of these countries, despite currently being at different stages of democratization, have had various kinds of problems of inclusion and exclusion of ethnic/religious minorities into their cities and polities. One paradoxical difference in terms of inclusion is important to note in this respect: Muslims are the *minority* discriminated against in secular Germany, whereas pious Muslims used to be the marginalized (and victimized) *majority* in staunchly secular Turkey, but no longer are. As discussed in previous chapters, pious Muslims have, in fact, acquired both political and economic power in Turkey over the past decade, which shifted power dynamics between the pious and the secular.

As Roger Brubaker (1992) emphasizes in his comparative work on Germany and France, the former's ethnic nationalism and ethnically determined notions of citizenship stand out. After decades of controversy and debates, Germany gave immigrants of Turkish descent the right to choose German citizenship on the condition that they gave up their Turkish citizenship. At the same time, the persistently strong German economy began attracting other immigrants from economically weaker parts of Europe. Unlike immigrants of Turkish descent, the newcomers, for the most part, neither spoke German nor had any sense of belonging to Germany. How is Kreuzberg affected by these different political processes in the host country and homeland?

"[S]ocial life . . . suffused by state practices not only extends the apparent *spatial reach of state power*, but also reveals its geographical unevenness," Joe Painter observes.[25] On the one hand, how do the power/authority of both homeland and host country operate in ethnically concentrated Kreuzberg? On the other hand, how far do the urban fault lines manifest in Kreuzberg stretch within and between the homeland and the host country?

MULTISCALAR CONTESTATION IN DIASPORIC SPACE

Kreuzberg provides a puzzle to politics of scale because fault lines traveling both ways between Turkey and Germany collide and intertwine in this ethnic neighborhood. Called "little Turkey," Kreuzberg provides a challenge to our preestablished spatial bias in terms of belonging and political membership. Common wisdom identifies belonging to a polity with national territory and the imagined community of the nation.[26] Kreuzbergers' primary attachment to their neighborhood defies conventional norms of belonging to either the German or the Turkish nation. Most Kreuzbergers claim only Kreuzberg as their home territory and community. Many are born, live, go to school, and socialize within this ethnically concentrated neighborhood all their lives.

Candan Turan's autobiographical film *Canım Kreuzberg* (Kreuzberg my love) is telling in this regard. The film begins in a Turkish village, where Candan, a third-generation Turkish German, is visiting her grandmother, who moved back to Turkey for good (*kesin dönüş*).[27] Although she has feelings for her grandmother's village and home country, it is obvious that Candan is simply a temporary visitor, a foreigner there. The film ends in Kreuzberg on a note that Candan does not belong to Germany either, since she does not feel welcomed to do so. Clearly, her associations with space/place in both Germany and Turkey are weak, but her belonging to Kreuzberg comes out clear, strong, and unquestioned. It is her neighborhood that takes on the central role of being the hub of belonging, membership, contestation, and inclusion, as well as other political and affective ties.

The primacy of Kreuzberg for the sense of belonging of its Turkish German residents is one of the several manifestations of divisive immigration issues. Recently gentrified, Kreuzberg has, like several highly contested sites in Istanbul, become difficult to share—in this case, not between secularists and devout Muslims as in Teşvikiye—but *within and between* antagonistic ethnic German and Turkish-descent residents. Divided immigrant groups as well as native Germans contest, claim, and negotiate for Kreuzberg by displaying various forms of territoriality. When Thilo Sarrazin visited "Kotti" (Kottbusser Tor) in Kreuzberg in July 2011, a year after his provocative book came out, Kreuzbergers reacted emotionally. Some called for him to be kicked out of the neighborhood, yelling: "Sarrazin muss weg aus Kreuzberg!" (Sarrazin must get out of Kreuzberg). Others engaged in heated debates about claims to space, belonging, and other rights of immigrants. In response, Sarrazin and his like-minded followers have accused the Kreuzbergers of not being able to engage in dialogue and of being undemocratic. For the right-wing, anti-immigrant political leaders, the divisive event became yet another token to argue for the incompatibility between Muslims and democracy.

While Kreuzberg is entirely vulnerable to these large-scale divides in the German state and society, it is also split by the major fault lines that divide Turkey and the Turkish state. However, since studies of immigrant neighborhoods have primarily shown interest in assimilation and integration, existing scholarship has not paid much attention to the multiscalar quality of conteststions in the immigrant neighborhood. More specifically, although we heard a lot about the scale of global capitalism, state spaces, contentious politics, and transnational movements,[28] little has been said about the scale of urban contestation (fault lines and alliances) over freedoms in the context of the immigrant neighborhood. Moreover, the defense of one scale over the others has also obscured our understanding of the centrality of the multiscalar politics of diasporic place.[29]

Most recently, the increasing frequency and visibility of urban uprisings has reinforced romanticism about the local scale. Critical of attributing something inherently "good" to the local scale, Mark Purcell rightly warns us:

> [I]t is dangerous to make any assumption about any scale. Scales are not independent entities with pre-given characteristics. Instead, they are socially constructed strategies to achieve particular ends. Therefore, any scale or scalar strategy can result in any outcome. Localization can lead to a more democratic city, or a less democratic one. *All depends on the agenda of those empowered by a given scalar strategy.*[30]

As Purcell puts it, neither the local nor the (inter)national scales produce *inherently* authoritarian or democratic politics.[31] These characteristics are contingent on many factors, including but not limited to historical, political, and socioeconomic conditions, and how these conditions are appropriated by nonstate or state actors. To complicate scalar politics further, one can highlight discord between different scales; even in deep democracies, we can find authoritarian localities that violate liberties, such as neighborhoods or organizations that master rigid exclusion and/or repression without prior planning or strategizing. In sharp contrast, microzones of freedom may be carved out abruptly in authoritarian regimes, such as underground organizations and the private domestic parties of the residents of Tehran under the Islamist regime.

But if local politics are not inherently better than that at other levels, contrary to what many activists for radical democracy argue, then what makes

highly contested places important in democratization? Bringing contested diasporic space into a rich literature on immigration and democracies enables us
to see what we cannot see otherwise: diaspora politics, the multiscalar spatiality of freedom and rights, and the democratic contestation over them. If contestations over freedoms do not reach other levels, local politics, as in Taksim
in Istanbul or Kreuzberg in Berlin, is unlikely to empower deeper democracy
overall.[32] Moreover, urban space that generates contestation beyond the national boundaries onto the international level is further empowered by virtue
of new global audiences, participants, and alliances. Hence, the interlocks between various scales of politics are indicative of the "spatial reach" and thereby
the power of democratic contestation.

6 KREUZBERG'S DIVIDED DIASPORA

SOME 40 PERCENT of Kreuzberg's residents may be Turkish Germans, but behind the neighborhood's claims to ethnic and cultural diversity, everything seems to come apart: the people, groups, associations, and the landscape. Kreuzberg creates the impression that Turks all arrive on German soil loaded down with ancient antagonisms from their homeland. Groupings of Turkish descent segregate themselves, each to its own "ghetto." Secular Alawites cannot get along with Islamists, who are in turn divided into the mutually non-cooperative Millî Görüş (National Vision)[1] and Gülen Movements. The LGBT community and the Islamists cannot get along easily, and the Kurds and the nationalists are traditionally antagonistic. What makes Kreuzberg remarkable is that the deep fault lines that divide the immigrant community are compressed into a small, overpopulated area. Located in the heart of Kreuzberg, Kotti is home to the congregations of both Islamist Millî Görüş and Alawite Cemevi mosques, as well as to LGBT clubs and associations. Clearly, none of these are friends or allies, but they cohabit on the same dense and crowded streets without any safety problems. On an ordinary day in Kotti, drug users and punks may mingle at one end of the street while Turkish-descent mothers push their children's strollers at the other, and feminists can be seen organizing outside all-male Turkish coffee shops.

Kreuzbergers from all walks of life and every ethnicity and class almost always defend their neighborhood proudly as a peacefully diverse haven. During my visit in 2012, I was chatting with Matthias, a PhD student in German history and a proud Kreuzberger. Matthias was also working for a company of tour guides in Berlin. I wondered how Germans all over the country viewed

Kreuzberg. I asked: "Would they consider it a ghetto?" He responded: "No, absolutely not a ghetto. Its image is liberal and diverse. Haven't you heard the term *Kreuzberg Mischung* [Kreuzberg mixture]? It's a place where everyone mixes *voluntarily*."[2]

On a beautiful summer day, I went for a long walk along the canal in Kreuzberg with several young second- and third-generation Turkish Germans, whose families lived in various parts of Germany. Several of them had moved from different German cities to Kreuzberg to study and/or work in Berlin. We discussed their different perspectives on the so-called Turkish neighborhoods across Germany. Osman, a second-generation Turkish German, proudly promoted *his* Turkish neighborhood in Cologne, saying that it was "a little bit outside the city but much better than Kreuzberg." In Osman's well-off neighborhood in Cologne, Turkish Germans lived in big houses with higher standards and well-groomed backyards. Faruk, a Berliner by birth, looked at Osman skeptically. Faruk clearly held Kreuzberg in much higher regard. He seemed reluctant to compare it, not only to any other Turkish neighborhood in Germany, but also to any other Muslim neighborhood in Europe. "The Turks in Kreuzberg are diverse. . . . the key is that they all live peacefully side by side with one another and Germans here," Faruk said. "We are also proud that Kreuzbergers have different class, ethnic, religious, and professional backgrounds. These [things] make Kreuzberg different from other immigrant neighborhoods."[3]

Regardless of the various motivations for living in or moving to Kreuzberg, one thing was clear. This exciting, rapidly gentrifying popular downtown neighborhood was no longer seen by Germans and the German state as a segregated ghetto or an enclave inhabited largely by an immigrant group. But, from the official point of view, an ethnically concentrated immigrant neighborhood that is in the most popular and central part of the city is a contradiction in terms.[4] To the extent that Kreuzberg stands out as "an anomaly" among other ethnically concentrated neighborhoods, it puzzles and confuses politicians and urban planners. As the term "Kreuzberg mixture" makes clear, Kreuzberg stands out as a strikingly inclusive place. It attracts artists and yuppies not only from all over Germany but from all over Europe and the world. Hence, rather than failure of integration, the unexpected and unaccustomed nature of mixing in Kreuzberg is likely to puzzle and discomfort policymakers. But officially the lack or failure of integration is still identified as the major problem. As a prominent Turkish German theater director who lives in Kreuzberg observed to me: "When German policymakers do not understand and fail to explain a process or a phenomenon regarding immigration, they opt to make a 'problem' out of it."[5] Most Kreuzberg residents whom I talked to, both immigrant and native German, concur that most political parties failed to attend to and handle the so-called Kreuzberg question with sociopolitical insight and socioeconomic sensitivity. They identify one exception—the Green Party, whose candidates have been consistently successful in local elections in Kreuzberg over the past two decades.

The discomfort with unusual forms of mixing in contested urban sites can be compared to the AKP government's picking on freedom-seeking, liberal university campuses, Gezi Park in Taksim Square, or Asmalı Mescit. Do diasporic urban sites in Germany simply stand for a curious and ambiguous mix of people, referred superficially as *diversity*? More bluntly, does this so-called diversity in Kreuzberg consist of parallel but disconnected lives that coexist although divided and alienated from one another? Or does this highly contested and deeply divided urban space generate *a new alchemy*, new forms of interaction between previously antagonistic ways of life? Do these contestations occasion peaceful cohabitation and culminate in democratic pluralism by pushing for democratic liberties and the rights of minorities?

BERLIN AND KREUZBERG
AT THE INTERSECTION OF FAULT LINES

Since the 1990s, Western democracies have become more and more self-conscious and concerned about the increasing presence of Islam in Europe. Reasons include the mushrooming of Islamic movements in urban space[6] after the Iranian revolution and the ongoing disputes over the head scarf, particularly in France and in Germany, since the late 1980s.[7] As a result, Germany's persistent problem with Turkish immigrants since the 1960s has gradually resolved into an "encounter with Islam." Put differently, with the new centrality of Islam as a threat to peace in world politics, the "immigration problem" in Germany has acquired a Muslim face.

In West Berlin, the larger effects of the reunification in 1989 went hand in hand with a major realization that the Muslim immigrants were not only there to stay, but also to become part of the urban life and even politics.[8] Particularly after 9/11, Berlin's notorious immigrant neighborhoods came to be seen as "Muslim neighborhoods." Over the past decade in Germany, as in other European democracies, the immigration issue has become overwhelmingly about "Islam" and its presumed incompatibility with secular Europe.[9] Yet different democracies have responded differently to the "threat of Islam."[10] Not surprisingly, the German media capitalized on the controversy growing out of its largest immigrant population—the conflict between secularist and pious Muslim Turkish immigrants. In recent years, heated debates in which secularist Turkish Germans have articulated anti-Islamist and even Islamophobic arguments have become popular on German television channels.[11] Meanwhile, liberal-minded Turkish Germans have shown themselves more open to dialogue with pious Muslims.[12] Currently, this divide between secularists and Islamists is the most visible split in the Turkish-descent immigrant community. In Kreuzberg, it is manifested most often between the secular Alawite community and Turkish German supporters of the AKP government.

Until the demise of the USSR in 1991, Europe's major divide was between the communist Eastern Bloc and the liberal democracies. The fall of the Berlin Wall in 1989 made that city paradigmatic of "mixing."[13] Elizabeth Strom asks, "What happens . . . if you take a city, draw a hostile border down the middle, create contrasting economic and political systems on either side, and then remove the border two generations later?" After 1989, when the previous border was abolished, the Berlin Wall became a "wall in [the] mind" between East and West Germans.[14] As with the spatial transgressions between Islamist and secular spaces in Istanbul in late 1990s, East and West Berliners may have crossed over spatially, but they maintained different sensibilities and practices in daily life. Many of them diverged in their lifestyles and consumption patterns. However, like the pious and secular citizens of Istanbul, they eventually mixed for practical reasons, such as commuting to work, education, shopping, and housing preferences.[15] Although they had different visions and memories of the city and attached different symbolic meanings to neighborhoods, buildings, and public spaces, they gradually ended up mixing and mingling—albeit often with reservation and hesitation.

Clearly, unlike the unspoken borders between Islamist and secular neighborhoods that divided Istanbul in the 1990s, the Berlin Wall had been a material barricade until its demolition in 1990. Although different politics (communism versus capitalism; Islamism versus secularism) divided both the society and the urban landscape, the dispute was over the relationship between urban space and power politics in each case. Like Istanbul, Berlin witnessed a shift from broader politically hostile fences dividing the city into micro fault lines that divided people based on their different lifestyles, habits, and practices. When I first visited Berlin in the fall of 1999, the city was still very much in perplexity and trying to figure out reunification. The historical pain and political burden of the wall was still heavy almost ten years after its demolition, and its imprint was still stamped on city life.

When I began conducting fieldwork in Kreuzberg just a decade later in 2010, Berlin was a much more festive and dynamic place. It had evolved into a haven for internationally renowned artists, intellectuals, and musicians. By the end of the first decade of the new millennium, Berlin has inarguably become a major center of European culture, civilization, and art. Moreover, many fans of Berlin were very explicit about their preference for Kreuzberg.

After being the most heavily populated and industrialized area of Berlin since the second half of the nineteenth century, Kreuzberg had many impoverished inhabitants. Many longtime immigrant residents I interviewed had vivid memories of the neighborhood from a few decades ago. Not long after construction of the Wall was begun in 1961, Kreuzberg gave shelter to the first wave of immigration from Turkey, becoming a "Turkish ghetto." Squatting in houses that were abandoned after the Wall was erected, a variety of anarchists, drug addicts, gays, lesbians, punks, and other "outcasts" of the 1960s made their homes alongside the Turks in this marginal place. Lying as it did on the outskirts of West Berlin, Kreuzberg sat physically at the barrier between the East and West. In this sense, the Turkish ghetto was born at a fault line between the worlds of communism and capitalism. Like other immigrant ghettos in Europe, Kreuzberg was a deprived, rundown place with substandard housing. Unlike the ghettos in the downtowns of American cities, the ethnically segregated places in European cities have typically been located at the city's outskirts, like the banlieue in France.[16]

By 1975, Turkish immigrants were attracted to "Berlin's relatively convenient housing-market condition and the subsidies provided for the inhabitants of this [then] isolated city."[17] Enclosed by the Berlin Wall on three sides, Kreuzberg seemed an efficient place for the segregation of the Turkish workers, referred to at that time as *Gastarbeiter* (guest workers). They were guests who were expected to go back to their homeland eventually. Housing conditions were so bad that three or four apartments in a building were sharing the same bathroom. In the mid-1970s, politicians began to object to the ethnic concentration in Kreuzberg, arguing that it would hinder integration. Between 1975 and 1990, "somewhat discriminatory regulation" was in place, which limited the movement of foreigners into other ethnically concentrated areas.[18]

For a long time, Kreuzberg had the stigma of a poor Turkish ghetto that the German politicians would have rather gotten rid of. In fact, many politicians tried to eradicate it from the maps by proposing various urban development projects that would destroy Kotti, the hub of Turkish diaspora. Until the Wall came down, many ruling parties tried to tear down the buildings in Kotti to build a highway connecting the Wall zone with the rest of the city. Plans were made for a highway from Kotti at the Wall to Neukölln and Wedding. However, I was told in my interviews with the longtime Kreuzbergers that "the resistance from the Turkish residents of Kotti was so strong and persistent that no political force could touch the neighborhood, no matter how much they tried." Most of the German Kreuzbergers that I talked to also gave a lot of credit to the Turkish immigrants in this strong urban resistance.

In most parts of Europe, urban policy and democratic ideals have often come into conflict in dealing with immigration issues. For example, in France, "urban policy . . . became increasingly concerned with issues of immigration and insecurity often to the detriment of its initial social and democratic ideals."[19] In contrast, Kreuzberg's major political and spatial transformation was *not* triggered by a change in the German state's urban planning policy. Rather, the abolition of the Berlin Wall put Kreuzberg right in the middle of the unified city.[20] This was unintended. The centrality of *unforeseen* political shifts to spatial transformations is often conveniently neglected in policy studies. Kreuzberg provides a precious laboratory to study the shift from a ghetto to a flourishing ethnic neighborhood that was not the result of policy and deliberate collective action. This is analytically noteworthy, since it also shows that the difference between the "bad" ghetto and the "good" ethnic neighborhood is *not* necessarily caused by the failures of the immigrants, but mainly by other unintentional external factors.

Highlighting the paradoxical and dialectical nature of segregation and mixing, Andreas Glaeser writes: "German unification . . . has divided the country."[21] However, the ironic divisiveness of the country's reunification had a positive effect on Kreuzberg. Although spatial and sociopolitical change did not pick up immediately,[22] over the next decade the segregated Turkish ghetto turned into a diverse, hip neighborhood that cherished the predominant Turkish culture of the immigrants.[23] While economic constraints and gentrification put pressure on and forced out many old residents, who persisted in staying put there for decades,[24] Kreuzberg has become highly attractive to many who can afford the rising costs of housing. Its "countercultural" image has persisted, but the meaning attached to that image has changed dramatically: formerly seen as a dumping ground for the unwanted poor, it has emerged as a fashionable middle-class neighborhood.[25]

The long-term effects of German reunification on Kreuzberg are multi-faceted and beyond the scope of this study.[26] But architecturally, old buildings were gradually renovated, and the streets began to look much different. Most of this urban renewal was not premediated or strategized in advance by either the Turkish diaspora or the urban planners. It all came by surprise in the aftermath of reunification. By 1990, 134,000 of the 1.7 million Turkish Germans were living in Berlin. Today, there are some 200,000 in Kreuzberg alone. Rapid gentrification has led to a new compartmentalization—Kreuzberg now has rich and poor ends. At the rich end, Bergmannstraße (Bergmann Street), with its fashionable boutiques, restaurants, and bars, stands out, attracting a population whose clothes, food preferences, and lifestyles make clear statements about their opinion of themselves. Some Turks who originally came to Germany for higher education, graduate studies, or career reasons have also moved to this fancier part of Kreuzberg, as have some lawyers, doctors, and academics of Turkish descent. On the less well-off side of the district, Kotti's popular streets, such as Oranienstraße, attract by reason of their diversity and vivid 24/7 life.

"NEIGHBORHOOD PRESSURE TRAVELS INTERNATIONALLY!"

I met Özcan Mutlu, a leading member of the Green Party since 2000 and a Bundestag MP, on a panel at the Staatlichen Europa-Schule Berlin (SESB; State European School) in Kreuzberg. German, Turkish, and children of parents from other countries attend the European school together. During the panel, Mutlu and spokespeople from other political parties discussed their policies and agendas with the high-school students. Afterwards Mutlu and I walked to the Landwehr Canal, which borders the school and runs through Kreuzberg and Neukölln. We chatted about Mutlu's life and politics over brunch at a boat-restaurant on the river. The son of a family that emigrated to Germany in 1973 from Gümüşhane in Turkey, Mutlu is a prominent political figure in Germany and something of a local fixture in Kreuzberg. He has strong feelings of belonging to the neighborhood.

Mutlu began his conversation with me by emphasizing that Kreuzberg was a microcosm of the homeland, Turkey.[27] He went on:

> I was bike-riding with my daughter on Unter den Linden [one of Berlin's most affluent boulevards]. We stopped at the Imbiss and ordered currywurst [pork sausage topped with curry ketchup, fast food typical of Berlin]. They charged two euros. I paid but asked in German if this was not too much for sausage.

Not having realized that I was from Turkey, the guys who served me began to talk to each other in Turkish, complaining, "The pork-eater does not want to pay for it." Only then did I realize that they were from Turkey. They did not recognize me, so they can't have been into politics. When they started grumbling in Turkish, I asked for my money back in Turkish. They started swearing at me in Turkish, so the other people at the counter could not understand their insults and be witnesses.

The controversy had gotten out of control. More Germans were watching and trying to understand what was happening. Then they called the police and made mutual complaints. Mutlu continued:

But I realized what the real problem was much later. The guys who served me the food were upset, not only because I ate pork during Ramadan, but also because they had sworn at me, and every time they swore, they violated their fast. They were angry at me for ruining their fast. When the police came, they asked them, "If eating pork is a sin, isn't selling it during Ramadan one too?"[28]

Like many secular Turks, Mutlu, a secular Alawite, did not observe the Ramadan fast. He is a well-respected resident of Kreuzberg, where he has lived for thirty-seven years, and has served the Turkish community in many ways. This has made him a well-known figure on the German political scene.[29] However, since the currywurst incident, he has been called temperamental and charges have been leveled at him regarding a conflict he had with the police ten years ago. His opponents say his temper caused the trouble. Mutlu denied this to me, calling it nonsensical and saying that it was aimed at countering his claim that "neighborhood pressure" is a major new problem in Berlin.[30]

Mutlu felt pressured by the Sunni Turkish community in Berlin. Religion was becoming more visible and self-imposing in Turkish immigrant communities in Germany, he observed to me. It has become a common practice to associate the pressure exerted by the pious on the secular with the neighborhood in Turkey. But, it is particularly striking that the currywurst incident happened on Unter den Linden, a nonethnic "white" street of Berlin. When I asked what neighborhood pressure had to do with a "white" nonimmigrant neighborhood in Berlin, Mutlu smiled and said:

Well, you know . . . what we refer as *mahalle baskısı* (neighborhood pressure) does not only take place only within the *mahalle* (neighborhood). In fact, neighborhood pressure is impossible in our neighborhood in Kreuzberg. It is defeated by the diversity and willpower of local Kreuzbergers. You know why? Because people know and trust each other in that neighborhood. People know me. Familiarity makes a sin "your sin," and nobody would interfere with that in my neighborhood.

Here, Mutlu puts his finger on the core of neighborhood politics. Kreuzberg was *his territory*, to which he feels a strong belonging. In his own neighborhood, he feels safe, recognized, and respected. The sense of belonging to a place gives a strong sense of empowerment and emancipation, even to a Bundestag member. In diasporic Kreuzberg, which is so unlike not only his hometown in Turkey but any other neighborhood in Germany, he feels free, sheltered, and in control of his own personal sphere. As discussed earlier, the strong claim to a certain urban space lies at the heart of the spatiality of freedom. Whether it is within the borders of the homeland or abroad, this spatiality largely underlies a sense of self-actualization, privacy, and freedom to adopt one's own lifestyle and indulge one's own tastes. The intimacy of place is the key to the ongoing political contestation over the "ownership," control, and utilization of territory. The *exclusionary* social and political conditions for Muslim immigrants render the *inclusive* neighborhood a rare privilege, which becomes a magnet for immigrants and other marginalized groups who feel discriminated against.

Mutlu is a strong advocate of the rights of Turkish and other immigrants in Germany and beyond. He is highly informed, well spoken, and very experienced in both the problems and solutions of the immigration question in Europe and Turkish-immigrant issues in Germany. In this respect, it is thought provoking to hear him argue that he feels *no pressure* in his neighborhood, while a few miles away from his "nest," he was pressured and harassed by pious Muslim Turks. In the heart of a global city in one of the strongest and most stable democracies of the world, the conditions of Mutlu's freedom seemed to depend on the local—the streets and neighborhoods of his territory. This is ironic. How can the perception and practices of freedom and rights change from one neighborhood to the next, where the overarching rule of law is supposed to apply consistently across Berlin and Germany (and in certain respects even across the supranational EU)?

The increasing importance of neighborhood politics analyzed here has little to do with the delegation of decision-making authority from the centralized state to local authorities and grassroots activists. On the contrary, unlike strategic community building or activism in urban democracy, the neighborhood politics in question seems to be a rather unintended aspect of ordinary people's ways of life and discontent. In the case of Germany, the accommodation of Turkish immigrants and their rights and liberties present a major challenge to the depth of democracy. But could the neighborhood pressure be blamed on the German government if Turkish Germans are pressuring, harassing, and offending each other at the local level? How could the German state be held responsible for pious Muslims pressuring secular Alawites on the streets of Berlin (or vice versa)?

Mutlu explains neighborhood pressure and the related urban unrest primarily on the basis of homeland politics in Turkey.[31] According to him, the unprecedented third term of the pro-Islamic AKP government has given pious Turkish immigrants in Germany a sense of entitlement to interfere in or dominate the lives of the secular Turkish diaspora. Mutlu's stories suggest that the *reach* of AKP's hegemony had a major impact on urban life in the Turkish neighborhood. Later, in my conversations with other Turkish German Alawites, I noted similar opposition to the AKP government, which they saw as oppressive of the Alawite minority.

Mutlu paused and took a sip of his Turkish coffee. How, I asked him, had neighborhood pressure, "an apparent Turkish export," moved to Germany? He gave me a compelling response: "Neighborhood pressure travels internationally!" But how and why could the spatial political patterns in an Istanbul neighborhood "jump" to a place in Europe? How far could the concurrent fault lines extend by cutting across, not only the neighborhoods, but the borders of the Turkish state?

> In topographical terms, the greater the distance that powers are dispersed or decentralized, the more spatially *extensive* is the reach of the state's authority. Reach, here, can be measured in miles and kilometers, but in practice the "reach of government" more often than not refers to its *pervasive quality*; the ability of the state to permeate everyday life.[32]

The capacity of states and governments to permeate and shape both societies and urban space has been discussed widely in existing literature.[33] But the sphere and scale of influence of the states on the diaspora and diasporic space are less thoroughly studied. How does the immigrant-sending state impact diasporic spaces in the host country? What is the interplay between the government in the homeland and the ethnic neighborhood in the immigrant-receiving country?

The immigrant neighborhood in the host country further complicates democratic contestation by dumping the fault lines of homeland on top of the existing conflicts in the host land. These various fault lines deepen in the ethnic neighborhood, since the conflicts in both states intersect and often clash and grow inflamed in the ethnic neighborhood. This is why this meeting point reinforces the depth of democratic contestation in a cross-section, where the struggle over rights and freedoms multiplies. Hence, the *spatially extensive* reach of the immigrant-sending state and *politically intensive* democratic contestation in diasporic urban space mutually constitute each other.

THE "UMBRELLA" OF DEVOUT MUSLIMS
AND ITS DESIGNATED "OUTCASTS"

Tarhan Bey, the director of a major Turkish immigrant association based in Kotti, proudly told me that his organization represented more than half of the Turkish immigrant associations in Berlin. I wondered why, and which ones they *didn't* represent. Instead of directly answering my question, Tarhan Bey went around the issue I was digging in. Not having a straightforward response, I inquired one by one about individual organizations and, in doing so, found out a major divide in Kreuzberg. I learned that the LGBT, Kurdish, and Alawite organizations were not part of this self-claimed "umbrella" organization. "We only represent the associations that organize and behave according to our national values, norms, and conventions [*adet*]," Tarhan Bey explained.

I probed a little further: "But I visited GLADT [Gays & Lesbians aus der Türkei][34] and met several spokespeople for LGBT Turkish Germans. For example, two young gay members of GLADT, Serkan and Berk seemed to be quite accepted and respected in the Turkish community." Rather irritated by my comment, Tarhan Bey snapped: "Just because a Mr. Serkan and a Mr. Berk see themselves as respectable public figures, it does not mean that their *behavior* is accepted by *our* community."

Later, several leading members of the Turkish community told me that many groups left this self-claimed umbrella organization (henceforth UO)[35] after Tarhan Bey took over. He was the first religiously oriented director of UO. My interviews with the people who refused to be under the umbrella indicated that his directorship overlapped with AKP's electoral victories in Turkey. Particularly, in my interviews with the members of the Turkish LGBT and Alawite communities, I was told that UO has gradually become insignificant and irrelevant for them. They advised me that there was no need to waste time talking to

UO. Clearly, the feelings at both ends of the fault line in the neighborhood were mutually unfriendly.

Tarhan Bey's generalization about national identity was explicitly about inclusion and exclusion: His UO was deciding which groups and organizations were a good fit for national values and conventions? Who stood out, was left out, or failed to integrate into so-called Turkish national unity? Ironically, the exclusion exerted by the pious Muslims against nonreligious or secular Turkish immigrants reminds one of the Islamophobic exclusion of Muslim immigrants by the German right-wing groups. Put differently, UO's new hostility to the LGBT and secular Alawites seems like the mirror image of the CDU's prejudice against pious Muslim immigrants. While right-wing anti-immigrant Germans claim to represent and be the gatekeepers of the dominant culture (*Leitkultur*) in Germany, the UO adopts the AKP's efforts to "Islamize" the national culture outside of Turkey. As the host country accuses Turkish immigrants of not acclimatizing and behaving according to dominant German culture, the self-proclaimed UO blames the nonreligious or Turkey's minority groups for not observing the ways of life and worldview of the pious Muslim majority in Turkey. The fault lines of the two countries intersect and often reinforce each other in spatially complicated and politically compounded ways.

SPLITS AMONG PIOUS MUSLIM IMMIGRANTS?

When I hung out with Alawite friends in Kreuzberg, I realized that most of them were offended to be categorized as "Muslim Turks," and preferred to be referred as "secular Turks." All Alawites that I chatted and socialized with expressed feelings of being oppressed by the Turkish state, particularly by the AKP government. On my visit to their Cemevi mosque in Kreuzberg, I was presented with their heavy historical baggage of victimhood in addition to the latest forms of oppression they faced from the AKP regime. The spokesperson in the Cemevi, a highly educated Turkish immigrant proficient in German, English, and Turkish, reminded me that the young people who were killed by the police during the Gezi protests were mostly Alawites. The Turkish German Alawite community's relations with the German state were much more amicable than Alawite relations with the Turkish state and the AKP. They felt treated with more dignity on German soil, since they did not feel discriminated against because of their secular religion.

Sunni Muslim immigrants from Turkey had a very different relationship with the German state than Alawites. The spokesperson for the Kreuzberg branch of the Islamist Millî Görüş (National Vision) movement, Ahmet Bey, began his conversation with me by emphasizing the level of Islamophobia in Germany. During my visit to their organization near Hermannplatz in Kreuzberg, he and his co-workers complained about nonrecognition and discrimination against Muslims. One of the major problems for them was the German state's rigid limitations on opening ethnic or religious minority schools. In addition, they complained about the law that restricted the height of minarets. Two female members of the Millî Görüş emphasized the discrimination against head-scarved women in public services. My conversation with this small group of devout Muslims became even more heated when they angrily brought up the recent failed attempt to ban circumcision in Cologne. The devout Muslims of Millî Görüş were outraged by the current politics of the host country.

Our conversation at Millî Görüş moved from stories of repression of and discrimination against Muslims to promotion of their organization. Ahmet Bey explained to me that Millî Görüş offered courses on the Turkish language and Quran teachings despite the German state's inflexibility in curriculum and educational policy. He proudly praised their preschools and the elementary and high schools as the main outlets for proper education for Turkish children. German teachers taught all courses, including religion, in these schools. I had difficulty understanding what made Millî Görüş schools different from other German schools, and Ahmet Bey was disturbed by my questions. Unsure as to whether my inquiries were simply cynical or naïve, he explained in great detail that there were not enough Turkish German teachers who could teach in German. He also added: "Since the German state does not permit head-scarved immigrants to teach, it is harder to find Turkish teachers."

The difficulty of finding Turkish teachers reveals yet another incident of how fault lines at home and in the host country overlap and reinforce each other. Due to his or her political orientation, a secular or nonreligious uncovered Turkish immigrant would not accept a position in Millî Görüş schools. Shared nationality or ethnicity of Turkish immigrants was not enough to overcome the split between pious and secular Muslims, or between the followers and opponents of the AKP. Hence, the difficulty of finding a Turkish teacher was not entirely owing to the German state's policy but also arose from the rift between secular and pious Turkish immigrants.

Similar patterns of fault lines and anxieties can thus be observed in a neighborhood in Turkey—still in the process of democratization—and Germany, an advanced democracy. Parallel and concurrent contestations in neighborhood politics between neighborhoods of Istanbul and Berlin cannot be explained by a focus strictly either on the local or national level.[36] Although institutional political reform is often associated with the nation-state, the impact of the local level in political transformation should not merely be seen as a mirror image of the national level. The multilevel nature of democratic contestation is inadequately captured by either a top-down or a bottom-up analysis.[37]

Despite my insistent probing, Ahmet Bey did not mention any initiatives of Turkish Muslim schools other than those of Millî Görüş's own schools. A week later, I went to visit the Gülen Movement's Forum für Interkulturellen Dialog (Forum for Intercultural Dialogue, FID). Unlike the rest of the associations founded by Turkish Germans, FID was not located in Kreuzberg or in any ethnically concentrated location but in a nicely decorated large flat on the border of Mitte, close to Potsdamer Platz, known as the new business center of Berlin. The spacious flat had a lot of light, new furniture, and a very large meeting room. Macit Bey, a second-generation Turkish German citizen, was in charge of the Forum. He was born into a religious Turkish family. When he was a student, members of the Gülen Movement had contacted him. They asked him to work in the *Nachhilfe* (after-school) courses to help Turkish children who were in need of educational support. When he accepted the offer, he joined the Gülen Movement. Later on, Macit Bey decided to pursue a PhD degree in sociology and wrote a thesis on transnationalism.

Needless to say, my chat with Macit Bey took a very different direction than my conversation with the members of Millî Görüş. Macit Bey and I moved back and forth between academic debates and publications and practical issues of everyday life in Berlin. We exchanged scholarly references from sociological literature written in German on this issue and discussed each other's academic interests and work. With his openness to questions and scientific inquiry, Macit Bey struck me as more of a social scientist and researcher than a follower of a religious movement.

Over coffee, I asked him why the Gülen Movement does not have a presence in religious matters in the Turkish scene in Berlin. Why had it not opened even one mosque? Why didn't we hear the voice of the movement in the context of religious conflicts, such as the much-contested issue of minarets' height? Unlike Millî Görüş's Ahmet Bey, who was intimidated by my politically sensitive questions, Macit Bey took no offense. He smiled and responded: "That is not what we do here. I don't think this city needs yet another mosque [he smiled again]. We keep our projects separate from religion. It is also a matter of expertise. Our global initiative is about education not religion."

Right there, he was in sharp disagreement with the spokespeople of Millî Görüş, who were primarily focused on the religious needs of the Turkish Muslim immigrant community. Macit Bey explained to me that the burning problem for Muslim and Turkish immigrants in Germany was education. "We focus on what our expertise requires us to do," he said. When I brought up the restrictions against Muslims' opening their own schools, Macit Bey confirmed most of them. But then he added that the Gülen Movement had opened twenty-six schools across Germany under these dire conditions. I was surprised to hear this because none of the people I had met at Millî Görüş had mentioned these Gülen schools. Macit Bey explained to me that half of the teachers at Gülen schools were *Almancı*, a term used to describe Turkish immigrants in Germany. The Gülen Movement recruited them, as they had recruited Macit Bey. He explained to me: "Bringing in Turkish teachers from Turkey is difficult, because they cannot pass the compatibility [*denklik*] tests to qualify as teachers in Germany." He also agreed with Ahmet Bey that it was difficult to find a sufficient number of qualified Turkish German teachers. Instead of emphasizing the head-scarf issue, his explanation of this problem was the language issue: "Many *Almancı* may not be proficient in German."

Briefly, both the Gülen Movement and Millî Görüş were cognizant of the schooling problem, but their responses and solutions to the issue were radically different. Having a good deal of global experience in education, the Gülen Movement seemed to find its way into German society by opting to stay entirely out of the highly contested religious domain. Avoiding this high-conflict political issue was the key in making a space for their schools in this country, which is clearly suspicious of Turkish immigrants and Islam.

Similarly, the spatial distance of the Gülen Movement's center from Kreuzberg is very revealing of its politics in Germany. Considering that the Gülen Movement built a reputation for building bridges and forming dialogues among antagonistic groups, its choice to stay out of Kreuzberg may suggest that it refuses to be part of the deep fault lines there.[38] Overall, the spokespeople of the Gülen Movement often choose to stay out of any "ethnic cloistering" and "religious conflict," since these spatial and political splits may jeopardize their rapport with the German state. The Gülen Movement avoids contentious issues, seeking rather to remain strongly engaged with the host state as part of its global mission (a source of recent conflict between it and the AKP government, discussed in the Conclusion below).[39]

When I asked Macit Bey if the Gülen Movement was cooperating with any of the Turkish associations in Kreuzberg, he told me:

> Our doors are open to everybody. I personally reach out to most of them. Some respond, and we do projects together. Others don't. For example, the most difficult have been the Alawite organizations. As a sociologist, and the director of FID, I am entirely open to different groups and views. I called their association several times to arrange a meeting. This is how Gülen Movement operates, you know. . . . We feel responsible to build bridges, especially where they have been burned down previously. They told me that I should not visit their center, since it would be inappropriate. I said OK. But when I invited them over, I was told that this would also be inappropriate and provoke the Alawite community.

Macit Bey spent a good deal of time trying to overcome the issue of *spatial appropriateness*: who was entitled to visit whom, and where. When he later suggested a meeting in a "neutral zone," such as a coffee shop, the person on the phone from the Alawite organization preferred another, and the conversation went on like this in a futile way. At the end of this long road of spatial politics, they met at an Alawite coffee shop. But Macit Bey told me that despite his efforts, the meeting had not led to any future cooperation.

When I inquired further about their efforts to be inclusive, I learned that the Gülen Movement had no contact or made any effort to be in touch with Turkish LGBT groups. Clearly, its doors were not really open to everybody as advertised. Regardless of any strategic efforts to avoid conflict and conflict-ridden urban space, the Gülen Movement was not immune to the deep splits in the homeland. But there was an important similarity between the urban and political divides in the home- and host lands. Contrary to the German public opinion, the fault lines were not only between pious and secular Turkish immigrants, but also within them.

My conversation with Macit Bey made it very clear that there were no obvious ties between pious Muslim groups in Berlin. On the contrary, I sensed an unspoken rift and mutual avoidance between the Millî Görüş and the Gülen Movement.[40] When I asked if the two Muslim groups cooperated in anything, Macit Bey said, "Not really." "Why?" I asked. He bluntly told me that Millî Görüş was considered a "radical Islamist organization here." When I reminded him of the close links that Millî Görüş had with the DITIB (Diyanet

İşleri Türk İslam Birliği; Türkisch-Islamische Union der Anstalt für Religion/ Turkish-Islamic Religious Association), an official extension of the religious directorate (Diyanet İşleri Başkanlığı)[41] in Turkey, Macit Bey smiled. He observed that the DITIB was a recognized organization linked to Turkish Republic, and Millî Görüş was an Islamist association that was distrusted by the German state.

A few days later, I experienced an event that made me rethink Macit Bey's story about his efforts to connect with non-Sunni secular Alawites. I met Nedim, a Kurdish-Alawite filmmaker from Erzurum, Turkey, in a group of several filmmakers and screenwriters in a neighborhood bar in Kotti. After hanging out at the bridge and other hot spots of Kreuzberg with them all night, we were having soup in a Turkish snack bar in Kotti. At some point, I was asking Nedim a question about his short film: "Were they all Alawites and/or Kurds?" Owing to a sudden moment of silence, my voice echoed unexpectedly in the snack bar. Hearing my question, Turkish-speaking people at the next table looked at me strangely. Following this odd moment, they immediately got ready to leave in a hurry. More strangely, it did not take another minute until the lights of the snack bar began going on and off to show us that the place was closing. It was strange, as we were not even done eating yet. We were also not at all intending to leave yet. It was almost 5:00 AM—*Sahur* time in the month of Ramadan. Fasting Muslims eat at Sahur for the last time before they start fasting again for the next day. Hence, my other friend from Istanbul and I looked at each other curiously trying to make sense of just what was happening there.

Seeming to expect this odd chain of events, Nedim was already up and ready to go, and told the owners by passing: "Allah kabul etsin" (God accept your fasting). He hastily walked toward the door. The rest of us were kind of slower than him, as it took us another minute or two to realize that we were literally being kicked out of the snack bar. Outside, Nedim told us that the snack bar was owned by a pious follower of the Gülen Movement. Apparently, when they accidentally heard my question on Alawites and Kurds, they felt irritated. This incident made me think that perhaps the LGBT community were not the only group that the followers of the Gülen Movement kept a distance from in Berlin. More important, no matter how strongly the Gülen's FID may be aiming at dissociating itself from the fault lines, its followers in Kreuzberg seem to be deeply embedded in these divides.

The next day, Nedim came to my class in Kreuzberg to screen and discuss his short film with my students. His short film was on mistreatment and discrimination against Kurdish Alawites at Diyarbakır in Turkey, the hub of the Kurdish conflict there. After the screening, one of my students asked about political cleavage and discrimination in Kreuzberg. In response, Nedim gave them the common introduction to the "peaceful heaven" of Kreuzberg. He said: "All of us are getting along quite well here. Kreuzberg is a close-knit neighborhood of strong feelings of belonging." As our shared experience one night ago made it clear, Nedim was all too aware and familiar with the deep fault lines of the neighborhood. This did not change his feelings about and representation of Kreuzberg as a harmonious place.

LOCAL AUTONOMY FROM NATIONAL GOVERNMENT: A BENEFICIAL DISAGREEMENT?

During my fieldwork, Kreuzberg provided a rich laboratory to explore the increasing importance of local politics under the increasingly anti-immigrant conservative CDU government. The German state has three levels of governance—federal, city, and local.[42] The three different levels of the German state sometimes have various agendas and may therefore come into conflict in their policies. "The Basic Law requires that all levels of governments (federal, city and local) be democratically governed; the specific structure of local government is otherwise left to state legislation. *Cities are, however, not 'creatures' of the state* and local autonomy is guaranteed by the Basic Law."[43]

The relative autonomy of local government can be observed in different outcomes in Germany. Against the backdrop of the recent triumphs of rightwing nationalist governments in Germany and Europe, Berlin and Kreuzberg have predominantly voted for and been ruled by center-left parties. Under the CDU's federal government, the Greens have for a long time run Kreuzberg, while Klaus Wowereit, the SPD mayor of Berlin, is currently serving a third term in office in coalition with the Left Party. The divide between the CDU in federal government and two center-left parties at local and city levels creates strong checks and balances, and a relatively more nested political climate for Turkish diasporic space.

Given the very low percentage of Turkish immigrants not only in political bodies such as the Bundestag, but in public service such as the police and fire department, their political involvement and participation in German society occurs in unofficial neighborhood politics. Since dual citizenship is not permitted, one must renounce one's prior citizenship in order to become a German citizen, and many Turks in Kreuzberg do not choose to do this.[44] Tension over this surfaced during a public panel discussion I attended in Südblok, a popular lounge-bar in Kreuzberg, soon before the local elections in 2011.

The panelists were the candidates of five major parties running for local elections in Kreuzberg—the CDU, the FDP (Freie Demokratische Partei; Free Democratic Party), the SPD, the Greens, and the Left Party—and the audience consisted mainly of Kreuzbergers of Turkish descent, who varied in party allegiance.[45] With the exception of the candidate for the business-friendly FDP, the candidates of all the other four parties were also of Turkish descent.[46] Unsurprisingly, the parties all differed in prioritizing the issues of unemployment, affordable housing, safety, and integration.

After the short presentations of the electoral candidates, there was a question-and-answer period. The heat of the discussion reflected central importance of local politics to the audience. Specifically, the most widely shared discontent expressed by the audience was that residents of Turkish descent who had resided in Kreuzberg for decades but were noncitizens still did not have the right to vote at the local level. This clearly undermined their "right to the city" that would enable them to access and have a voice in shaping urban space. Many people in the audience made agitated comments and pressing requests for the disassociation of local electoral rights—rights to participate in *their* neighborhood politics—from citizenship rights in the country. Unsurprisingly, issues relating to immigrants and citizenship were not at all divisive of the audience and panelists, since they all agreed on these.

As I had previously noted in Kreuzberg, local residents disagreed about the safety of their neighborhood. The CDU's candidate, Ertan Taşkıran, who had lived in Germany since 1979, and in Kreuzberg since 1980, stood out in his emphasis on safety, and in my interview with him, I asked him about what made safety such a major concern there. His list of concerns was quite long, and included the drug addicts who hang around at the entrances of metro stations and parks. He also complained about street art, mainly the graffiti that covered buildings across Kotti. In sharp contrast to members and voters of the center-left parties, Taşkıran thought that the graffiti made the neighborhood look run-down, ugly, and like a ghetto.

Taşkıran observed to me that these matters were mishandled and were treated lightly by the party in office locally, the Greens, whose willingness "to accommodate the drug addicts in Kreuzberg" particularly infuriated him. "The Green Party assigned a designated corner to the drug-users in order to enable the police to keep an eye on them," he said. "It provides clean syringes

and placebo drugs." According to Taşkıran, this policy was attracting and encouraging drug users from other areas to hang out at Kotti. Several other residents, particularly parents of youngsters, also problematized the issue of drug
users. They stated that this policy was an extension of the state's former policy of concentrating marginals in this neighborhood. Taşkıran criticized these
policies and proposed harsher measures to ban drugs and to get drug users
out of the neighborhood. "Look at the streets and subway entrances! We are
scared to use the sidewalks. Local government's policy makes the neighborhood look bad," he said.

In sharp contrast, the candidates of the opposition parties—Greens, the
SPD, and particularly the Left Party—entirely disagreed with Taşkıran. There
was a firm consensus among all shades of the leftists and social democrats that
Kreuzberg was one of the safest places in Berlin.[47] "How can one feel not safe,"
an artist asked me "when the streets are full of people at all hours of the day
or night, and there is no trouble, no fighting or violence. People are too busy
having fun." Similarly, the leftist students and gay residents of Kotti concurred
in my interviews that the drug users do no harm to the neighborhood. "They
do their own thing. They don't disturb anybody," said a photographer of ethnic German descent. At other times, in my interviews with the Greens' Özcan
Mutlu and Figen İzgi, the candidate from the Left Party, both elaborated on
how safe and secure Kreuzberg was. No doubt, the current reputation of Kreuzberg as a safe immigrant neighborhood has a lot to do with its recent gentrification, which has overcome, albeit not entirely eradicated, the previous image of
it as a ghetto prone to violence.[48]

The CDU's Taşkıran is a practicing Muslim and was fasting during the pre-
electoral panel discussion in Kreuzberg. As our conversation following the
panel stretched into *iftar* (breaking the fast) time, Taşkıran did not mind breaking his fast in Südblok, where other customers were drinking alcohol at the bar.
When he began talking about the mosques, he told me that Kreuzberg was a
multicultural neighborhood and therefore "Arabs come to *our* mosque here."
Following up with his security concerns, I asked whether there was any radical
Islamist activity in the mosques in and around Kreuzberg. He said that there
was no security problem there posed by any religious group or sects.

Taşkıran also dismissed the Greens' class politics as pretentious and insin-
cere. He referred to the "two faces of Kreuzberg," based on the two-faced nature
of the Greens' politics, saying: "The wanna-be leftist Greens live in the *other*
Kreuzberg, gentrified, affluent, safe, chic Bergmannstraße. It is easier to object

to gentrification in Kreuzberg when you are conveniently settled in the well-off part of the neighborhood."

However, the mutual distrust between Left and Right in the Turkish immigrant community gives rise to many myths about their respective political leaders. Bundestag members Cem Özdemir, the leader of the Green Party, and Özcan Mutlu have both lived in Kreuzberg for a long time, Özdemir in a building in Kotti celebrated for having formerly been occupied by squatters.

Overall, the electoral victories and political achievements of the Greens in Germany by far surpass their successes in other democracies. Most important, the efficient disagreement between the CDU and its strong leftist opposition distinguishes Germany from other European countries. In France, for example, "an unprecedented coalition between the Right and Left" was facilitated to a certain extent by their shared anti-immigrationism and Islamophobia.[49] Accordingly, the disagreement between the CDU in power at the federal level and the Green Party running local government in Kreuzberg may serve as a beneficial divide. Fruitful disagreement between these political parties facilitated and strengthened discussion on many levels about the rights and liberties of immigrants, particularly until the Grand Coalition was formed between the SPD and the CDU in 2013.

7 EMERGING SOLIDARITIES IN IMMIGRANT ZONES

"DÖRFLICH . . ." (RURAL), said Inke, "sehr dörflich . . ." (very rural) to describe what is probably one of the most diverse neighborhoods in Germany and Europe. Sitting at her dinner table, I asked Inke curiously which aspect of Kreuzberg reminded her of a small village. Wasn't the kind of diversity that Kreuzberg sheltered often associated with capital cities? Inke sarcastically looked at her partner, Jürgen, and said "Jürgen could have invited probably a hundred friends tonight, all of whom live very similar lives in Kreuzberg, and all of whom agree on almost everything." The group of seven longtime Kreuzbergers laughed in agreement at the dinner table. Hans, who was comfortable speaking Turkish, and occasionally switched from German to Turkish when talking to me, followed up Inke's comment by saying:

> It is true actually. We take pride in the diversity of our neighborhood, but I say hi to like-minded people in every corner. . . . I have known these Kreuzbergers for a long time. Despite its diversity, Kreuzberg feels like *my little village*. I don't feel like that in any other part of Germany. I don't feel like that in Spandau [everybody laughs] or anywhere else in Berlin.

Other guests continued making fun about other parts of Berlin, ridiculing certain places. Inke and Jürgen, Kreuzbergers since the 1980s, were my neighbors. They lived in a condo facing the same courtyard as the condo that I sublet for the second time during my stay in 2012. After a few casual conversations on the playground in the courtyard, where our children played, and at our doorsteps, they invited me for dinner to introduce their Kreuzberger friends to me.

Inke and Jürgen's friends admitted that evening that they were all "addicted" to Kreuzberg—the only place where they felt at home. Kreuzberg was irreplaceable for them because of their personal and political history in the neighborhood, but also because of their shared lifestyles and worldviews. The village-like quality described to me was not much different from how residents of Teşvikiye and the UF community felt about their *intimate* space. All of these urbanites of different nationalities in two different countries shared a very strong and proud sense of belonging to and familiarity with their neighborhood. More important, with an explicit sentiment of territoriality, they projected their unfulfilled political demands and needs from their government onto that place, which they could mold, and would defend at any cost.

Although all of the guests at the dinner party had moved from different parts of Germany in 1980s, they all ended up staying in Kreuzberg for decades, despite unpleasant changes and challenges. Clearly, Kreuzberg was deeply affected by the major historical breakthroughs that Germany has gone through over the past few decades. What attracted these people a few decades ago to Kreuzberg, a *Stadtteil* (urban district) that bore the stigma of a Turkish ghetto until the new millennium? And what was keeping them there? Why didn't they move, given the challenges of life in a contested ethnic neighborhood, such as schooling problems and the increasing costs of housing because of gentrification? Moreover, in an era of increasing Islamophobia, why were they still living in an area 40 to 80 percent of whose inhabitants were Turkish immigrants (depending on the neighborhood)?

Echoing my previous conversations with many other German Kreuzbergers, Jörg explained: "Kreuzberg is the *least German place* in Germany, hence the least conservative." He added with a smile, "It is heaven for anti-nationalists, anti-sexists, anti-fascists, and anti-racists." Jörg was a university professor and had a lot of contact with Turkish students. I asked why he liked the least German place and Jürgen jumped into the conversation: "Like most conscientious Germans, we are regretful and afraid of what a stronger Germany is capable of doing. We are ashamed of our history. We are stuck with its ghosts forever. Don't you feel similarly about Turkey?"

I needed a few minutes to put these strong statements into perspective. Discontent with ultranationalism is rather common in Turkey and Germany. This common reaction of democrats is owing to the strong ethnic tone of nationalist sentiments and the history of political violence associated with it. But there was something more than the critique of nationalism in this conversation.

Were these German Kreuzbergers escaping to this "ethnic island" from their own nation-state by *finding refuge* in a Turkish ethnic neighborhood? And, more important, why did they happily stay in this "Turkish zone" at a time when "Muslim cloisters" were increasingly distrusted and suspected as hotbeds of bigotry, disorder, and violence? I found it interesting that in an age of rising anti-immigrant sentiments, progressive German residents of Kreuzberg expressed a "fear of a bigger Germany"[1] while objecting to the weaknesses shown by German democracy in its accommodation of ethno-religious minorities both in the past and currently. At the same time, I learned that these longtime Kreuzbergers had collectively opposed reunification in 1989, soon after which the Berlin Wall came down. This opposition was in line with their fear and distrust of a more powerful German state and society.

The agreement on these issues was so strong that each person at the dinner table had to explain to me in different ways and words why they were not proud of being German. Listening to this conversation, I thought that Inke was right. As if these people were reading one another's minds, they were finishing each other's sentences. Who were these like-minded inhabitants of this "village-like" place? My insatiable curiosity was somehow satisfied when I learned that in the 1980s and 1990s, this group of people had belonged to the former Autonomous Movement (henceforth AM).[2] When I inquired about the history of the AM and their past in the neighborhood, Anna said: "We came here to Kreuzberg because it was the only place that accommodated us, the anarchists in the 1980s. With our multicolored hair, anarchist looks, and marginal getups, we couldn't set foot in a regular neighborhood at night. We merged with outcasts in Kreuzberg."

As we enjoyed the delicious food that Jürgen had cooked, Anna continued: "We came here because of our political agendas and activism. Both Berlin and Kreuzberg have always been a place for radicals, their marginal lives, marginal art, and anti-system politics. This place never lost that quality. But I have to also admit that when we first came here, I was immediately struck by the women, their short hair and sexy looks."

Anna had moved to Kreuzberg with her anarchist boyfriend, but upon her arrival in the neighborhood, she discovered her interest in women and embraced her bisexuality. For decades, Kreuzberg has had the reputation of being the focal point for the women's movement and the LGBT community. When the guests showed me a sample of the magazine they had published in the 1980s against patriarchy and male violence, I started to get a better picture of their group. From that night on, my fieldwork integrated a new layer of inquiry about this "other" German face of Kreuzberg. In today's Kreuzberg, the former anarchists were notable for their *ökologische* (environment-friendly) sensitivities. They were all strong advocates of gender equality, peace, and freedom. The more I learned about their lifestyle, the clearer it became to me why they took pleasure in living alongside other ethnic, sexual, and religious minorities who were excluded and discriminated against by their own state and society.

During my several trips to Kreuzberg, I gradually realized that the love and attachment of the former anarchists for Kreuzberg could not simply be explained by a specific ideological drive. This was not simply a critique or dislike of capitalism, since they were pursuing quite bourgeois ways of life. Neither were they defending communism or anarchism—a utopia with which the AM movement had identified in the past. The guests admitted that that fervor had faded away a long time ago.[3] Nor could their urban politics and territoriality be reduced to their allegiance to other political ideologies that they actually held, such as environmentalism and feminism.

Astonished by the strength of the consensus among these progressive Kreuzbergers, I often asked: "Why Kreuzberg among all the other mixed neighborhoods?" I received very similar answers: "There is only one Kreuzberg in Europe where I can *breathe freely*. This is a unique place. I have larger needs and demands for freedom and rights." Others said: "All my friends and comrades live here. Where and why would I go?" Kreuzberg's former anarchists represent a new class of German urbanites committed to a middle-class lifestyle with more freedoms, which German political culture has so far failed to give them. They felt betrayed and pushed to the margins as anarchists in the past and as feminists, environmentalists, LGBT supporters, or activists more recently. But throughout their past and present, they had all felt alienated and suffocated by orthodox German political culture.

The AM and the Turkish immigrant community had arrived there at around the same time. They had not mixed much originally, but both contributed to the formation of a "new" kind of urbanism—"new" in the sense that it was a safe and protected island. In this island, minorities shared their zeal for "rescuing" their rights and freedoms from the German state. Very much like the gay community and the Turkish immigrants, the former members of the AM defined themselves as "fugitives" in Germany. Kreuzberg enables them to escape the predominant political culture in Germany, which they despise and look down on as conservative, exclusionary, patriarchal, and anti-immigrant.

Although the Kreuzberg residents of ethnically German and Turkish descent seem to be negligent, or even sometimes in denial, about their shared urban politics and lifestyles, there is a very fundamental issue that ties both to this neighborhood: their sense of belonging is to Kreuzberg more than to their respective homelands. Although the CDU is not guilty of the kind of political repression and hegemony that characterizes the AKP in Turkey, the German state tradition has pushed these new urbanites to a neighborhood where they feel safe and free to express themselves. The increasing Islamophobia in Europe and the anti-immigrant attitudes of the CDU have brought the ethnically German and Turkish German residents of Kreuzberg closer together in their opposition to the conservative government.

My fieldwork revealed continuity between the seemingly mutually antagonistic lives of ethnically German and Turkish German Kreuzbergers. I heard multiple complaints from both sides that Germany's dominant culture (*Leitkultur*) left them no space to breathe outside Kreuzberg. The neighborhood was a safe space from which to engage with the German state, Turkey, and Europe—where they could live as they wanted to, but without avoiding the outside world and secluding themselves. Through their local attachments and lifestyles, these new German urbanites confronted national, regional, and world politics on multiple levels.

THE NEW AVENUES AND CHALLENGES OF INTERETHNIC BONDS

Friendship and Marriage

In an age of unsurmountable barriers between immigrants and the nationals of European states, Kreuzberg attracts and cultivates those who dislike and oppose the exclusionary practices of the German state and its discriminatory politics against minorities. Jürgen's friend Hans was a good example of a German who had learned Turkish and had several good Turkish friends. Hans has been working on trauma with Kurdish immigrants from Turkey. On the one hand, the Turkish language was useful for him in his work. From another perspective, he felt he needed to learn "the second language" in his country, which was perceived similar to the importance of Spanish in the United States or French in Canada. Hans added that he had many Turkish friends, some of whom were his political allies. Similarly, Michael, a squatter, mentioned Turkish German Kreuzbergers who were his political comrades in the squatter movement.

On a beautiful summer night, I went to the wedding party of Aslı and Dietrich on the communal terrace of an old building in Kotti. Aslı, a Turkish woman who had come to Berlin to pursue a graduate degree, had met Dietrich, a German musician, five years ago. As was not unusual in interethnic marriages, the guests included both ethnic and Turkish Germans, Turks, people from other European countries, and Americans. Many had interethnic bonds through friendships, romantic relationships, marriage, or work partnerships. One, Alex, an ethnic German Kreuzberger who was fluent in Turkish, with almost no accent, was a psychiatrist in a hospital that had a symbolic meaning for longtime residents of the neighborhood. He explained to me that being born and giving birth in this hospital was considered an important mark of recruitment into Kreuzberg community.[4] When I asked Alex why he had learned Turkish, he was surprised and asked me with a smile why I had learned German. After he told me about his visits to Turkey, I suspected that he had a partner who was from Turkey. Proving my guess wrong, Alex told me that there was no unusual or personal reason. He just had close Turkish friends and lived and worked in Kreuzberg. "It was as simple as that!"

At the wedding party, Turkish pop music was played almost exclusively, and the food was a mixture of Turkish dishes and barbequed German sausage. This kind of social mixing is not at all unusual in Kreuzberg. Moreover, these cross-national friendships and relationships should not be taken lightly, because they puncture the traditional barriers between immigrants and Germans—old barriers that are still the rule rather than an exception across Germany. These emerging bonds in Kreuzberg emerge relatively more easily between Germans and recently arrived Turks untouched by the heavy baggage of history of immigration in Germany. Yet a new generation of educated Turkish German Kreuzbergers is also breaking through the ancient fault lines with dates, relationships, and friendships. My findings on them challenge the bulk of existing scholarship that negatively associates residence in ethnic neighborhoods with friendships between nationals and immigrants.[5] However, these new bridges are emerging and therefore still rare, rather than the rule. Such bonds are difficult to establish, since they must overcome the effect of many decades of failure to accommodate Turkish immigrants.

Art as a Bridge: The New Creative Class

Art, particularly film and theater, has been one important means of creating new bonds between ethnic and Turkish Germans. The Ballhaus Naunynstraße theater in central Kotti, which symbolizes the "post-immigration" (*postmigrantische*) vision, has attracted a lot of attention, putting a stamp on the theater scene in Germany. It capitalizes on dark humor, sarcasm, and tackling politically unresolved issues, such as integration and racism, with the help of humor. The largest portion of the audience is ethnic German, but a striking number of actors, directors, and other people involved in the production of the plays at the Ballhaus have been Turkish. A Kreuzberger friend of mine jokingly remarked: "We [Turkish Germans] go to the receptions and parties at the bar on the first floor, and the [ethnic] Germans go to the plays." Nevertheless, the Ballhaus has overall been a great success. Recently, the former director of the Ballhaus, Shermin Langhoff, accepted a prominent position as the new director of the Maxim Gorki Theater.[6] She is regarded as "shaking up" German theater. Similarly, Neco Çelik, the director of *Schwarze Jungfrauen* (Black Virgins) and Tamer Yiğit, director of *Ein Warngedicht* (A Cautionary Poem), have received high recognition in Germany, helping to change the ancient stereotypes of Turkish Germans as an uneducated ethnic underclass.

But unsurprisingly, the cohabitation of immigrants and nationals in Kreuzberg has been far from smooth, and has presented multiple challenges to residents. Friendships and bonds across the native and Turkish German *Almancı* communities were not only rare, but also difficult to establish. A week after I met Neco Çelik through a Kreuzberger friend, Neco invited us to an *iftar* (fast-breaking) dinner at his place. There I met Neco's five children, all between the ages of three and seventeen, and his wife, who was also a theater player. They lived in a nice two-floor apartment overlooking a large private green playground area. As he cooked, I asked him why Turkish-German bonding in Kreuzberg was still difficult despite the similar middle-class lifestyles and shared taste in art, food, and so on. Without me mentioning a word about them, Neco sarcastically brought up the former anarchists of the AM. He said:

> When we were younger, both the AM and we [Turkish immigrants] had similar class backgrounds. But we did not squat, since it was a concept alien to our culture. They did. The former anarchists repaired the abandoned houses, and they later claimed ownership and fought for their rights to stay in the places where they squatted. Our parents did not have language, skills, and education to stand up for our rights. Now, some of these former squatter anarchists own beautiful condos in Kreuzberg with rapidly increasing values. They have quickly become bourgeois. On the other hand, their immigrant counterparts are still renters. Worst of all, with gentrification, the immigrant Turks are having a harder time every day paying the increasing rents. They are forced out of their own neighborhood. [He smiled.] Were you asking me why it is hard for us to become friends?

Unlike in the case of Teşvikiye in Istanbul, where the affluent move out to expensive gated communities and the middle class move into rented condos, Kreuzberg's gentrification typically forced out poor Turkish immigrants. In May 2012, to oppose rapid gentrification, a resistance movement, Kotti and Co., set up a tent in the middle of Kotti, which has since become a one-room flat that is recognized by, and has negotiated rent control with, the local authorities. While Kotti and Co. was mostly organized by religious Turkish immigrants, several ethnic German locals and internationals joined the resistance to gentrification. As usual, some opposing groups, including Alawites, did not join in.

In a conversation over lunch at a hip café-restaurant in Kotti, Neco agreed that both the former AM members and his Turkish German peers enjoy similar lifestyles, art, and food. However, he added: "I don't think they consider any of us as *ökologisch* [environment-friendly or eco-friendly] as themselves."

Subsequently, I began asking German Kreuzbergers, including the former AM members, how they perceived Turkish German residents. Almost all ethnic German Kreuzbergers that I talked to agreed that the newer generation(s) of the Turkish German community had produced an intellectual and creative class. Most of them told to me that these new artists and intellectuals were much closer to their own ways of life, politics, and taste for art than CDU voters. In my chats with German Kreuzbergers, they cited prominent Turkish German Kreuzbergers such as Shermin Langhoff, Neco Çelik, the internationally acclaimed DJ İpek İpekçioğlu, the writer Feridun Zaimoğlu, and the Green Party's Bundestag representatives Cem Özdemir and Özcan Mutlu. Most of my German respondents expressed personal familiarity with and sympathies for these local people. Strikingly, a high number of the new creative class of Turkish Germans were based in and/or born in Kreuzberg. Many of them stood out, not only in Berlin and Germany, but also in Europe and globally.

The Public Schooling Controversy

"There is definitely an issue in elementary school when 75 percent of students are immigrants and most of them cannot even speak proper German," Inke, the mother of two girls, told me. Hans disagreed and reminded her that his daughter's public school in Kreuzberg was a good one. This was not an immigration issue, he insisted. German policy-makers were to blame for failing to provide a good education. In response, Inke reminded us that many of their former anarchist friends had ended up sending their children to schools outside their neighborhood, or moved to the better parts of Kreuzberg, where the majority of children were not immigrants.[7] In most of my conversations about schooling in Kreuzberg, the ethnic German Kreuzbergers enthusiastically debated and disagreed with each other.

Turkish Germans and immigrants I spoke to were no less divided on the subject of schooling in Kreuzberg.[8] The politician Figen İzgi, a Left Party candidate in the local elections in Kreuzberg in 2011, told me that her children had a great education in Kreuzberg.[9] In contrast, the famous Turkish DJ İpek İpekçioğlu, the child of immigrants, had had to cope with persistent difficulties with the German language during her early education.[10] The disagreements about schooling were extremely complicated, and created ongoing disputes about education. However, rather than simply alienating and pitting ethnically German and Turkish German Kreuzbergers against one another, the school controversy divides *both* communities *from within*, cutting across the dichotomies of immigrant versus native and creating new agreements and solidarities *between* like-minded ethnic and Turkish Germans.[11]

My discussions on schooling controversies also revealed a striking spatial divide, a clear-cut division between bohemian Kotti in the east and gentrified, upscale, "mainstream" Kreuzberg. Historically, the divide had originated as merely an administrative distinction between the old SW 61 (Südwest 61, southwest 61) and SO 36 (Südost 36, southeast 36) postal codes. This division has, with time, however, lent itself to a socioeconomic line dividing the neighborhood along class/status lines. Unsurprisingly, the highly gentrified chic streets of SW 61 attract well-off Germans and Turks, while Kotti in SO 36 is much more mixed and marked by the visibility of diverse and economically less advantaged groups there. I was told by many Kreuzbergers across the national-immigrant divide that this spatial division makes a big difference in terms of the quality of schooling. The divided landscape attests to some of the most pivotal splits within both the ethnic and Turkish German communities, which also translate into new bondings between them in terms of taste, lifestyle, habits, education, art, and consumption.

SEXUAL POLITICS

The new debates on sexual politics stretch the boundaries of the more conventional concepts of citizenship. The debates on citizenship have conventionally been confined to the realm of political rights and freedoms of a presumably universal (heterosexual male) subject. Sexual politics extended the previous literature on citizenship, rights, and freedoms from the national to other levels of spatial politics. The idea of the "sexual citizen" helped make sexuality part of citizenship, "using the idea of citizenship as a space for thinking about sexual identities, desires and practices," David Bell and Jon Binni write.

> From the outset, it was clear that debates about sexual citizenship were and continue to be marked by *questions of geography*. From the mapping of the differential legal status of sexual minorities onwards, debates about sexual citizenship have explicitly been debates about space. Key issues have included the ways in which private space and public space get defined around sexual acts, national differences in sexual citizenship, the ways in which sexual citizenship works at *different spatial scales*, global flows of ideas about sexual citizenship, and the different discursive and material sites from which rights claims might be articulated.[12]

Sexual citizenship brings to the forefront the incongruent issues of national citizenship and urban residency. Concretely, civil rights and individual liberties associated with urban residency and the political rights associated with citizenship in the neighborhood meet and collide in Kreuzberg. Is Kreuzberg with a striking feminist history and LGBT visibility a meeting point or a battleground between host country and immigrants in terms of the politics of gender and sexuality?

Among many reasons for relocating in Kreuzberg,[13] several German families with children explained to me that they did not want to raise their children in the context of the patriarchal gender politics always evident on the crowded streets of Kotti. The stigma about Turkish men as patriarchal, abusive, and/ or macho wife-beaters is difficult to ignore in German society.[14] Previous research shows that "[c]ontradictory constructions of community among Germans and Turks intersect with differences in family ideals and gender roles. As a result, family and gender are a focal point of German-Turkish misunderstanding."[15] When we *emplace* (add place as a major dimension to the analysis of intersecting factors) these gender stereotypes, they become stronger. Ethnic ghettos are often directly associated with male domination and domestic violence committed by immigrant, and especially Muslim, men. From this perspective, the stigma persists, regardless of whether or not gender oppression is really higher there than in other neighborhoods of Berlin. Since racial profiling of Muslims has evidently become more pronounced,[16] the documentation and analysis of the cases must be analyzed by taking into account the likely bias.

This bias deepens an already existing fault line in gender politics. Then, what results when different fault lines that have their sources in the sexual politics in the homeland and the host country coincide in an immigrant neighborhood?

Fault lines and New Bridges Between Women: Queer Politics

Kreuzberg has historically been the midpoint of a vivid LGBT life as well as queer politics and arts of both Berlin and Europe. Lesbian and transgender women of Turkish descent have a strong visibility and voice, which contributes to Kreuzberg's reputation as a queer-friendly neighborhood. In particular, Club SO36, one of Kreuzberg's first nightclubs, is an LGBT beacon in the neighborhood.

Kreuzberg's sexual politics must be understood against the backdrop of the stigmas attached to being "Muslim Turkish." There seems to be a widely shared wisdom about sexuality and Islam: "[S]exuality remains as one of the cornerstones through which 'Muslimness' is reinforced," Anissa Hélie writes.[17] However, although Muslim women have been affected by multiple restrictions on their freedom of sexuality, these restrictions are rarely the sole effect of religion. Hence, pointing to Islam as the cause of violations of gender rights and sexual freedoms narrows our understanding of much larger political conflicts. Rather, most of these issues are often shaped by the social and political dynamics of place, the jurisdiction of a state, and/or the larger geography, regardless whether it is Muslim or not.[18]

We see a paradox when we situate the politics of sexuality in Kreuzberg in Germany's national gender politics and feminist movement. Although Germany has had a strong history of feminism and although German feminists have successfully stood up for their own rights against the German state, they are divided on the issue of Muslim immigrant women's freedoms and rights.[19] Some German feminists have insisted on leaving it to the state to decide on head-scarved women's rights, seeing the wearing of the head scarf as an issue concerning secularity, not a feminist one. This presents a double standard because the same feminists have refused to leave their own rights in the hands of the same secular German state, which bans the head scarf for teachers. More important, the absence of solidarity between German feminists and Muslim immigrant women is not really helping anybody, but weakening the prospects of a more inclusive and powerful feminist coalition in Germany.

Adding fault lines originating in Turkey to this divide in Germany, my interviews with members of the Turkish German LGBT community in Kreuzberg indicate that some of them agree with and ally themselves with anti-head-scarf German feminists in supporting the state's ban on head scarves for women in public service jobs, such as teachers. Like secularists in Turkey, they fear that pious Muslims are likely to show little or no respect for their lifestyles, rights, and freedoms.

Against the backdrop of anti-head-scarf alliances between German nationals and Turkish immigrants,[20] lesbians of Turkish descent have built solidarities across distant and/or previously antagonistic groups in Kreuzberg and beyond. İpek İpekçioğlu[21] and her music have put a stamp on SO 36 and the politics of gender and sexuality in Kreuzberg. In strong association with SO 36, DJ İpek's name echoes beyond Kotti and Germany into the international music scene. Since she travels frequently not only between Turkey and Germany but also all around the world to play her music, it was initially difficult for me to catch her in Berlin.

DJ İpek could not move with her girlfriend into a larger flat in the center of Kreuzberg, because "the larger apartments were all taken by Turkish mothers with many children." So she moved to the recently gentrified "Kreuzkölln" on the border between Kreuzberg and Neukölln. İpek studied pedagogy and in the past worked in social responsibility projects as a project manager with disabled and young girls who had experienced sexual harassment and abuse. During our long chat, İpek talked in detail about the ways in which she has worked toward a lesbian-friendly culture in Kreuzberg and said that she often had help and cooperation from other Turkish immigrant women. İpek regularly organized numerous events at SO 36, one of the many "lesbian clubs" in Kotti. Many of these events were not limited to lesbian parties, but were more inclusive.[22] To reach out widely to immigrant women, İpek also organized daylight parties for women, who were expected to be at home at night. She taught them dance classes and courses on how to become a DJ and to form support groups.

In my various conversations with her, İpek specifically emphasized the links that were generated in SO 36 *between* Turkish and ethnic Germans in Kreuzberg. No doubt, these links were facilitated by two important factors: striking lesbian visibility and the women's movement. İpek and her strong lesbian network in Kreuzberg showcase the fact that Muslim communities do not *inherently* police and restrict sexual freedoms and sabotage women's movements. The restrictions and violations of sexual freedoms and gender rights are the effect of several intersecting factors. First and foremost, the inclusiveness and accommodation of LGBT and women of ethnic minorities by the larger political milieu plays a major role. Second, democratic liberties depend largely on the presence of connections and cooperations between sexual citizens/residents of ethnic minorities and the gender politics of the homeland and host country.

On the Move Between Kreuzberg and Istanbul

DJ İpek İpekçioğlu's views on the issue of political membership and belonging are important to note, because they are the exact opposite of those of the former anarchists who define themselves as anti-German:

> I stopped long ago pretending to be anti-German. Just because I am an *Almancı* [Turkish immigrant], it does not mean that I am against Germany. It took me a long time to *come out* in every way . . . sexually and nationally. I could only identify what I liked about this place and come to terms with my feelings of belonging [here] after various international experiences.

After being schooled partly in Turkey and partly in Wedding in Berlin, İpek left Germany for Britain to work as a nanny, mainly because of her ongoing frustrations with persisting difficulty in learning the German language. She learned to speak fluent English and even got an offer to work in New York as a nanny. "But," she said, "I missed Germany. It was in London that I realized that I was as much German as I was Turkish."[23] As an internationally renowned DJ, İpek has strong links to both Istanbul and Berlin. To use Doreen Massey's terminology, she has a "global sense of place."[24] Her story highlights the new centrality of place in an increasingly globalized world.[25] When İpek returned to Germany, she made an extra effort to improve her German so that she could have a career in Kreuzberg. She said: "Language is power. So I learned it. I wanted to vote in this country. So I acquired German citizenship."

When we were having drinks at Café G. in Kreuzkölln, I asked her what specifically makes her attached to Kreuzberg. Given her fame as a DJ, she could live anywhere she liked in the world. She said, "Freedom and friendship." İpek clearly shares a similar passion for freedom and rights with many other residents of Kreuzberg. Ironically, however, her sense of belonging to Kreuzberg was sealed with her growing ties to both Germany and Turkey. Her case contradicts those of both many other *Almancıs* and the former anarchists of the AM, who are tied to Kreuzberg to the extent that they are critical of "German-ness" and domestic politics in Turkey.

One important similarity between the followers of AM and İpek was that they were all more capable of taking critical stances against their own homelands—Germany and Turkey—and their respective discriminatory policies against minorities. İpek talked about the intersections of the politics of space and sexuality in Turkey:

> Istanbul tires me out and tests me in many ways. I like it, but I also miss my "space" here in Berlin. I like the scale of space here. It is large and spacious [*ferah*]. It is also green. Nobody looks from next door into my bedroom. I am comfortable with the physical distance between the buildings, and love the social space people allow each other. Turkey makes it difficult to experiment with sexuality more freely and to experience more intimacy.

İpek's moves between Istanbul and Kreuzberg show how space and freedom co-constitute each other. Similar to mobility, "[s]paciousness is closely associated with the sense of being free. Freedom implies space; it means having the power and enough room in which to act," Yi-Fu Tuan observes.[26] İpek bought a condo in Kasımpaşa in Istanbul, where housing was more affordable than other neighborhoods. Contrary to the image of Kasımpaşa as an unsafe, lower-class neighborhood, it has been neither hostile nor unfriendly to her at all. Since İpek works late at night as a DJ, she comes back home late. When she had guests, nobody in the neighborhood seemed to bother, harass, or judge her.

But when she began making real friends in the neighborhood, a few issues were raised by them. For example, when she hung the colorful flag of gay pride on her window, one of her neighbors told her: "You know what? You should really take down that flag." İpek asked, "Why?" Trying to be helpful and protective of İpek, her friend warned her that locals had done a search on the Internet, and that they knew what it stood for. İpek laughed and responded: "So then, I have a better reason to keep it there. I hang the flag because I want the people to know."

A few days later, another friendly neighbor suggested timidly that it would be a good idea to change her drapes. Half surprised and half curious, İpek asked why, again thinking of different tastes. "These are a little small," her friend said. "They don't cover your windows entirely. [She sighed.] People are talking about your female guests, because they can see through your drapes." İpek took all of these comments with a positive attitude and open mind. She said they were not offensive and caused her no hurt feelings or anger. She said she was happy to have a place in Istanbul, and that it was important to her to spend a part of her life there. But, she added, she belonged to Kreuzberg, which has been a cornerstone of queer lifestyle and politics.

Everyday experiences of privacy and freedom are largely gendered practices. It is not surprising that İpek felt short of space in Istanbul, where lesbian visibility is remarkably low. In fact, one has to look for a lesbian place really hard in Istanbul, since the few gay coffee shops and bars are predominantly for homosexual men. For İpek, as a transgender woman, the right of public visibility and respect for privacy were fundamental. Hence, Kreuzberg seemed to win over Istanbul when it came to privacy and having one's own space.

As we continued comparing Istanbul's neighborhoods and their various politics, she switched to a discussion of the bumpy relations between *Almancı* like herself, Turkish internationals in Germany, and Istanbulites:

> I play all kinds of music, from techno to Turkish and ethnic, even Türkü [Turkish folk music]. . . . When I play these [kinds of music] here in Kreuzberg, Turkish internationals ask with disappointment whether I always play *like this*. When I play in Istanbul, it is a whole different story. In Istanbul, music equals distinction and cultural capital, which is associated with your class and status. People look down on their own [and thus on İpek's] music. In my parties in Kreuzberg, we dance and have fun with our own music [*kendi müziğimizle oynuyoruz ve coşuyoruz*]. In my parties here in Kreuzberg, there is no pretension, no class- or taste-related concerns. There is no showing off!

She paused for a second and said: "Kreuzberg is free of restraints in many ways. . . . we are proud that there is a sex shop next to the halal food market." I asked İpek how it was that Kreuzbergers seemed to get along happily, when so many conflicting groups, ideologies, and lifestyles coexisted side by side in Kreuzberg. She said:

> Kreuzberg was not like this before. When we lived in Wedding a long time ago during my childhood, I was scared of coming to Kreuzberg. Things changed a lot. Now, rich Germans and the upper middle class have become big fans of Kreuzberg. Tourists go to Mitte—the old center of the city. . . . Kreuzberg is *the new center for cool locals* in Berlin. Despite our differences, we are cool here.

Contemporary Kreuzberg is a mixture of many "cool" trends, albeit (or because) many of these trends contradict each other. Kreuzberg is hipster, punk, gay, increasingly pious Muslim, gentrified, but also increasingly inclusive and mixed. Currently Kreuzberg is in flux, and its urban and political transformations unsettle old stereotypes about identity groups and immigrants. But most important, Kreuzberg is a breathing space and a zone of freedom for both

Turkish and ethnic Germans who seek their freedom and always want a better, deeper democracy.

CONCLUSION

The two aspects of democracy, the *spatial reach* of democratic contestation and the *depth* of freedoms, do not cease to interact, whether a democracy is deemed "consolidated" or not.[27] These two aspects need to be aligned constantly, mainly because democracies, including advanced ones such as Germany, also face the challenge of accommodating rights and freedoms of minorities.[28]

This ethnography of contested urban space suggests that splits have a much stronger impact in shaping the depth of democracy when they cut across different scales—local, national, and international.[29] The stretch of fault lines between Teşvikiye in Istanbul and Kreuzberg in Berlin is telling in this regard. The linkage between urban discontents in Turkey and Germany is an important aspect of how Erdoğan and the AKP came to be perceived negatively in the West.

The contestations in Turkey and Germany resound from one country to the other, with the help of activists, public figures, academics, politicians, filmmakers, and other artists, many of whom reside in Kreuzberg.[30] As a highly contested site, Kreuzberg demands and struggles for "openness, porosity, heterogeneity, fallibility, unevenness and creativity of state practices," in Joe Painter's words.[31] Although Kreuzbergers prioritize their belonging to their neighborhood above any other sense of membership and loyalty,[32] they address the nation-state in their urban contestation—and not just local Kreuzbergers or the international community.

During and after the Gezi protests, contestation and protests in the two countries resonated more explicitly with each other. Although the Turkish community did not unite either in Kreuzberg or Germany over the Gezi protests in Istanbul, various groups, particularly Alawites, voiced their support for the Gezi protestors separately. This, is turn, created a public opinion critical of Erdoğan, which culminated in Merkel's negative remarks about the AKP's handling of the protests. Hence, despite the lack of cross-ideological alliances, the meeting of the fault lines of homeland and host land challenged exclusions and undermined violations of freedoms and rights in each country. John Allen and Allan Cochrane write:

> Authority may be detached from the "centre", but it is re-embedded in regions and urban areas as part of a "national regional" or "urban" assemblage. Yet, in

this topological landscape, what works for central government in terms of its hierarchical powers of reach also has the, perhaps, unintended consequence of opening up that authority to negotiation and displacement.[33]

The increasing mobility of immigrants between Turkey and Germany also strengthens the ties and political momentum of resistance and democratic contestation in each country. But the divides among Kreuzbergers of Turkish descent remain too deep for them to unite, despite the fact that the status of Turks as an ethnic underclass persists in Germany. Nevertheless, intense disagreement and contestation in Kreuzberg advances the struggle against this discrimination against minorities, and generates a yearning for democratic liberties and rights. Although the German government does not recognize the divides among the Turkish diaspora and treats them simply as Turkish immigrants, these divided groups interact and engage separately with the German state and society. Since they have different agendas that do not align, their interactions with the host state remain specific to their goals and agendas. As discussed, Alawites in Kreuzberg seem to form relatively better bonds with ethnic German Kreuzbergers than pious Muslims, who are most exposed to the Islamophobic tendencies of German society and the government.

Like the Islamist groups, the Kurds are divided among themselves. Unsurprisingly, the PKK (Partiya Karkerên Kurdistan; Kurdistan Workers' Party) and nonmilitant Kurds do not cooperate.[34] Hence, their engagement and bonds with ethnic German Kreuzbergers remain on a personal level, and it is more difficult to generalize about them. Although the relations of these groups to Turkey and Germany vary widely, both states have a tendency to see these diasporas as monolithic. As is explicit in Merkel's and Erdoğan's discourses, the fact that there are deep fault lines within the Turkish immigrant community puzzles the two governments and their political leaders.

Out of the deep divides compounded by fault lines in both home and host countries, the agentic diaspora neighborhood, unlike many other ethnically concentrated neighborhoods, generates new friendships and shared lifestyles and sensitivities across the ancient divide between Turkish immigrants and native Germans. This is how diasporic space disrupts and interrupts governments' discriminatory policies against minorities and marginalized groups.[35] Since "prosaic geographies of the state"[36] involve wide-ranging interactions with both ordinary nonstate and state actors, these intense state-space negotiations contribute to a critical rethinking of the political culture and drive potential political reforms.

Paradoxically, to the extent that progressive Kreuzbergers—whether German nationals or Turkish immigrants—are less trusting of the German or the Turkish state,[37] they put more effort into demanding deeper democracy and more freedoms. But rather than informing us about the declining sovereignty of the state over the immigrant population in an age of globalization,[38] the experience of Kreuzberg shows the spatiality of freedoms and democratic contestations.

CONCLUSION

Unified Opposition to the Divided Supremacy of the AKP

JUST TWO MONTHS after the brutal expulsion of the Gezi protestors in 2013, many Istanbul sites were painted in rainbow colors after the pro-Islamist local government had the rainbow-colored Fındıklı stairs in Beyoğlu repainted gray.[1] In a single day, provoked by the hostility of the AKP to freedom of sexuality, a city that had consistently witnessed numerous homo- and transphobic incidents came to support the LGBT community.[2] Invigorated by the Gezi spirit, Istanbulites needed only a little spark to rise above previous ideological divides to defend rights and freedoms for all. Painting stairs and sidewalks swept across several Turkish cities.

Similarly, the AKP's repression of the Gezi protests culminated in another, unusually overarching alliance. It connected rival soccer fanatics, who had strong allegiances to competing sport clubs, and who were therefore seemingly fated to be lifelong enemies. Given the macho character of soccer fanaticism, the support for the Gezi spirit of the Fenerbahçe and Beşiktaş sports clubs' fan base was particularly surprising. What brought Turkish society to this point of an unprecedented anti-government alliance, an alliance that bridged the deepest fault lines of all sorts, ideological, identitarian, and spatial?

"WE ARE NOT ACTIVISTS, WE ARE THE PEOPLE"

"We are not activists, we are the people" was one of the slogans of demonstrators protesting against the undemocratic acts of the AKP government.[3] With the largest number of cases under review at the European Court of Human Rights in 2013, Erdoğan's Turkey is considered one of the region's top violators of human rights and freedoms, along with Putin's Russia. The violations in

Turkey are closely tied to Erdoğan's ever-increasing paternalism and "moral micromanagement"[4] of urban ways of life.[5] Since "paternalism is undertaken for the *good of* or *the sake of* its target, . . . [it] appears to be very broadly speaking benevolent," Christian Coons and Michael Weber observe.[6] "We don't want a youth of drunkards under the influence,"[7] Erdoğan declares, for example, presenting his moralistic dictates as aimed at preserving the health of the nation's youth.

From his failed attempts to criminalize abortion to restrictions on alcohol and encouragement of women to have three children, all Erdoğan's encroachments on ways of life, particularly urban lifestyles, must be seen in the context of rising paternalism and an assault on civil liberties. As Şeyla Benhabib points out: "The real problem, in a country where alcoholism is minimal, is Mr. Erdoğan's 'culture war' against the country's secular classes, and the illiberal form of democracy that he is advancing."[8] Especially in the context of the current strengthening of national security measures and surveillance, AKP paternalism amounts to a free pass for political authoritarianism. It is simply a pretext for violating civil rights. The real threat of paternalism, which is neglected in most of the ongoing debates,[9] is its capacity to encapsulate and present sheer power struggles between the conservatives and progressives as moral and ethical debates. Along these lines, a leading columnist in Turkey, Ahmet Hakan, criticized Erdoğan's paternalism and his failure to acknowledge and respond to youth's yearning for freedoms and rights:

> The children who took to the streets. . . . Those children tell you this: Leave me alone. Don't interfere with how I sit, how I behave in the subway, how I live, how I talk, how I dress, how I think, how I eat and drink. Do not express your opinion about all of these issues with or without respect. Do not scold me. Do not talk down on me. You are not our father. Do not play the role of patriarchal father with us.[10]

The Gezi protests thus differ from the bulk of the Occupy movement protests. First, unlike the other Occupy protests, with their incoherent or vague agendas, the protestors in Turkey have had a clearly defined and widely shared goal and a target: they united in defense of freedoms and rights against a political authoritarianism based on persistent paternalism. Political dictates as to how people should live go back to the early Republican era, but they have reached a new extreme under the AKP. The words of a feminist Gezi protestor in Ankara capture both the continuity from the Republican elite tradition into the AKP era and the refreshing change that was born out of urban space and surfaced most strikingly with the Gezi spirit:

> [I]t is heartening that women, especially Kemalist women, are rising against the *real and symbolic fathers* who have constantly told them *how to live*. I am excited to transform the street into a place of resistance and solidarity alongside the women of my neighborhood . . . we should lay claim to our neighborhoods.[11]

THE POLITICS OF YOUTH?

It should not be surprising that Erdoğan's paternalism disturbed and provoked the youth more intensely than other age groups. The contested sites studied in this book, including the Gezi protests, all manifest a striking *age factor*. Although the protests bonded people across generations, the visibility of the generation of the 1980s and 1990s was central to both mundane everyday life in contested sites and to the protests.[12] Until the Gezi protests, a misperception based on ideological commitment and political partisanship stereotyped young Turks, including those in their twenties and thirties, as "apolitical." However, in the protests across the nation, the youth showed that rejection of ideological divides must not be conflated with being apolitical or indifferent to politics. The young Gezi protestors in the contested urban space and campuses rose above ideological fault lines and united in defense of freedoms and rights.

There are several historical, political, and socio-psychological factors that distinguish this generation from their elders. Unlike their parents and grandparents, they did not experience the traumatizing clashes between Left and Right that ended in state violence, torture, and other atrocities. Unlike the generation born in the 1970s, they did not have to problematize and struggle with the remnants of secularist Kemalist authoritarianism, the repression of religious freedom for and discrimination against pious Muslims and religious and ethnic minorities. Moreover, unlike all previous generations, they did not experience military coups and their traumatizing aftermaths. On the contrary, they are the product of a rather democratic era marked by a series of political reforms in Turkey, during which civil society flourished, along with expansion of freedoms and rights. Hence, the youth born in 1980s and 1990s found the opportunity to experiment with their civil and individual liberties. Unscarred by the violent conflict between Left and Right in 1970s and the confrontation between Islamism and secularism in the 1990s, the new generation learned to rise above ideological fault lines.

Moreover, born after feminist consciousness bloomed in Turkey's big cities, this generation had a greater chance of being raised in households that were relatively "free" of paternal heads. They have become the pioneers of lifestyle politics, in which they are used to being heard, respected, responded to, and taken seriously in the family.

Hence, this youth is integral in shifting our understanding of politics from a primarily ideological (leftist, communist, fascist, Islamist, and so on) power struggle to the prioritization of freedoms for all. They constitute the reason and agency to correct the ancient conflation of ideological partisanship with politics. Unintentionally, they have become the key in freeing freedom-seekers from the cages of ideological and identitarian allegiances.

Furthermore, the technology-savvy young Gezi protestors were by no means alone in their quest for freedom. The younger generation uniting against Erdoğan's "intrusions" have been taught, supported, and backed, not only by their professors, who were pioneers in shaping sites of contestation, and their mothers, who are naturally protective of their children, but ironically also even by the soccer fanatics of Beşiktaş Market (Çarşı).[13] In addition, various occupational groups cutting across the generations—particularly artists, lawyers, and doctors—were already boiling with rage before the Gezi demonstrations began on May 27, 2013, which made them natural supporters of the dissenting youth.

While urban circumstances that culminated in these alliances were long *in formation* and simmering at contested urban sites for many years, the tension climbed rapidly in the weeks preceding the Gezi protests. Over the last ten days of May 2013, I was surrounded by infuriated Istanbulites across wide-ranging neighborhoods, from Teşvikiye to Bebek, from Taksim to Kadıköy, and from Eminönü and Beşiktaş. When Erdoğan declared that *ayran* (a yogurt beverage) was Turkey's "national drink" (*milli içecek*), after hastily pushing through yet another law limiting the hours of alcohol sale, furious nonobserving Istanbulites raised glasses of *rakı* (Turkish anisette) to toast their nation.

To back up his much-resented restrictions on the sale and consumption of alcohol, Erdoğan offensively demanded: "How come the law issued by two drunkards is in force, but the *law ordered by religion* has to be rejected?"[14] Erdoğan's statement was received with fury by Turkish society, which understandably interpreted the "two drunkards" to be modern Turkey's two founding fathers, Kemal Atatürk and İsmet İnönü. Erdoğan's huge U-turn away from his previous speeches must be noted in relation to these recent statements. In his talks in 2002–3, Erdoğan had impressed the secular and diversified his constituency by making a commitment to and guaranteeing secular law and the secular regime. Just one week before the Gezi protests exploded, his words "law ordered by religion" informed of a dramatic change in his discourse on the rules of the game.

May 2013 witnessed more rage in Istanbul. Along with large-scale violations of freedom, Erdoğan continued to insult drinkers of alcohol, the youth, the LGBT community, sex workers, and even art lovers publicly. In his efforts to justify his goal of closing down state-subsidized theaters (*Şehir ve devlet tiyatroları*), he affronted and marginalized artists: "These [actors] are the *elite* people with alcoholic beverages in their hands, who look down on people. . . . The state runs theaters nowhere on earth."[15] Erdoğan did not hesitate to wage *war* on the un-Islamic ways of urbanites from all walks of life. Under overt attacks on the dignity of its residents Istanbul took on a new defensive face wracked with discontent and fury. The same week, a "kissing protest" took place in an Ankara subway station after a police officer using a loudspeaker cautioned a young couple against kissing in public.

POLITICS OF CLASS?

Gezi protests need to be understood in the larger context of history and politics. Urban protests and movements are no novelty,[16] but the endemic quality of the Occupy movements that express their discontents by laying claim to urban sites across the globe, South and North, seems to be today's zeitgeist. The Gezi protests were immediately compared to a series of recent urban protests ranging from the Occupy movements to the so-called Arab Spring, the Green Movement in Iran, and many others. No doubt, the Gezi protests also had grassroots objections to "neoliberal restructuring" in common with other urban protests. Undoubtedly, cities have become increasingly dominated by neoliberal forces, which have created potentially irreversible socioeconomic inequalities and injustices almost indiscriminately across the world. However, previous social research, particularly in urban studies, falls short of explaining other strategic causes and motivations of these protests. Similarly, for an in-depth understanding of the Turkish case, one needs, in Kerem Öktem's words, to address the question of "why such large-scale protests could erupt under the conditions of rapid economic growth . . . [and] decreasing unemployment and urban poverty rates" in Turkey.[17]

Although cities and neighborhoods concurrently have pressing "material concerns" such as gentrification, the issue of rights and freedoms must not be overshadowed by an exclusive focus on the AKP's socioeconomic policies and neoliberal agendas.[18] Most of the alliances depicted in this book, including those among the Gezi protestors, owed a great deal to available material resources, such as cutting-edge technology, competitive (and often expensive) educations, consumption, and privileged lifestyles. Although the Gezi protests were initiated by a small group of leftist urban activists, they rapidly turned into a genuinely cross-class resistance.[19] Similarly, students on contested campuses, such as UF and ODTÜ, and Kreuzbergers, such as German AM and the German Turkish LGBT or Greens, may often identify with the left spectrum of politics. Nevertheless, the predominant political culture in these urban sites, and the leading lifestyles there, speak to and reflect a middle-class ethos with a heavy emphasis on liberties.

Although youth from various class backgrounds participated in the contestations, the middle class played a highly visible role in leading the struggles. Along with a shared dislike of the AKP government's neoliberal policies, the crowds were able to formulate their grievances very clearly: they were uniting to stand up against violations of freedoms, injustices, and Erdoğan's authoritarianism. Like the other contested sites discussed in this book, Gezi Park was agentic inasmuch as the formation of new alliances bridged the ancient divides between secularists and pious Muslims. This is why and how Muslims of various ideological standpoints, particularly feminist, liberal, and anti-capitalist Muslims, joined the protests.

My findings on the sociospatial political inclusivity that is a constant theme throughout this book illustrate these nonideological alliances. I argue that both the divides and the collaborations that came out of these divided places were motivated by a "politics of lifestyle" and flourished owing to shared demands for liberties. More concretely, at the heart of this urban politics were contestations over ways of life associated largely with the middle class. This explains why the main actors of this new urban politics identify easily with gay politics or environmentalists, as in the contexts of both Gezi and Kreuzberg. This may also explain why they appear less likely to be motivated by class-related ideologies. This is why the trees of Gezi Park sparked a nationwide uprising against AKP authoritarianism, while the more than three hundred casualties in the Soma mining disaster in May 2014 did not lead to such a large-scale uprising. Turkey's new urbanites were horrified and infuriated by the Soma disaster, blamed the AKP for it, and lamented the abuse of labor rights, but Soma did not trigger a nationwide upheaval the way Gezi did.[20] The language and practices of the new urbanism are primarily nonideological.

DIFFERENTIATING URBAN PROTESTS FROM URBAN
CONTESTATION ENGRAINED IN WAYS OF LIFE

Just a few years ago, when I spoke of lack of freedoms as one of the major shortcomings and problems of Turkish and Middle Eastern politics, I was often interrupted and corrected by colleagues. "Turkish society and freedoms don't fit. These are apples and oranges," they said. "Freedom is a foreign, Western concept for Turkey. You are importing the term inappropriately." One of the many accomplishments of the Gezi protests was the breakthrough from this misleading discourse—a misperception that denied the place of freedom and freedom seekers from all walks of life in Turkish society.

However, the victory of the Gezi spirit in terms of establishing lasting bonds and new alliances over rights and freedoms did not prevent the gradual fading away of the protests. Many demonstrators yearned for ongoing solidarity as the protests slowly died away during the long, hot summer days, when Istanbul is largely abandoned particularly by its middle- and upper-middle class residents. Was the resistance really defeated by the government and the police despite the forcefulness of its voice and the impact it had on multiple levels? Do not the "stair revolution" and frequent campus protests indicate the persistence of the Gezi spirit long after Gezi Park was emptied? Since short-lived demonstrations are not sufficient to make a substantial political change, how are these sudden protests to be translated into a more permanent political achievement?

The most common way of thinking about the success of an urban upheaval is its immediate and tangible impact on the government. Did the upheaval or revolution succeed in "overthrowing" the state or bringing the government down? Or did the government back down and/or respond to the protestors' demands? In the Turkish case, most of the answers to these questions have been negative. Since Turkey has experienced many decades of free and fair elections, with a strong civil society allowing some voice to its citizens, a revolutionary end to the regime was also very unlikely.[21] Erdoğan made no effort either to reach a mutual understanding with the protestors or to acknowledge the grievances of his opponents. On the contrary, rejecting the large-scale grievances of society, he insistently continued to call the protestors "plunderers" (*çapulcular*), drunkards, and the marginal. By dismissing their needs and demands, he relentlessly redefined the word "marginal" in the process. For Erdoğan, it seems, it encompasses everybody who disagrees with his rule, policies, and worldview. Moreover, relying on his constituents' majority vote, Erdoğan did not hesitate to polarize Turkish society and provoke his voters to confront the opposition.

In doing so, he took advantage of *majoritarian procedural democracy* to hammer down a fragile young pluralist *civil democracy.*[22] As Nilüfer Göle notes, "if the Arab Spring demanded the majority's voice in democracy, the Turkish movement [rose] up against democratic majoritarianism."[23]

Nevertheless, indexing democratization *exclusively* to the immediate results of protests may be misleading, mainly because protests *are just one* manifestation of urban politics among contestations at many places and on multiple levels that have more lasting, longer-term impacts on the political trajectory of a country. Sudden protests are often most flashy, but also short-lived and incoherent. Most often, their initial pulse fades away through exhaustion, because eruptive, emotional outbursts cannot be routinized and maintained as a regular lifestyle. Nowadays, the protests disappear even faster in the face of heightened security measures and overempowered law enforcement. Ironically, this happens both in authoritarian states and democracies, since most regimes use potential threats of terror and national security to crush urban protests.

Saskia Sassen sees a global pattern in current world politics—the growing significance of "the global street" in political transitions. But, she adds, these streets and squares should be understood separately from the classic European "boulevard and piazza" model of public space and activity. Juxtaposing the latter with today's global street, she argues that contemporary urban contestation is distinguished from earlier urban politics, not by empowerment, but by the increasing "complication of powerlessness."[24] In other words, globally endemic protests are not making a difference in enabling the dissenters, minorities, or any opposition to power structures, but only render their situation more complex. Sassen's argument is solid, but also ambiguous on one issue. Her two claims contradict one another: that the global trend may not necessarily empower the powerless, but the powerless make "politics" and "history" across the world. If making and shaping history and political trajectories are not about power, then what is? I suggest that we need a broader definition of power to recognize the power of divisions, splits and contestation in mundane places—the power that is generated by urban divides and alliances.[25] Ethnographic evidence suggests that contested sites have the power to impact social reality and political processes. Hence, places and people associated with urban contestation in daily life (as opposed to urban protest) are not necessarily entirely powerless.

Recently, world politics has been shaken up by numerous urban protests, most of which have exploded over a local issue- and/or event-based conflict, and have had large-scale impacts across regions and continents. Social scientists, particularly urbanists, have been thinking and theorizing this new form of global politics through comparative lenses.[26] But as most of the recent protests, including the Occupy and Gezi movements, were quickly suppressed in front of our eyes, we know that abrupt uprisings here and there across the world may often *not* lend themselves to long-lasting coherent movements, and even less so to substantial institutional change. Then, to what extent should we take these abrupt protests seriously, if not central, with regard to democratization? More concretely, will the new global urban uprisings have an influence on reforming majoritarian democracies that fail to truly represent large sections of their citizens? Probably not. However, one must not lose perspective about the subtle links between the urban protests and the transformative effects of urban space and city life. Long after Gezi has died away, the new urbanism remains still strong in city life.

Although the mundane dynamics of urban contestation and abrupt urban protests are not disconnected, and although they periodically feed each other, they cannot be reduced to each other. The lines between sudden protests and nondeliberate acts in urban politics are fuzzy and always in flux. For example, when anti-government protests erupted at the Middle East Technical University in Ankara in December 2012, the rough treatment of the nonviolent student protestors by the police led to their expansion to other oppositional campuses in major cities across the country. Yet beyond the inflammatory effect of campus protests, which were soon repressed, the AKP found itself positioned against a more lasting, organized alliance between established elite institutions of high education. Once the flames of the campus protests faded away, these privileged universities remained self-consciously part of a strong alliance against the government. Not only are they hotbeds of knowledge production, scientific inquiry, and critical thinking, but their alumni are often in elite positions both inside and outside of Turkey. These contested sites are thus anything but entirely powerless. Opposition continued in daily life on campus and in the neighborhood without necessarily translating into upheavals, which are vulnerable, fragile, and often immobilized by law enforcement.

Luckily, the democratic opposition does not rely solely on the actual and immediate outcomes of protests. The impact of urban politics can be found in new forms of urbanism at contested sites, showcased in Teşvikiye, UF, and Kreuzberg. These contested sites withstand the authoritarian, exclusive, and/or discriminatory tendencies of the governments of Turkey and Germany. At times when the parliament is incapable of generating efficient contestation and negotiation, the new urbanisms at contested sites take over that role. Unlike the emotional outburst in uprisings, this new urbanism stays put; it grows on the basis of urban ways of life that are resilient, persistent, and assertive of democratic practices. The long-lasting effects of opposition flourish in the most quotidian venues that residents claim and belong to—rather than at protest sites occupied for a short period and then invaded by law enforcement.

More concretely, discontented urbanites negotiate and ally over rights and freedoms nonstrategically, not just by organizing protests at temporarily occupied urban sites, but by living their lives in urban space that they already feel territorial and often proud about. The police who repress and eradicate protests cannot get rid of or eradicate the contested quarters or campuses, which are in the "possession" of local urbanites. These urban sites generate democratic contestation and alliances by remaining inclusive and accommodating others' ways of life. Unlike parliament, which further polarizes government and opposition, contested urban space bridges ideological and identitarian cleavages through quotidian living. Put differently, unlike the failure of the political elite to find strategic ways to agree and cooperate, the contested quarter and campus nondeliberately generate affinities and bonds across ancient divides. This is how urban residents take what belongs to them, their city, gaining their freedoms and rights in those claimed and rescued territories. This is why scholarship must look beyond ostentatious protests and study the mundane understated but persisting qualities and strengths of contested urban space, the zones of freedom.

Both contested urban space and protest sites divert conflict from the state and contain and dilute it. Moreover, both urban protests and the politics of lifestyle at contested sites are nurtured by a politics of place that includes and accommodates previously clashing ways of life. Numerous protestors had previously been *rehearsing* democratic contestation, both disagreement/splits and consent/alliances, in contested quarters, campuses, and street discussed in this book. No doubt, struggles over the city and urban ways of life are more indirect and diffuse than abrupt protests. This is why they are harder for the government to detect, attack, or even overtly undermine. By the same token, they are more elusive and harder for researchers to study. A deeper understanding of urban politics therefore requires an in-depth look at the quotidian dynamics of contested urban sites. Unsurprisingly, the politics of space/place and lifestyle are often neglected, not only by laypeople and policymakers, but also by scholars of democratization, particularly those with an exclusive focus on institutional and/or quantitative indicators.[27]

THE CENTRALITY OF THE PLACE

Richard Sennett highlights a major characteristic of the Occupy movement, which compares well with other protests, including the Gezi protest: "The Occupy Sanctuaries were at best semi-legal: you had to fight the authorities for that space."[28] Hence, unlike contestations at everyday urban sites, they are consistently targeted by law enforcement, courts, and intelligence. Police find it much easier to access occupied protest zones and attack protestors there than in everyday life on contested streets, neighborhoods, or campuses. Contested safe campuses similar to UF have proven successful in keeping police forces out, as the presidents of Turkish universities are empowered to decide whether or not there should be a police presence on campus. Compared to the free zones of campuses and quarters, protest sites remain under strict law-enforcement surveillance even long after the protest has come to an end. In fact, they often turn into lost castles of urban contestation. In the aftermath of the Gezi protests, for example, Taksim Square and adjacent areas, such as Beyoğlu and İstiklal Street, have been targeted, or "stigmatized," by the police as unruly places. Taksim Square has even been physically transformed to make it less accessible to protestors and more accessible for police and tanks.

Place is a central definer of the characteristics of a protest. The quality of the Gezi protests changed remarkably even when they expanded from Gezi Park to the larger Taksim Square and beyond. Gezi Park was temporarily a "haven of peace, freedom and happiness,"[29] until the protestors were expelled. However, when the protest spread into Taksim Square, surrounding neighborhoods, and the city as a whole, ideological fault lines changed the Gezi spirit and led to confrontation. Violent struggles took place, not only between the protestors and the police but also among bystanders.

In contrast, when Taksim was evacuated and the Gezi demonstrators were pushed out of Taksim Square and toward Nişantaşi and Teşvikiye, the color of confrontation changed again in the neighborly territory of Teşvikiye. Police brutality became much more difficult when ordinary residents of Teşvikiye not involved in the protest—who included the CEOs of companies, some of the country's major entrepreneurs, leading politicians, and intellectuals—poured into the streets and confronted the police face to face on their doorsteps. Wearing their pajamas rather than gas masks, the locals yelled things like: "Get out of our neighborhood! Get off our streets and sidewalks! We lived happily [here] before you showed up! Leave our streets and kids alone! We were here before you and we'll be safe without you!" It was noticeably easier for the residents to protect what was theirs from the police invasion than it was for the protestors in the temporarily occupied protest zones.

No doubt, the protests and more mundane contestations in neighborhoods and campuses have much in common. However, compared to confrontational protestors, the residents of a contested neighborhood have a major advantage because of their sense of belonging, ownership, and habitual claim to their territory.[30] They are empowered by their sense of self-entitlement to the place where they live, work, and socialize. This is different from actual legal ownership of a place. In September 2013, when the police intervened in the protests in secular quarters such as Kadıköy and Moda, the local residents struck back with slogans such as "The apartment is a rental but the neighborhood is ours." Unlike temporarily claimed or occupied squares in protests, people's deeply rooted feelings of belonging and sense of entitlement to shape the politics of their neighborhoods, campuses, shops, and so on empower them in claiming their right to the city. This territoriality facilitates the contestation over freedom and rights by equipping the residents with self-confidence in their own *natural habitat*, where they feel safe and stronger. Rather than the arbitrary impositions of the government, their ways of life become pivotal in determining what will prevail in city life and politics.

After the brutal attacks of the police in Gezi Park, the inclusivity of the protests was challenged to a certain extent. The implications of this temporary regression could be best observed in the forums held in neighborhood parks, which aimed at political mobilization in the aftermath of the Gezi protests. Despite the intention to keep the Gezi spirit alive, the park forums relapsed into exclusivity and the comforting familiarity of the like-minded. For example, unlike the contested urban spaces analyzed in this book, park forums failed to attract and integrate pious Muslims. The devout did not join, and the discussions never materialized beyond the momentary pleasure of agreement by the like-minded. My participant observations suggested that these forums failed to preserve the previous victory of *unintended* mixing across ideological lines. The Gezi protest succeeded to the extent that it merged into urban contestation as a way of life and lifestyle politics. Urban contestation is thus a major asset and a victory for democratization, always provided that the alliances that have been negotiated in the process persist and flourish.

Hence, in Sassen's words, "the contested city is where the civic is made."[31] The new global politics is about a particular kind of emancipation—a liberation from polarizing fault lines and the cages that compartmentalize urbanites into ideological and identitarian clusters. Ironically, this emancipation does not come from the calming down or disappearance of disagreement and conflict. Deeper freedoms, I argue, come from further disagreement and conflict that divide presumably homogeneous ideological or identitarian camps, including the secular, the pious, the middle class, and the leftists.

WILL DEVOUT MUSLIMS ALSO DIVIDE INSIDE AND ALLY OUTSIDE?

One question persists in the aftermath of Gezi protests—the precarious link between urban contestation and the ballot box. Neither the expansion of the zones of and for freedom nor the persistence of the Gezi spirit can guarantee their short-term effect on electoral outcomes. Despite accusations of vast corruption, the AKP won the local elections in most of Turkey's cities in March 2014. Party politics, particularly the government and its secularist opposition, the CHP, continues to fail in representing the political needs, yearning, and agendas of the discontented masses.[32] Considering that the leading freedom-seekers in this book are mostly university students and youth backed up by their mothers, professors, and the creative class, the hope of forming a new opposition party likely to win the upcoming elections seems dim. During my post-Gezi fieldwork in the summer of 2013, I met several enthusiastic and politically conscientious residents of Istanbul who were trying to mobilize people for the formation of a new political party. Most of these very small-scale grassroots activities, in which new enthusiasts were emerging, were taking place in parks, cafes, and at get-togethers at people's homes. These conscientious Istanbulites included CEOs of companies, entrepreneurs, young activists, and students. Clearly, none had Erdoğan's longtime experience in politics, particularly his decades-long involvement with grassroots and local urban politics as the protégé of Necmettin Erbakan.

Despite the goodwill, the immediate political initiatives in the post-Gezi period have been largely immature. The formation of a powerful opposition party that could take the AKP down may take a longer time period until the freedom-seeking youth grow older and develop their own party politics. For now, Turkey faces the persistence of the hegemonic AKP and its weak opposition, the CHP, both of which are equally uninterested and unskilled in protecting and expanding rights and liberties. Hence, the efforts to mobilize electoral support for the CHP or any of the older parties in park forums and streets do not seem to provide a way out of Turkey's stagnant party politics. Erdoğan's easy victory in the presidential elections in 2014 confirms this dark picture. What, then, seems to be a way out? On the basis of my findings on the divides among secular residents in Turkey, I suggest that the key is likely to be in the emerging disagreement and the potential deepening of divides among the devout Muslims.

The main contribution of this book is to subvert the negative or skeptical view of political divides and urban splits by showing how urban contestation can open the way for new and shifting alliances between previously antagonistic groups. When conflict is better accommodated and contained in contested sites of the city (than between the branches of the state), urban space takes on a primary role in politics. Under these conditions, the creation of safe zones in contested urban space becomes pivotal for political divisions.

The AKP's hegemony has yet to be significantly punctured by emerging and potential divisions among both Erdoğan's supporters and various pious Muslim groups. Well-educated urban middle-class Muslims have been involved, however, both in recent corruption scandals and in collusion with Erdoğan's increasing violations of rights and freedoms. Although discontent with the AKP among pious Muslims is relatively new and indecisive, some AKP voters are already changing their minds and sides. If Erdoğan fails to control his authoritarian attitudes and repression of ordinary citizens, his supporters from various class backgrounds may also switch their allegiance.[33] For example, although Manisa is a largely conservative town and supported the AKP, many people there turned against Erdoğan after the Soma mining disaster. During Erdoğan's visit to the mine a few days after the explosion, Manisa residents heckled him harshly on the streets, blaming him for the deaths of their relatives and neighbors. Surprised by the hostility of locals in a pro-AKP town, it has been reported, Erdoğan slapped an ordinary citizen in the crowd.

Just as shared secular lifestyles did not suffice to unite secular Turks behind a secularist politics, piety and faith-based ways of life may no longer be sufficient to unify devout Muslims under the AKP's pro-Islamic authoritarian rule. Their shared interest in participating in a free-market economy and adoption of bourgeois lifestyles has involved pious Muslims in power struggles and economic conflict. If religiosity and secularity are no longer to be the main axis of conflict, political divisions are likely to occur among devout Muslims along the continuum between democracy and authoritarianism.

In fact, this scenario about splits among the devout Muslims is more than just a normative wish or a prescriptive analysis. Such divides among devout Muslims have already been emerging over the past few years.[34] Along with the demise of the EU dream, two parallel developments have taken place in the two most influential pious groups, the AKP and the Gülen Movement (GM), the largest and most internationally mobilized Islamic organization. While the AKP's economic and political reforms slowed down during its second term (2007–11), the GM gradually turned its international networks into a "global empire." Although the GM stood by the AKP in its war against the military under the rubric of Ergenekon trials, the post-2010 period saw tensions between them. Disputes initially erupted over infrequent and trivial events, but as of 2011, a deeper fault line and distrust have begun to define the relations between the AKP and the GM.[35]

To the extent that the AKP has become more authoritarian and adopted confrontational politics, the GM has distanced itself from Erdoğan's increasingly hegemonic rule. The leader of the GM, Fethullah Gülen, who has resided in Pennsylvania since 1999, has made several public statements critical of AKP's increasing authoritarianism.[36] GM adherents have consistently emphasized that its conflict-avoiding politics does not welcome displays of temper and acts of aggression, mainly because they don't believe that these ever solve problems and end political conflicts. This worldview stands in sharp contrast to Erdoğan's aggressive tones, which surface frequently in international settings. The GM has never approved of Erdoğan's uncompromising politics, such as his aggressive stance toward Israel and his storming out in anger at Shimon Peres and vowing never to attend the annual Davos meeting again.[37]

A good deal of the conflict between the AKP and the GM arises from their conflicting worldviews and perspectives on world politics. The GM's international exposure and acclimatization have brought it into closer contact and collaboration with global powers. This global expansion infuses the movement with new worldviews and new powerful friends, such as the United States. For example, the GM's U.S. branch has developed dialogues with evangelicals and the Jewish lobby in the United States, and its adherents there have had hands-on close-up experience of interactions and negotiations with international actors.

This situation has led to sharp disputes between the GM and the AKP, notably over the flotilla from Turkey that aimed at breaking the Gaza blockade to bring aid to the Palestinians. The flotilla was attacked by Israeli military forces in international waters, leading to the death of nine Turkish civilians. It was supported by the AKP and organized mainly by the Turkish Foundation for Human Rights and Freedoms and Humanitarian Relief (referred to as İHH in Turkish), which has a reputation as an "Islamist" organization in the eyes of

Fethullah Gülen's followers. Gülen disapproved of the action, accusing the AKP government in U.S. media of jeopardizing the lives of civilians in a hopeless cause, given clear warnings from Israel.[38]

There is no doubt that the GM's global networks baffle the increasingly authoritarian AKP, since it cannot control such a well-recognized international network. The GM is thus empowered vis-à-vis the government, and constitutes the loudest Islamic opposition to the AKP, by virtue of its international outreach. In addition to conflicts with regard to international politics, conflict arises between the AKP and the GM because of the power struggle in domestic politics. There is an overarching consensus in the GM that non-state actors can and must sit at the table with states for negotiation instead of using violence, and it refuses to engage or cooperate with terrorist groups.[39] This explains how and why the GM may differ from the AKP in prioritizing policies that deal with the Kurdish question. While both the AKP and the GM regarded the PKK as a terrorist threat to the Turkish state, and although both agree on the urgency of a resolution to the conflict, the GM seems to remain distrustful of the AKP's methods and efforts, undercover or latent, in handling the Kurdish problem.[40]

The divides and rivalry between the GM and the AKP go beyond the Kurdish issue. Infuriated by Erdoğan's plan to build a mosque on the Çamlıca Hill, a popular public park in Istanbul, a GM spokesman snapped: "[Such a] display of political grandiosity is un-Islamic, since it violates the principle of modesty. It's like an imitation of Anıtkabir [Atatürk's mausoleum in Ankara]."[41]

When I asked if the government was undermining the GM's economic self-interest, I heard very similar responses from followers:

The government decided to close our *dersanes* [preparatory schools for the university entrance examination], and people think that we despise the government for it. Honestly, in terms of the larger context of our educational institutions, it does no harm to us. We can easily turn the *dersanes* into schools. But the government makes all these hasty policy changes without really bringing about educational reform. We need genuine reform, not impulsive, immature changes. Our children go to school in this country and suffer from previous and ongoing problems created by the AKP. If they are closing *dersanes*, they should lift the university exam. Or if they keep the university entrance exam, they'll have to replace the *dersane* with a different option for preparation. By doing none of these things, the government sets the stage for increasing private tutoring, which is likely to lead to a boost in the informal economy. Worse than that, all of this only works for the affluent, who can afford private tutors. We are accused of neoliberalism, but look what they are doing.[42]

The distrust is mutual. In my interviews with adherents of the AKP, I heard similar tales of discontent and frustration with the GM. Many complained about how the Gülen Movement had become a capitalist enterprise by only looking out for its own economic interests:

"They only do business with each other, and favor each other. This is called monopoly."[43]

"If you give your hand, you cannot get your arm back [*Elini versen, kolunu alamıyorsun*]. They stick like glue for charity to their own causes, and when you need them they are nowhere to be found."

"Money speaks in the GM. When they ask for your money, they also ask for unconditional submission. You are not supposed to think for yourself."

While the GM's international expansion is a major discomfort for many AKP followers, the leader's residency in the United States seems to irritate them even more. One said:

Prime Minister Erdoğan invites the leader of the GM back home to Turkey. If he is such a patriot, why does he insist so much on staying away? He is acquitted and welcomed by the prime minister. What else does one need? I really think that the movement keeps him away to turn him into a mythical figure, to make a mysterious hero out of him.

Years of close engagements with the Turkish state and many host states across the world have smoothed and eased relations between the GM and various branches of the Turkish state.[44] These engagements have also provided this previously nonstate community movement with a platform for familiarizing and experimenting with formal institutions of state. Although the GM has consistently refused to mix party politics with religion, and thereby refrained from forming a political party, its members have increasingly taken positions in state bureaucracy. Several branches of the state witnessed a concentration of the followers of the GM, including but not limited to law enforcement. The access of the GM to the branches of the state has reinforced power struggles between the elected officials of the AKP and the appointed officials of the GM. These two groups have become increasingly distrustful rivals, unable to share the means of control and the resources of the state, even including intelligence.[45] When the police and the government show erratic signs of competition, it is highly alarming that both the police and the intelligence service are politicized. Similarly, hastily passed bills turn the legislature into a political body, while unsubstantiated arrests and long prison sentences for military officials without following proper procedures cast doubt on the judiciary as a politicized institution.

The pressing problem in Turkey is *not* the fact that there seems to be conflict between the branches of the state, and thereby between Islamist leaders in these branches. Leading political sociologists argue that the state is not a monolithic institution, and that its branches can come into conflict.[46] The question is *how* these conflicts emerge and are handled and contained. The wiretapping of the prime minister's office suggests that there is lack of commitment to the rules of the game not only by the government but also by different branches of the state. The findings of this study suggest that the deep conflict between the Islamist elite that divides the state can be deflected from formal political institutions to urban space. Divisions among the devout are thus likely to lead to further alliances across the Islamist-secularist dichotomy, debilitating the AKP's hegemony and potentially reducing its electoral constituency.

On the basis of empirical evidence on splits between the two main Islamic organizations, I argue that the major problem is not disagreement or distrust between Muslims, but the ways in which power struggles deeply divide different branches of the state. While disagreements can be handled within the rules of the game, violation of the major principles of democracy politicizes the governing institutions of the state.

Paradoxically, a certain degree of distrust among social actors who share similar lifestyles—pious Muslims in this case—gives them an incentive to rely more on political institutions than on their own community. Once people can no longer take for granted communal reciprocal ties or identitarian bondings, their need and yearning for political institutional reform increases.[47] The decline of close-knit communal trust often goes hand in hand with decreasing clientelism,[48] while also raising the importance of having stronger democratic institutions. Recent splits among devout Muslim women are a good example. Strong objections were voiced by some educated head-scarved Muslim women against the AKP's (failed) attempt to ban abortions and caesarian births.[49] These devout discontented adherents of the AKP have taken sides with secular feminists in defense of women's rights over their bodies. Instead of trusting the judgment of pious Muslim men or collaborating with the Muslim community, these progressive Muslims voiced their support of institutionalized gender reform and equality. They thereby supported the legality of abortion, despite the fact that they would not have abortions themselves.

A similar example comes from the most recent tensions within the GM. My most recent observations within the movement in Turkey and the United States reveal that the GM has put increasing emphasis on its rapidly growing branch in the United States. Appreciating graduate degrees from respectable American universities and a good command of English (and other languages), the GM has created new power hierarchies and privileges within the communal movement. Unsurprisingly, these new inequalities have led to discomforts and tensions within the GM in Turkey. Consequently, both pious women and Turkey-based followers of the GM are learning to prioritize institutional contractual arrangements rather than relying solely on informal assurances of reciprocity and communal commitments. Hence, inner splits are likely to constitute one big step toward respect and commitment to institutional rules even within the same Islamic community movement.

Like Turkish secularism, neither Muslim piety nor Islamism are fixed, monolithic categories. In contemporary Turkey and many other post–Arab Spring countries, such as Egypt, Muslims are divided by intense power struggles, which lead to distrust. They differ along the lines of class, gender, ethnicity, and worldview. Accordingly, in addition to the GM, several other devout groups have also parted ways with or criticized the AKP. For example, anti-capitalist Muslims became more visible during the Gezi protests and allied with the protestors in their objection to the AKP's neoliberal policies.

These splits among the devout and their new alliances with nonreligious groups did not appear suddenly during the Gezi protests, but have been under way for several years. To the extent that Muslims were included in secular sites, their allegiance to the AKP became conditional. The more accommodated they were in mixed urban sites, the more they were able to develop new, shifting alliances with other residents. For example, when the leader of the GM publicly announced his discontentment with the AKP shortly before the local elections in March 2014, the most educated strata of the GM openly advocated voting for the secularist opposition party, the CHP. Although the results of the elections suggest that GM adherents did not transfer their votes collectively to the CHP, the movement's leaders and spokesmen publicly displayed strong opposition to the AKP.[50]

These emerging splits among Muslim actors serve as a propellant of democratization for several reasons. In the first place, they encourage tolerance of individual differences and a desire for institutional reform to bolster individual rights and democratic liberties. The divides among the pious thereby move the debates on predominantly cultural or identitarian issues toward political pluralism at the institutional level. More specifically, the splits within Muslim groups shift the axis of conflict. Do both secular and pious Muslims divide along the axis of authoritarianism versus democracy? The remarks of President Gül—one of the founders of the AKP—to government during the Gezi protests were highly significant in this respect. He warned the AKP that its political success, earned over a decade, might disintegrate overnight if it mishandled the protests.[51]

However, the political inclinations and actions of Erdoğan, particularly after he won the presidentail elections in 2014—silencing oppositional voices, repressing protest, and, perhaps worst of all, polarizing Turkish society through divide-and-rule tactics—remain a serious impediment to democratization.[52] Preaching hostility that could potentially overshadow the new alliances in Turkey's cities risks leading the country into deeper political disorder. Erdoğan has made statements like: "I can summon a million people to my support against a hundred protestors" and "We are keeping 50 percent [of my supporters] at home." This became particularly problematic when half the society was in despair and felt disrespected, unheard, mistreated, repressed, and oppressed.[53] By silencing the media, he cut off and isolated the other half—his own constituents—from the injustices and police brutality against protestors and opposition. Moreover, while he deprived 50 percent, his opposition, of their rights to assemble and protest, the other half, his followers, were allowed to protest without police intervention. The police did not intervene, for example, when a large group of Muslims demonstrated in front of Hagia Sofia in Istanbul on the anniversary of the Gezi protests on May 31, 2014, demanding that the former Byzantine basilica (converted into a museum in 1935) be opened for worship as a mosque, whereas on that day only a year earlier anti-government protestors had been blocked, tear-gassed, and detained.[54]

Only time will tell whether divisions among the devout and urban alliances will help defeat the AKP, which is betting on the unconditional unity and loyalty of its followers. This is why the opposition must prioritize forming links and alliances with various Muslim groups. Erdoğan plans to remain in power as a president for another term, during which his immunity protects him from any law suits. As Şeyla Benhabib has observed, his proposal to change the system would give the president "extremely empowering and potentially dangerous privileges," in a country where checks and balances are remarkably weak. Comparing this presidential system with Putinism, rather than with Western democracies, Benhabib raised the most pressing concern: "Given the weakness of the opposition, Turkey is sliding into a model of plebiscitary, charismatic leadership, with a 'supreme leader,' who is elected with majority support."[55] Similarly, other scholars have engaged in debates on Turkey's majoritarian or "electoral dictatorship,"[56] arguing that electoral democracy can be misused for authoritarian ends.

In my participation in a closed private discussion with President Gül and a small group of academics during his visit to Boston in May 2014, several Turkish academics asked the former president about violations of freedom, corruption allegations, the upcoming presidential elections, and his withdrawal from contention in them. While acknowledging the dark situation and gloomy times, he made one important comment. Referring briefly to "The Failed Autocrat," an article published in *Foreign Affairs* by Daron Acemoğlu,[57] who was in the room, Gül said: "The society is ahead of politics [*toplum siyasetin önünde*]." He insisted that this temporary dark situation would "have to pass."

Turkey's future will be bright in the hands of its highly educated, freedom-loving youth, who have genuine passion for democracy. That is why this book is dedicated first and foremost to them. However, in the very short run, new political alliances may fall short of defeating Erdoğan's AKP. For the moment, a better outlet for opposition may be found outside the realm of collective action, party politics, and political society. Even civil society, which I have heavily focused on in my previous writings, does not provide the creative dynamics and spontaneous strengths that urban space offers under AKP's supremacy.

While civil society activities and associations became targets of the authoritarian government and brutal law enforcement, ordinary everyday outlets in Turkey's cities that fall outside the government's hegemony and escape it are growing rapidly. Since civil societies are entwined with the states, a strong civil society belongs to, flourishes, and acts efficiently in a deeper democracy. During the authoritarian rule of the AKP, which is hostile to civic disobedience and rights, contested urban sites have themselves partly taken over the pivotal role of democratic opposition from civil society.[58] Urban and place-based improvisations become imperative for efficient opposition, since the police excel in hands-on repression of anti-government protests. On May 31, 2014, the first anniversary of the Gezi protests, a massive concentration of police, brought in from different cities, temporarily blocked Taksim Square, as well as access to pedestrian İstiklal Street from many side streets and ferry transportation across the Bosphorus. Istanbulites sarcastically noted: "'If I were a dictator,' Erdoğan said, 'you would not be able to stroll in squares!' He's kept his word!"

An efficient opposition is likely to develop through understanding, connecting with, and forming mutual understandings and new alliances in the city with ordinary Muslim residents who object to Erdoğan's authoritarianism and hold their commitment to a deeper democracy higher than ideological partisanship. These emerging bonds and potential alliances with Muslim urbanites, particularly Muslim youth and women, are extremely important for the near future. Enthusiastic participants in post-Gezi forums in parks and well-intentioned newcomers to party politics seem to downplay, if not neglect, the centrality of such urban alliances. It would, however, be a mistake not to capitalize on affinities with educated, pro-democratic Muslim residents, because like all people and places at the fault lines, they have the potential to go either way.

REFERENCE MATTER

NOTES

INTRODUCTION: THE CITY AND THE GOVERNMENT

1. See Cassano 2013. On May 28, the group petitioned Istanbul's Council to Protect Culture Heritage as a coalition of Right to the City associations.

2. As the bulldozers started uprooting the trees, tension arose between the protestors and the police. At about 5:00 a.m. on May 30, the peaceful protestors were caught by surprise facing the disproportional use of force and violence by the police. Taking advantage of his parliamentary immunity, Sırrı Süreyya Önder, representing the Kurdish Peace and Democracy Party (BDP) faced off a bulldozer to stop it from destroying the park. However, the Kurdish presence remained low and less visible in the protests overall, since they did not wish to endanger the peace process under Erdoğan's regime.

3. Originally, the protest was closely associated with a residents' group called Taksim Platform, established in January 2012, which has been in a dialogue with both Taksim area residents and local government in the city in order to form public opinion about several projects, such as the construction of an underground tunnel.

4. According to a KONDA survey, the average age of the protestors was twenty-eight. http://t24.com.tr/haber/konda-gezi-parki-anketi-cikardi,231889 (in Turkish).

5. *Economist*, June 6, 2013.

6. "Turkey's 'Standing Man' Wins German Award," *Al Jazeera*, August 26, 2013; "Turkey's Standing Man Wins German Rights Award," *Hürriyet*, August 26, 2013. The Turkish choreographer has become an icon of peaceful resistance by standing motionless for hours and starting a new form of anti-government resistance in Istanbul.

7. "Gezi Protestolarındaki cesareti için dev ödül" [Giant award to Divan Hotel for its bravery during Gezi protests]. *Hürriyet*, October 8, 2013.

8. Davis and Libertun de Duren 2011: 2.

9. Ibid.: 4.

10. See esp. Sennett 1998: 12.

11. See, e.g., Davis and Libertun de Duren 2011.

12. While scholarship has been rich in analyses of the spatiality of socioeconomic processes, the spatial turn in exploring political issues, such as citizenship, democracy,

and social justice, has been rather recent and scant. See, for exceptions, Işın 2000; Sassen 2006; Soja 2010.

13. No doubt, space is not the only factor that shapes freedoms, but it is a largely neglected factor even in intersectional studies, which take the intersection of various social and political variables seriously. I use "spatiality of freedom" not as a merely negative or positive quality of politics, but as a *conditional* aspect of it. Depending on sociopolitical conditions, governments and political forces, including both progressive/democratic and conservative/authoritarian ones, all interact with urban space.

14. Throughout this book, to differentiate the ordinary believing, practicing residents whom I refer to as "pious Muslims" from the Islamist political elite, I switch between the terms "pious Muslims," "pro-Islamic," and "Islamist." Pious Muslims are identified primarily by their faith-based ways of life (rather than a unifying Islamist political ideology), whereas the AKP represents a conservative, right-wing, neoliberal, pro-Islamic political ideology. Although overlaps between the two categories may exist, it would be a sweeping generalization to identify religious urbanites from all classes and walks of life with the increasingly paternalist and authoritarian party ideology of the AKP.

15. Turam 2012a, 2012b. See also Ağırdır 2013.

16. With regard to methodological improvisations, see Zussman 2004; Pierce 2003; Nelson 2001; Trouille 2012. Though I hadn't arrived in the field with a distinct agenda, I was spontaneously pulled into studying the street-level contestations. "Many of the [scholars who do sociology of place] do not seem to have started, as Burawoy (1998) would have it, with their favorite theory, then gone out looking for places to reconstruct it. . . . Adie Nelson seems to have found herself at ballet classes more as a mother than a sociologist, and then, a good sociologist as well as a mother, began to think about what her experience told her about 'dream work.' Jennifer Pierce's tenure trials were not an issue she sought: They were something that happened to her" (Zussman 2004: 358). For striking methodological examples, see Nelson 2001; Pierce 2003.

17. Turam 2008a, 2008b.

18. Author's interviews in the aftermath of Republican Marches in 2007. I have argued elsewhere (Turam 2008b) that the secularist opposition Republican People's Party (CHP) was doomed to failing in forming efficient opposition because the secularist Kemalists were accustomed to claiming "custody" of the state and never learned to engage or share power with rival political forces.

19. Davis and Libertun de Duren 2011: 4.

20. On the shifting political allegiance of Turkish business and entrepreneurs, see Yavuz 2012.

21. Öniş 2012; Kadıoğlu 2012: 55.

22. The presidential crisis put a sharp end to the period of smooth engagement between pious Muslims in the parliament and the secular branches of the state, which lasted over a decade.

23. In its second and third terms in office, the AKP waged war on the military, accusing it of an anti-government conspiracy committed by an extralegal network, referred to as the "Ergenekon network." A large number of military officers of different ranks were detained for extended periods without trial and when they were eventually tried received long or life sentences, suggesting that the judiciary had lost its independence.

24. See esp. Bayar 2014.

25. "[O]ne should not underestimate the elements of exclusion, which appeared to underpin the 'old regime,' and to some extent new elements of inclusion have been built into the 'new regime,'" the prominent political economist Ziya Öniş writes. "While the old regime provided little leeway for the religious and conservative segments to express their identity claims, the new system has similarly limited the claims of secularists or minority groups," (Öniş 2013: 106–7). See also Tombuş 2013.

26. I use the terms "lifestyle" and "ways of life" interchangeably throughout the book in the context of freedoms and rights.

27. Ağırdır 2013 provides the best account of the centrality of lifestyle in polarized Turkey.

28. "Turkish TV Presenter Fired for Revealing Cleavage," *Hürriyet*, October 9, 2013. www.france24.com/en/20131009-turkish-tv-presenter-fired-revealing-cleavage-veliaht -gozde-kansu-celik/

29. Commentators have criticized the "mentality of the judiciary" (*yargının zihniyeti*) or used the term "judicial activism" (*yargısal aktivism*) to describe the increasingly political and authoritarian attitude of the judiciary. See Berkan 2013; Taha 2013b. A large number of military officers, including top-ranking generals and the chief of the General Staff (*Genelkurmay Başkanı*), İlker Başbuğ, were sentenced to decades in prison. Although the AKP lifted some of these sentences before the local elections in March 2014, the judiciary remains questionable, as it deferred political rulings to special courts rather than pursuing fair trials.

30. Özbudun 2012; Belge 2012. Conference paper. "Dismantling Turkey's Juristocracy: AK Party and the Transformation of Political Power in Turkey," Middle East Studies Association Annual Meeting, Denver, Colorado, November 2012. See also Taha 2013a, 2013b.

31. I thank Yeşim Bayar for suggesting the term "searching for freedom."

32. For comprehensive discussion, see Polletta 2002, 2006. Previous scholarship on democratic contestation has largely focused on grassroots activism, collective action, and social movements. Similarly, the bulk of existing work in urban studies has been on urban democracy that entailed local governance, community-building, and strategic networking in cities. See, e.g., Singerman 1996.

33. Bayat 2007.

34. Tilly and Blockmans 1994; Tilly and Tarrow 2006; McAdam, Tarrow, and Tilly 2001. Mundane everyday life lacks both strategic mobilization and collective action. Unlike

these wide-ranging forms of abrupt or long-term organizing, the new urbanism is manifested in the ways of life and thereby unconventional parameters of power contestations.

35. In contrast to the predominant neglect of power struggles in many theories of symbolic interaction and the public sphere, recent ethnographies have paid attention to "the actual processes through which open territories are claimed, controlled, and contested" (Trouille 2012: 2). See also Turam 2012a; Gökarıksel 2012.

36. These places were regarded as "secular spaces" because of secular ways of life, as well as subjectivities and identities associated largely with nonreligiosity or secularism.

37. Although being a "devout Muslim" was not sufficient to define the identity of the newcomers, their reception at secular sites mainly focused on piety as the main identifier of their identity. Unsurprisingly, through this process of downplaying the other aspects of lifestyle of the devout newcomers, the head scarf has become the most central identification because of its gendered visibility.

38. On liberal higher education in the Middle East, see Betty Anderson 2008.

39. I conducted some one hundred and fifty ethnographic interviews in the three highly contested urban sites. Between 2007 and 2013, I conducted twelve field trips to Istanbul and three field trips to Berlin, which became the basis of Part 3 of this book. The length of each trip ranged between two weeks and two months. Since I was studying a spatial and political *process*, multiple field trips were necessary to trace and capture the dynamics of gradual change. While most of my interviews with the locals were ethnographic, and thus informal and often spontaneous, I also scheduled open-ended interviews, at least on initial contact. In addition to participant observation, I also conducted group discussions in Istanbul.

40. Hinze 2013.

41. In each part of this book, the first chapter on splits is followed by a second chapter that illustrates the new bonds and cooperations that grew on the basis of struggles for freedoms and rights.

42. This shift was due neither to deliberation nor protest or another form of collective action, but merely to mundane daily practices. This finding differs from the deliberative politics exercised in the public sites of q'at chewing discussed in Wedeen 2007.

43. Casanova 1994, 2001.

44. Horowitz 1993: 33–34.

45. Cemal Kafadar, interview by Serkan Ayazoğlu, "Haliç Metro Köprüsü uykularımı kaçırıyor" [Losing sleep over the Golden Horn Metro Bridge], *Taraf*, January 9, 2013. Horrified by the reduction of such historic places to kitsch, Kafadar questioned whether a respectable film director would treat St. Peter's Basilica in Rome like that.

46. Ibid., author's translation.

47. Agency is the ability to act and bring about change (Charrad 2010). Contested and divided urban sites often attract, cope with, and may generate strong alliances, mak-

ing them pivotal players in power struggles and putting them at the agentic end of the continuum.

48 Clearly, these qualities are not inherent in a place, but are often negotiated through power dynamics.

49. Placing power dynamics at the center of analysis, this book treats agentic places and what Cemal Kafadar calls a "noplace" as the two ends of the continuum. Hence, most places are not static but move along this axis, attracting, accommodating, reinforcing, or diffusing power and conflict.

50. Clearly, this argument stands in sharp contrast with predominant views and conventional thinking that sees highly contested and deeply divided urban space as a threat to political stability and national security.

51. Charrad 2010: 517.

52. Power does not manifest itself as a zero-sum game between agency and structure, but rather as an ongoing, and often vexing, process of negotiation. See esp. Giddens 1991; Charrad 2010.

53. As Zussman brilliantly argues (2004: 355): "A focus on people in places, then, makes no assumptions about whether the macro precedes the micro or the micro precedes the macro . . . A focus on people in places is, perhaps at the most abstract level, a way to look at *both* structure and agency, without assuming the priority of either."

54. Zussman (2004: 354) rightly argues that "places are typically the manifestations, or, perhaps more precisely, the *instantiations* of institutions and policies" (emphasis added). But they are also powerful actors that shape policies and institutional politics, whether strategically through urban mobilization or unintentionally in everyday urban life.

55. One prioritizes the structuralist aspects of urban politics by focusing on the power of the state, focusing on the ways in which different states and governments impose themselves on urban space. See, e.g., Brenner 2004.

56. The structuralist school has been criticized for downplaying issues of agency in respect to the place and residents' capacity to strategize, mobilize, resist, and/or transform power structures. See, e.g., Koenraad 2012: 256. Other studies emphasize the importance of urban contestation by bringing to the forefront alternative, dissenting, or oppositional voices "from below." Low 2000; Dikeç 2007: 5, 127–47; Öz and Eder 2012; Turam 2012a.

57. Many urbanists prioritize residents, their local participation, and their claims to the right to the city under the rubric of urban or radical democracy.

58. This tendency, found in many debates on the right to the city, is criticized by Purcell as "the local trap." See Purcell 2006; Purcell and Brown 2005.

59. See, e.g., Hasson and Ley 1994; Read 2012; Read and Pekkanen 2009.

60. On two plazas that "are continuously reconceived, redefined, and reworked by citizens and the state" see Low 2000: 123.

61. Binali Yıldırım quoted in "*Bu sözler sosyal medyayı salladı*" (These words shook up social media), *Hürriyet*, January 29, 2013, trans. and emphasis by author.

62. "Binali'nin Üniversite tercihi" (Binali's choice of university), *Penguen*, no. 542 (February 7, 2013), cover.

63. Performances at the Atatürk Cultural Center had in the past been interrupted only by natural or political disasters—military coups and a fire in 1970.

64. During the Gezi protests, demonstrators entered the AKM building and filmed the interior, revealing that it had been gutted. Erdoğan then admitted that, contrary to the impression that had been given to the public, it was in fact scheduled to be demolished, like many other much-loved buildings in Istanbul. In speeches, he subsequently offered various suggestions as to what might replace it, but nothing was done. Eventually, Güler Sabancı, a world-famous entrepreneur and a member of one of Turkey's top-ranking families, donated 30 million Turkish lira to renovate it. See "Sabancı'dan AKM'ye 30 milyon" [Thirty million from Sabancı to AKM], *Radikal*, February 16, 2012.

65. "AKM'ye Sabancı Desteği" [Sabancı's support of AKM], *Milliyet*, February 16, 2012. A prominent philanthropist and the chair of the board of Sabancı Holdings, Güler Sabancı worked admirably with Ertuğrul Günay, the minister of art and culture, who had transferred from the secularist opposition party. Unfortunately, their partnership came to an end in February 2013 when Günay's position as a minister was terminated.

66. I thank Valentine Moghadam for her question about how disturbing these places are for urban residents who support conservative or authoritarian governments.

67. Dikeç 2007.

68. "In your speeches, you give orders to the judiciary. We see that the judiciary, security, bureaucracy, media and business are under your command. In what kind of regime does one find such scenarios?" Danzikyan Yetvart demanded of the prime minister (Yetvart, "Çığırından çıkan rejim" [The regime out of its mind], *Radikal*, June 7, 2013).

69. Unsurprisingly, much urban space remains uncontested and undivided, including strictly Islamic neighborhoods, such as Fatih, staunchly secular neighborhoods of Izmir and Ankara, gated communities, and rigidly secular university campuses.

70. Some places remain persistently segregated and therefore fall out of the scope of this book's interests. However, neatly segregated places have been in decline in many big cities in Turkey.

71. "Önünde cami dahi olsa ... " [Even if there is a mosque ...], *Vatan*, October 23, 2013; "Erdoğan: Yol geçecekse camiyi de yıkarız" [Erdoğan: We would knock down even the mosque if a road is being built," *Radikal*, October 22, 2013. Erdoğan said that his government was serving the public overall rather than individual interests.

72. Turam 2012a.

73. Lefebvre 1996: 195; Purcell 2008: 94–96.

74. Harvey 2012: 4; emphasis added.

75. In addition, the advocacy of right to the city is overwhelmingly motivated by a shared objection against the *exclusionary* "neoliberal idea of city-as-property." Purcell 2008: 106. See also, e.g., Brenner, Madden, and Wachsmut 2012; Harvey 2012. Along

these lines, the contested urban spaces discussed in this book promote an *inclusionary* ideal of the city-as-inhabited or the city-as-equally-shared across lines of class, religion, ethnicity, gender, and age.

76. In the face of new exclusionary and authoritarian tendencies of democracies with heightened security-related measures, these new urbanites form new alliances against violation of rights and freedoms that go beyond the scope of right to the city. As Harvey (2012: xii) *emphasizes*, these democratic outcomes originate from the *actual practices* of urbanites and not from Lefebvre's or others' ideas of the right to the city. Urban space generates new motives and power, as the new inhabitants come up with a new language, humor, and vision to oppose political hegemony.

77. As the ideological does not define the political, the nonideological does not imply apolitical.

78. Weber shows that democracy grew (out of feudalism) in the cities thanks to the burgher's participation and demands. The burgher is not just an accidental urban figure for Weber; his main quality is freedom—freedom earned through the acquisition of citizenship by taking advantage of urban space. "City air makes man free," writes Weber, quite literally in the context of the end of serfdom in central and northern European cities (Weber 1958: 100). As "the city became an autonomous and autocephalous institutional association," citizenship came to be evaluated as "an individual right" (ibid.: 113).

79. Ibid.: 574.

80. "[T]he current uprisings in the cities of the MENA region are quite different from what might have been in the medieval city of Weber," Saskia Sassen (2011: 574) rightly argues. Despite the different historical contexts, this book builds upon Weber's work conceptually, since *The City* set the stage for revealing and theorizing the ways in which urban space, freedom, and democracy are mutually dependent.

81. Bayat [2010] 2013.

82. Turam 2012a.

83. Schwedler 2011.

84. E.g., Sassen 2011: 574; Harvey 2003, 2012.

85. Craiutu and Jennings 2009.

86. Ibid.: 21.

87. Tocqueville [1835–40] 2000. Whereas the first volume of Tocqueville's *Democracy in America* exalts self-government and local administration, his second volume includes praise for the art of self-organization and association, mutual respect between religion and politics, individual freedoms, and "self-interest rightly understood."

88. This is much different from the predominant view in political science that sees democratization as a linear "transition" that is expected to reach a finale—an end point referred to as "consolidated democracy." See, e.g., Diamond, Plattner, and Brumberg 2003; Schmitter 2010: 19; Carothers 2000.

89. The most common use of the term "scale" in political studies is to indicate the

level of governance, whether global, national, regional, or local. Since this book is not about governance, however, but about urban democratic contestation, it differs from this usage. "[R]ecent scale research has generated a greater appreciation of the inherently spatial aspect of politics," Adam Moore writes (2008: 204). This enables us to engage spatial scale more smoothly with political theory. See also Purcell 2006.

90. For exceptions, see Migdal 2001; Migdal, Kohli, and Shue 1994; Wedeen 2008; Bayat 2007.

91. Hall 1995; Mann 1993; Arjomand 1989; Zubaida 2009.

92. Sassen 2011.

93. The same need for engagement applies to the divide between political and urban sociology. For works by scholars who bridge these two fields, see Peter Evans 2002; Brenner 2004; Brenner, Jessop, Jones, and Macleod 2003; Davis 1994; Davis and Libertun de Duren 2011; Weinstein 2014, 2009; Bayat 1997, [2010] 2013.

94. Hence, the exhaustion or annihilation of the protest must also not be confused with defeat of democratic contestation.

95. Harvey 2012: 162. "What Tahrir Square showed to the world was an obvious truth: that it is *bodies on the street* and the squares, not the babble of sentiments on Twitter or Facebook, that really matter" (ibid.).

CHAPTER 1. BETWEEN STATE SPACES AND AUTONOMOUS PLACES

1. Cemal Kafadar, interview by Serkan Ayazoğlu, "Haliç Metro Köprüsü Uykularımı Kaçırıyor" (Losing sleep over the Golden Horn Metro Bridge), *Taraf*, January 9, 2013 (author's translation, emphasis added). The Golden Horn Metro Bridge opened in February 2014.

2. Tocqueville [1856] 1955; Mann 1993.

3. See esp. Painter 2005.

4. Dikeç 2007; Turam 2012b.

5. Dikeç 2007; Turam 2012a.

6. See esp. Kafescioğlu 2009: 1.

7. "The idea of an association, which could unite the city into a corporate unit was missing in Mecca . . . in Asiatic and Oriental settlements of an urban economic character, normally only extended families and professional associations were vehicles of communal actions. Communal action was not the product of an urban burgher stratum as such" (Weber 1958: 96) While Weber's work was more complete on India and China, his comments on the Islamic city were mostly restricted to the Arab world. The problem with taking a place like Mecca as reference point is that from the fourteenth to the twentieth centuries, the Ottoman Empire, which was hardly typified by the Arab cities it colonized, comprised the largest part of the Muslim world.

8. Weber's work reveals that the urban politics in Constantinople goes beyond the "extended family and tribes" that he associates with the "Islamic city." From the time of

the Islamic Middle Ages until the sixteenth century in Constantinople, "merchants, corporations and guilds" represented "the interests of the burghers beside purely military associations such as the *Janitscharen* [janissaries; Turkish, *yeniçeri*] and *Sipahis*, and the religious organizations of the *Ulemas* and *Dervishes*" (Weber 1958: 88). Nevertheless, his accounts fail to do justice to the rich and complex sociopolitical cultural and architectural heritage of the Ottoman Empire, whose army, trade, and *waqf* (foundations) provided a platform for people's civic participation, in addition to many other formations that Weber's "Occidental city" did not have. As Reşat Kasaba argues, the Ottoman port cities generated vibrant commercial activity. However, because Weber read the Islamic cities through the lens of the Occidental ones, rather than capturing and analyzing what was actually happening in the cities of the Ottoman Empire, his work points, in a "sociology of absence," to what was missing in the Orient. See Kasaba 1994; Zubaida 2005.

9. "On the one hand, the 'Islamization' of the Byzantine city following the Ottoman conquest meant establishing new urban policies, a new type of urban administration, and new institutions and organizations, as well as the promotion of new building types." On the other hand, however, the modernization efforts interrupted this Islamization process as "the change in Istanbul's urban form . . . took place incrementally and resulted in a patchy and eclectic regularity" (Çelik 1993: xvi).

10. Bozdoğan 2001.

11. Dayaratne 2012: 310. In his study of Bahrain, Dayaratne differentiates *architectural landscapes*, which are powerful tools to create a sense of belonging to the nation, from *landscapes*, which he identifies as "contested realms." But architectural landscapes that are the cornerstones of nation-building are, of course, also contested by shifting ties of power elite throughout the history, as we see in present-day Turkey.

12. Houston 2005: 107: "In this understanding the environment's random sovereignty over human activity is replaced by its regulated sovereignty as the planner-expert."

13. See, e.g., Painter 2006.

14. Bozdoğan 2001: 298.

15. Ismail 2000.

16. Bora 1999: 49; Çinar 2005; Özyürek 2006; Mills 2010.

17. Çinar 2005; Özyürek 2006. Over the past few decades, Islamists have celebrated the day of the conquest of Byzantine Constantinople, while secularists celebrate the day of the founding of the Turkish Republic. Most recently, the AKP government's disrespect for and cancellation of secular national celebrations has infuriated secular residents of Istanbul. Many Istanbulites have begun showing heightened feelings for these national days and there is much more pronounced mourning on December 10, the day of founding father Kemal Atatürk's death.

18. See Dikeç 2007: 14 and 74. Dikeç highlights the spontaneity of the rise of Republican nationalism and the increasing uneasiness about Islam in the *banlieue* in France throughout the 1990s.

19. Bora, 1999: 48.

20. Secor 2001.

21. Bora, 1999: 52.

22. Keyder 2005.

23. Bora 1999: 55.

24. Ibid.: 55–56; Keyder 1999.

25. White 2002; Turam 2007; Tuğal 2009.

26. Here "secular space" refers to urban public sites that are defensively associated with secular ways of life and nonreligious activities and symbols. By virtue of objections to or discouragement of public display of religious symbols, such as the head scarf, in these places, they were regarded as a secularist monopoly until the 2000s. The term "Islamic space" is conversely used to refer to sites where symbols of and references to Islam are ubiquitous in lifestyles, sartorial choices, music played or sold in the stores, and so on.

27. See, e.g., Genel and Karaosmanoğlu 2006: 475.

28. Migdal, Kohli, and Shue 1994; Migdal 2001.

29. Houston 2005: 103.

30. Harvey 2012: xvii.

31. Ahmet Hakan, "Neden böyle yapıyor?" [Why is he doing this?], *Hürriyet*, November 8, 2013.

32. Houston 2005: 102.

33. İnci Pastanesi's owners and staff were expelled on a workday by the police, some of whom did not even bother to show ID. Customers protested vigorously, and film of the physical and verbal altercations quickly appeared on YouTube.

34. Linz and Stepan 1996.

35. Trouille 2012: 2–3.

36. On violent spaces, see, e.g., Davis forthcoming.

37. Çakmak 2013.

38. Polletta 1999: 3.

39. Sara Evans and Harry Boyte discuss the physicality of space in their book *Free Spaces: Sources of Democratic Change in America* (1992), but most of the debate that followed its publication was either vague or negligent on the subject.

40. Polletta 1999: 7.

41. See, e.g., Sassen 2006; Escobar 2001. Francesca Polletta concludes that the nature of the ties is "established or reinforced" by web sites, rather than the physical space itself being transformed (Polletta 1999: 25).

42. Polletta sees "the free space concepts as an attempt to capture the social structural dimensions of several cultural dynamics" (1999: 7) Concretely, she links associative structures (transmovement, indigenous, and prefigurative, all of which are referred to as free spaces) with the tasks of mobilization. She is quite right in suggesting this, be-

cause, paradoxically, the inflation of the terminology of space in this literature has gone hand in hand with reducing space to the characteristics of social groups, networks, and associations.

43. Zussman 2004: 354.

PART 1. ON NEIGHBORHOOD POLITICS

1. Bayat 2007.

2. I thank Nilüfer Isvan for bringing the broader uses of the term "social pressure" to my attention.

3. See Şerif Mardin's paper submitted to the 2009 annual meeting of the Middle East Studies Association in Boston, where there were four panels on "neighborhood pressure" in Turkey. And see also Altınordu 2009.

4. Çakır 2008; Şerif Mardin, unpublished paper.

5. See esp. Toprak et al., 2008. Toprak and her collaborators also revealed that the neighborhood was joining forces with religious communities and the pro-Islamic government in pressuring "Others" to conform and intervening in their un-Islamic lifestyles and personal spheres.

6. Turam 2012a.

7. Ruşen Çakır, "Neighborhood → State → Neighborhood → State," *Vatan*, November 7, 2013.

8. Tophane became the target neighborhood for police raids on mixed-gender student housing, for example, because the contrast between the students' lifestyles and those of the conservative locals was more pronounced there than elsewhere in Istanbul.

9. See, e.g., Read 2012.

10. See esp. Majd 2008.

11. Read 2012; Read and Pekkanen 2009. Other studies of neighborhoods also showed how Islamists were absorbed into the capitalist system or mobilized at the local grassroots level. See White 2002; Tuğal 2009.

12. For inclusive debates on consumption, the city, and politics, see also Reynolds 2012; Ley 1996. Reynolds's historical analysis of urban consumption culture in Egypt situates the political transformation in the larger context of "modernization" under the imperial rule. In contrast, my analysis of high-spending, fashion-conscious head-scarved women in Teşvikiye locates urban politics in larger processes of democratization.

13. Escobar 2001: 158.

14. For a remarkable analysis of urbanites' politics of lifestyle, consumption, and attraction to the city center, see Ley 1996.

15. On the agentic powers of the middle class, see esp. Gershoni and Jankowski 1995 and spatial turn literature, e.g., Warf and Arias 2009.

16. The predominant reduction of political dynamics to socioeconomic factors in urban politics is also caused by the largely space-blind attitude of political studies.

A large majority of political scientists and political sociologists maintain their suspicion of—and thereby underestimate—the centrality of space in political processes (for exceptions, see Evans 2002; Davis 1994; Brenner 2004). Furthermore, even scholars in the subfields of these disciplines often talk past each other and thereby fail to link political processes and urban space. For example, urban sociologists, in disconnect from political sociology, have often prioritized the socioeconomic aspects of urban space over its political facets. In turn, political sociologists, in disconnect from urban sociologists, have often ignored the importance of space at the expense of class, gender, ethnicity, and race.

17. The debate around Lefebvre's notion of the right to the city deserves notice here. The bulk of the analysis in this debate juxtaposes neoliberal urbanism against democracy, because neoliberalism is viewed as "negatively affecting the enfranchisement of urban citizens" (Purcell 2003: 99). From this perspective, it can be argued that although the new, built-in consumption sites of Teşvikiye were attracting socially and politically heterogeneous crowds, these places were failing in integrating and creating peaceful cohabitation in the neighborhood. Subsequently, the neighborhood turned into a hub for clashes and resentment despite (or due to) its ability to draw different lifestyles together. However, an in-depth ethnographic look reveals other, more nuanced aspects of an emerging neighborhood politics. Accordingly, Part 1 of this book complicates the presumably inevitable tension between a free market economy and democracy by bringing diverse dynamics of power and yearnings for freedom into the analysis. Although I agree with the critiques of neoliberalization as a spatial process (for a good example, see Brenner, Peck, and Theodore 2010) and urban space as a primarily neoliberal realm (Sassen 1991; Logan and Molotch 2007; see also Gökarıksel, 2007 for a similar perspective in the Turkish context), this book shifts the focus to the urban alliances over civil liberties and individual freedoms.

18. Without underestimating the centrality of global capitalism in the city, I focus on people's yearning and struggle for freedoms and rights. These struggles are not exclusively shaped by socioeconomic factors. Similarly, "ongoing production and signification of space and built environments by the nation-state . . . is not cancelled out by the global logic of capital" (Houston 2005: 117).

19. As Purcell (2003: 106) states, "The struggles of inhabitants against marginalization are struggles against an array of social and spatial structures of which capitalism is only one." Contestations in and over urban space intersect with multiple struggles over religion, gender, ethnicity, and so on. (Urban) space and contestation are explicitly intersectional, which must not be obscured under the rubric of the city as a hotbed of class inequalities and neoliberal regimes. Hence, an exclusive or narrow focus on socioeconomic factors may obscure a multiplicity of conflicts, such as between religious and secular ways of life. Although lifestyle politics is often shaped by class-related issues, there is no reason to ignore other aspects of it. Ethnographic evidence in Part 1 suggests

that the issue of inclusion/exclusion and power struggles are largely shaped by clashing of lifestyles and defense of conflicting freedoms.

20. Soja 2010: 2, 11. Clearly, this analysis parts ways with the rich literature in the United States on the neighborhood as a hub of crime, poverty, ghettoization, segregation, and other problems caused by urbanization. The predominant sociological interest in the neighborhood is largely motivated by social problems and/or crime, often associated with urbanization and urban poverty. Specifically in American sociology, the leading themes are racial segregation, class inequalities, ghettoization, and public services—often backed up by a critique of neoliberal economy. See, e.g., Bruch and Mare 2006; Peterson and Kriva 2010; see also Bartu and Kolluoğlu 2008 on similar issues in the Turkish context. The ethnography of Teşvikiye shows how power struggles and neighborhood space are mapped onto each other in negotiating rights and freedoms. This is what Hosam Sholom and David Ley (1994) refer to as a "post-material" aspect of neighborhood organizing, which refers to primarily political factors.

CHAPTER 2. A NEIGHBORHOOD DIVIDED BY LIFESTYLES

1. "The residential area was connected to the Taksim Şişli artery at Harbiye in 1865" (Çelik 1993: 42).

2. For two different perspectives on the "communal" basis and strong networks of pious society, see Gellner 1996 and Singerman 1996.

3. For a similar analysis of "imaginary geographies of consumption" that were also "places to be seen" in colonial Egypt, see Reynolds 2012: 8.

4. For an analysis of the links between consumption and politics, see, e.g., Daunton and Hilton 2001.

5. Öncü and Weyland 1997; Keyder 2005.

6. Trouille 2012: 3.

7. With regard to the "'extension" of the private sphere to the streets in a neighborhood setting, see also Mills 2007.

8. Lefebvre 1996: 144.

9. Reynolds 2012.

10. Trouille 2012: 3.

11. Although the park has been gentrified over the past decade, most status-conscious longtime Teşvikiyeli don't go in for picnicking in public parks. Frequently, too, they spend their leisure time in expensive gyms.

12. In his study of a highly contested soccer field in Los Angeles, David Trouille notes that the "categories of insider and outsider require constant renegotiation by regulars [i.e., regular visitors] who feel powerful on the [site] yet marginal in the . . . residential setting" (2012: 3).

13. Bora, 1999: 53. See also Lefebvre 1996.

14. See, e.g., Aydınlı 2012; Turam 2012a, 2012b.

15. Ismail 2000.

16. Soja 2010: 197–98.

17. Lefebvre 1996: 195.

18. See also Harb 2009; Deab and Harb 2014; and other articles in the *International Journal of Urban and Regional Research* 33 (4).

19. Featherstone 1987: 55

20. Author's interview, June 10, 2007. Emphasis added.

21. Turam 2008a.

22. Trouille 2012: 3. Emphases added.

23. On political decency, see esp. Hall 2013.

CHAPTER 3. AFFINITIES IN THE ZONES OF FREEDOM

1. Öniş 2013. See also Turam 2012b; Öktem 2012; Kadıoğlu 2012.

2. See esp. Özbudun 2012.

3. Kuru and Stepan 2012: 9.

4. Almost three-fifths (58 percent) of Turkey's citizens voted yes in the 2010 referendum, changing no fewer than twenty-four constitutional provisions. With the exception of a few amendments—recognition of affirmative action for women, children, the elderly, and the disabled; a ban on secret state surveillance of personal data; and higher barriers to the Constitutional Court's ability to dissolve parties—most of the changes were concerned with structures and procedures, not matters of individual liberties and civil rights.

5. See Turam 2012b.

6. Keyder 2005: 124; Bartu and Kolluoğlu 2008.

7. In physics, the concept of "cross section" is used to express the *likelihood of interaction* between particles. This basic concept is then extended to the cases where the interaction probability in the targeted area assumes intermediate values—because the target itself is *not homogeneous,* or because a nonuniform field mediates the interaction.

8. See esp. Gellner 1981, 1996.

9. Hall 2013.

10. It is worth pointing out that this spatial analysis must not be confused with special determinism. There is nothing inherent in these places other than what is created by historical and social conditions and through political contestation. Put differently, it is the social interactions, power dynamics, and politics of contestation that endow a political agency to these hybrid places.

11. In 2009, Uğur Derman was awarded the Presidential Culture and Art Grand Award in the field of Traditional Arts (Geleneksel Sanatlar). www.tccb.gov.tr/haberler /170/48586/cumhurbaskanligi-kultur-ve-sanat-buyuk-odulleri-sahiplerini-buldu.html (in Turkish).

12. Interview with Uğur Derman, July 2010.

13. The construction company Keten İnşaat buys old buildings in Teşvikiye and in their place builds relatively more affordable smaller condominium units. This plays a major role in material transformation of the neighborhood. See www.keteninsaat.com (in Turkish).

14. Purcell 2008: 66; emphasis added.

15. Different places may produce a good deal of resistance on the basis of shared political goals of cultural homogeneity and/or shared past, Peter Evans notes (2002: 223–25). But his book *Livable Cities?* also indicates that some places do *not* produce this kind of community-based unified collective action. Instead, it highlights the agency taken on by certain places that are inclusive and thereby highly contested.

16. Purcell 2008: 63, 74. His work parts with the bulk of the previous scholarship on urban democracy, which claims that local-level decision-making and consensus building is *necessarily* generated through "conscious mobilization" or various kinds of network building and "assemblage" formation. For a critical engagement with theories that see cities as bundles of networks and assemblages, see Brenner, Madden, and Wachsmuth 2012: 123–24. The literature on grassroots organizing that generates social networks and cultural capital is rich. See, e.g., White 1997; Clark 2004; Singerman 1996. In addition to mobilization, networks, and assemblages, the literature highlights civic virtue, communal spirit, shared history (of urban residents), and/or shared ideological goals, such as nationalism or Islamism, as strengths of urban politics.

17. On the politics of presence, see esp. Bayat 2007.

18. Putnam 1995.

19. Bayat [2010] 2013; Turam 2012a.

20. For a compelling analysis of the weaknesses of the CHP, see Öniş 2013: 116–17. "The extraordinary rise of the AKP that allowed it to occupy a disproportionately large share of the center was in part due to the weakness of the principal opposition party, the CHP. Effective and responsible opposition can often play an important and constructive role in pushing the governing party in a reformist direction. In the Turkish context, the CHP during the course of the past decade has failed to fulfill this function" (116).

21. This interlocutor's view calls to mind the reluctance to deemphasize or give up freedoms so as to prioritize equality expressed by Tocqueville [1835–40] 2000: 482.

22. Turam 2012b.

23. It is important to remember Tocqueville's observations on "self-interest rightly understood" and Adam Smith's *Theory of Moral Sentiments* (1759). It has long been ignored that the theory of political liberalism as developed by Smith and Tocqueville does not sit well with either aggressive forms of neoliberalism or libertarians' unconditional prioritizing of the self over the society.

24. On the passion for democratic liberties, see esp. Tocqueville [1835–40] 2000, [1856] 1955.

25. Escobar 2001: 153.

26. Brenner 2004: 181.

27. Keyder 1999: 25.

28. In relation to the interplay between place and institutions, note Zussman's (2004: 354) notion of places as *"instantiations* of institutions and policies" (my emphasis).

29. Lefebvre 1996: 195.

PART 2. ON CAMPUS POLITICS

1. Interview with a Turkish social scientist at a major state university in Istanbul, October 14, 2012.

2. For confidentiality's sake, the individuals mentioned and the university itself are identified with pseudonyms here.

3. See, for exceptions, Anderson 2008, 2011; Altbach 1989.

4. Weber [1946b] 1991. This also explains why the bulk of the literature on universities has been produced by educationalists, rather than political scientists and sociologists.

5. McMillen 2010.

6. Weber [1908] 1973.

7. Ibid., 6.

8. See esp. McEldowney et al. 2009; Gaffikin et al. 2008.

9. Barber 2001.

10. Cohen and Zelnik 2002; Freeman 2004.

11. See, for an exception, Betty Anderson 2008.

12. Bayat [2010] 2013: 11.

13. "ODTÜ olaylarına YÖK'ten soruşturma" [YÖK investigation of ODTÜ incidents], *Hürriyet*, December 25, 2012.

14. Weber 1946a: 146.

15. Calhoun 2006 (author's emphasis).

16. Barber 2001.

17. Evans and Boyte 1992; Polletta 1999.

18. Gamson 1989; Tetreault 1993.

19. The social movements literature leaves these important questions unanswered; see, for a critical view, Polletta 1999. There remains a major gap between the interest in collective action and the theorization of the political space.

20. See, e.g., Fisher and Sloan 1995.

21. Mann 1993 counterposes top-down despotic power "over" society, such as that embodied in the YÖK, with the infrastructural power of a responsive, accountable state that penetrates and interacts with the society and thus rules "through" it.

22. Özbudun 2012: 43.

23. Gülap, "Rektör: Tebaasını kendisi oluşturan kral" (Rector: The king who established his own subjects), *Radikal*, February 1, 2010.

24. See Kaplan 1999: 384; Güçlü 1993.

25. See İsmet Berkan, *Radikal*, February 27, 2008. When the AKP attempted to lift

the head-scarf ban in 2008, secularist faculty, such as Professor Mustafa Aydın, the head of ÜAK (Üniversiteler Arası Kurul; Council of Interuniversity Affairs) criticized the collusion between YÖK, the AKP government, and President Gül. According to Aydın, YÖK was responsible for the chaos, and the rectors were "unintentionally violating the law" by permitting head scarves on campus. He accused YÖK's chair, who was appointed by the AKP, Professor Ziya Özcan, of violating the principle of laicism and asked him to apologize for his unconstitutional ruling in lifting the ban. He also added "ÜAK warned YÖK about this potential chaos. . . . Now, law has become so elastic, everybody interprets it according to himself."

26. Sami Selçuk, *Star*, January 29, 2008. Some jurists, like Selçuk, argued that the head-scarf ban could have been rescinded under the Constitution even before it was altered, and that the precedents supporting the ban in previous cases were not binding on the universities.

CHAPTER 4. FAULT LINES ON CAMPUS

1. Author's interviews with faculty from other universities.

2. Author's interviews with secularist faculty. For example, discomfort was noted at several university sites and functions with regard to the observance of fasting during Ramadan.

3. While certain departments, such as sociology, political science, and some departments of engineering, were more intensely caught up in the polarization, others, such as economics, seemed to remain less drawn into the contestation. Obviously, although the entire campus community felt quite strongly about the head-scarf ban and other issues concerning Islam, not everyone expressed an opinion loudly.

4. Author's interview with Professor Aydın in 2008.

5. Since 2007, not only have the branches of the Turkish government contradicted and overruled each other's decisions, as we observed in the head-scarf policies, but on March 14, 2008, soon after the AKP's second electoral victory in 2007, the Constitutional Court heard a lawsuit to ban the AKP from constituting a government because of its presumed anti-secular activities. Since the international community was watching very closely, the court decided not to close down the AKP in power by a six-to-five vote by its members on July 31, 2008. Since 2007, Turkey has witnessed the gradual formation of fault lines that cut across every sphere of state and society.

6. The shifting tides of government-university relations have altered the influence of YÖK and the police on campuses. Whereas the police were after leftist terrorists in the 1970s, since the 1980s, they have often aimed at turning the campus into an apolitical space. Since 1998, they have worked more carefully to prevent head-scarved students from having access to campuses. The much-contested head-scarf controversy continued until the AKP's third term in office, when the government lifted the ban entirely.

7. This conversation took place during my first interview with President Narin in May 2008. I discussed this event with several other faculty who were present in the event.

8. In my interview with President Narin, she also added that the street divided not only the campus but also two Istanbul neighborhoods. This border-like quality of the street complicated the issue further. The police in one neighborhood were more cooperative than those of the other, who were more punitive and harsh. Hence, the university was always careful and cognizant of which police it was interacting with. The demonstration over the assassination of the Turkish Armenian writer Hrant Dink was confronted by the uncooperative police.

9. For a more defensive view on the material centrality of place, see Gieryn 2002.

10. As Poletta points out, the intangible usages of space, such as "ideological room" (Poletta 1999: 1, 4) or the social space of the movement (Evans and Boyte 1992) reduces concrete material places to an abstract idea. Subsequently, the abstraction obscures the power that a place is capable of generating, and the conflict it can either diffuse or fuel.

11. Benhabib 2009.

12. There are very few pious male faculty on campus, none of whom were part of these political discussions.

13. One university campus I visited in a religious city near Istanbul was a perfect example of the rule of fear on campus. Knowing that he would not be reelected in upcoming elections, the hard-core secularist rector went so far as to get his wife to run in his stead. A professor whom I interviewed on this campus cautioned me to stop talking about political issues once we stepped out of his office. I had used the word "Islamist," and as we walked to the elevators, he looked around nervously to see who might be listening and signaled me to be quiet. We did not subsequently exchange a word in publicly shared campus space.

14. On this issue, President Narin faced strong opposition from anti-scarf faculty. My interviews showed that some anti-scarf faculty were putting a lot of pressure on the university senate in order to save face in the eyes of the state and secular society. Other anti-scarf faculty argued that it was their right to be represented by an active senate, the duty of which was to represent the faculty on matters that "involve faculty." The pro-scarf camp disagreed and supported President Narin by stating that there was nothing in the handbook requiring the senate to make statements about public and political issues. Backing Narin up, they emphasized that the senate's announcements would violate academic principles by reducing the university's view to a one united voice at a time when there was deep disagreement. Moreover, it would break with the UF tradition, because no UF rector or senate had made such political announcements in the past.

15. Author's interviews, June 2008.

16. Despite a lot of pressure from secularist faculty, the university senate followed the UF's tradition and did not issue a public announcement. Hence, both camps tried

to come up with a petition. Differences owing to gender, space, and age rendered the head-scarf conflict unsolvable.

The petition respected the right to wear a head scarf, but not before college—that is, only for female students who were above the age of eighteen. The petition objected to it in elementary and high school education and public offices. Yet nothing was easy for the highly sophisticated, analytical, and argumentative UF professors. An anti-scarf faculty member brought up the issue that the age eighteen would not mean much for the Islamists, who married off girls at unusually early ages. And what about university students who were under eighteen and high school students who were older? Could they wear head scarves in high schools?

17. "There must . . . be boundary-crossing: physicists must sometimes question chemists, sociologists must sometimes question economists. . . . Fields and subfields that police their borders too well are apt to become stultifying and to imprison their members within established paradigms increasingly ripe for challenge" (Calhoun 2006: 35).

18. In my interview with Professor Bilgin, he objected to my use of the term *Kemalist* to describe his political orientation. I then asked who the Kemalists were. Were the ruling elite who had carried out the military coups Kemalists? Or were the intelligence and police forces that tortured political prisoners after the coups the Kemalists? He disagreed irritably. Instead of concretely identifying who might be considered a present-day Kemalist, he said that currently the CHP (the secularist opposition party) could be referred to as Kemalists. But he also disagreed with some anti-democratic views defended by them, saying, "they are wrong in their distrust of democracy. 'Kemalism' as a term and ideology has been used, misused, and abused a lot nowadays."

19. Erdem Tarhan, "Gündelik yaşamda din laiklik ve türban" (Religion, laicism and the head scarf in everyday life), *Milliyet*, December 4–10, 2007, states: "In Turkey, 73 percent of women say that they chose to wear a head scarf because of their own religious beliefs. Only 2.7 percent say that they cover [their heads] by their husbands' choice, and 2.9 percent mention family elders' expectations. The rest wear a head scarf because they see it as custom (13.79 percent) or out of habit (4.9 percent)."

20. Bilgin got 170 faculty votes; Narin, 140.

21. Author's interview, 2008.

22. Most of the pro-scarf faculty, including President Narin, were struggling to maintain this free space, resisting an agreement on a binding sartorial rule over women's bodies. In fact, all pro-scarf faculty of UF would object the head scarf if it was identified as the sartorial rule of the campus or in Turkey. Objection to obligatory head covering was an unspoken agreement, perhaps the only one, between the pro- and anti-scarf faculty members, but no one brought this up given their mutual animosity.

23. More often, the e-mail server that connected all faculty hosted burning debates in the manner of a town hall meeting. The e-mail exchanges amounted to open insults and offenses at some point. When I asked about the growing resentment on campus,

President Narin opined that, unlike face-to-face chats, virtual conversations (e-mails) have a negative effect, deepening disagreements. "Those e-mails are kept in the mail accounts and preserve the rage," she said, "whereas an argument over lunch might end with a joke and quickly be forgotten." Professor C herself capitalized this in her e-mail to the faculty as a whole, which she shared with me.

24. Arat 2010: 869–70.

25. Calhoun 2006: 36.

26. In the past, the Young Civils had organized a series of collective actions demanding peace and justice for Kurds, Armenians, gays, and the youth, particularly for students who were taking the university placement exam. In my field visits to their association in Taksim Square and interviews with several followers, they told me how they have organized protests, press releases, and visits to other cities in the Eastern Kurdish region, which have attracted a lot of attention both from the media and in Turkish society. They have been the most visible student activists in the country and have earned much respect and support from other activist groups. Although the Young Civils have mainly organized across campuses, the UF culture clearly has the potential to expand beyond them.

27. Author's interviews, 2010.

28. Author's interviews with an education professor, May 2009,

29. Author's interviews in the education faculty, May–June 2009.

30. Gaffikin et al. 2008.

31. On the right to change urban space, see Harvey 2003: 939.

CHAPTER 5. NEW COALITIONS IN SAFE ZONES

1. I have had several chats and collaborate on other projects with Fatma (pseudonym) over the past few years. I refrain from quoting her writings here in order to protect the anonymity.

2. "Dog Experts Bite Back at Turkey's Pit Bull Ban" (in English), *Hürriyet*, June 29, 2010. After a few incidents in which people were bitten by pit bulls in 2010, the AKP made a move to ban certain breeds. At some point, the government went so far as to propose the removal of pets from private homes if there were complaints from occasional guests. As already experienced on the UF campus, pious citizens of Turkey, including head-scarved women, have occasionally joined against the AKP's failed attempts to ban certain pets.

3. Özgür Mumcu. "ODTÜ yalnız değildir" [ODTÜ is not alone], *Radikal*, December 27, 2012.

4. While leftist media accused AKP of creating hegemony over the universities through YÖK (originally created by secularist authoritarianism), pro-Islamic newspapers blamed the students for causing disorder.

5. McGill students who carried banners reading "No Cops on Campus" were not the

only ones who encountered police brutality on campuses in Canada. www.cbc.ca/news/canada/montreal/story/2011/11/15/quebec-mcgill-protest.html

6. "ODTÜ'de boykot var" [There is a boycott at ODTÜ], *Radikal*, December 20, 2012.

7. "ODTÜ'de iddialar bitmiyor, ambulans gelmedi, taciz yapıldı" [The complaints don't stop at ODTÜ: Ambulance didn't arrive, and there was harassment"], *Radikal*, December 20, 2012.

8. "Gözaltındaki ODTÜ'lüler için açıklama" [Announcement about the arrested ODTÜ students], *Radikal*, December 21, 2012; "ODTÜ olaylarına YÖK'ten soruşturma" [YÖK investigation of ODTÜ incidents], *Hürriyet*, December 25, 2012:

9. Bulutsuzluk Özlemi is a protest rock group. See www.ntvmsnbc.com/id/25409561 (in Turkish).

10. In conflict with their rectors, the faculty of some of these universities, such as Galatasaray University, condemned YÖK and the police.

11. "Bilgi Üniversiteli akademisyenlerinden ODTÜ açıklaması" (Bilgi University faculty explain about the ODTÜ incident), *Hürriyet*, December 27, 2012.

12. Hacettepe University, Afyon Kocatepe University, Bingöl University, Sabahattin Zaim University, Uşak University, and Bezmialem Vakıf University supported the government and criticized the ODTÜ protestors.

13. Özgür Mumcu. "ODTÜ yalnız değildir" [ODTÜ is not alone], *Radikal*, December 27, 2012.

14. "ODTÜ'deki eylemci öğrencilere operasyon" [Operation against the student protestors at ODTÜ], *Zaman*, December 21, 2012.

15. See, e.g., Cohen and Zelnik 2002; Freeman 2004. Note the cases of the student movement in the 1960s and the Occupy movement in 2010–11.

16. See, e.g., Betty Anderson 2011.

PART 3. ON "ETHNIC" NEIGHBORHOODS

1. "De facto ein Einreiseverbot" [A de facto travel ban], *Die Welt*, May 30, 2014, www.welt.de/print/welt_kompakt/print_politik/article128542303/De-facto-ein-Einrei severbot.html. "Cem Özdemir'den başbakana üslup elestirisi [Cem Özdemir criticizes prime minister's style of language), *Radikal*, May 28, 2014. Erdoğan responded: "You are not at liberty to talk like this to the prime minister of your homeland. . . . Wherever you are a member of the parliament, you have to know your place." Erdoğan added that he would not like to see Özdemir in Turkey anymore.

2. Brubaker 2005; Moore 2008: 203–4.

3. Leitner et al. 2008.

4. See esp. Dikeç 2007.

5. Mass immigration from Turkey started in 1961 after the Ankara agreement was signed between Germany and Turkey and intensified between 1968 and 1973.

6. Sarrazin 2010. The book displays a strong anti-immigrant bias in regard to what

the author refers to as the "immigration problem." Sarrazin is a member of the German Social Democratic Party (SPD).

7. Testimonies were heard from some six hundred witnesses on a terrorist "National Socialist Underground" that claimed to have murdered nine immigrants—eight of them Turks. See "First Day of Historic Trial: German Court Adjourns Neo-Nazi Case Until May 14," *Spiegel*, May 6, 2013, www.spiegel.de/international/germany/german-nsu-neo-nazi-trial-starts-in-munich-a-898287.html.

8. See, e.g., "Merkel Walks a Tightrope on German Immigration," *Time*, October 21, 2010: "Chancellor Angela Merkel's pronouncement . . . that attempts to build a 'multicultural' Germany had 'failed, absolutely failed' was hardly the first such tirade against immigrants." The main groups in the German opposition are the Social Democratic Party (Sozialdemokratische Partei Deutschlands; SPD), the Greens, and the Left Party. Sigmar Gabriel, leader of the SPD, denounced both Merkel and her supporters in government on the immigration issue. Renate Künast, the Green Party's parliamentary leader, blamed Merkel for "looking for an enemy" in order to "distract attention away from the problems in her party."

9. This presents a clear contrast with the current Turkish case, in which the AKP has no strong opposition and there is thus not much dispute in parliament or the governing party.

10. Statements by the German Chambers of Commerce about the need for skilled workers triggered further objections from liberal-minded CDU ministers. Economy minister Rainer Brüderle called for "a points-based system of immigration" like that of Canada or Australia. "For several years, more people have been leaving our country than entering it. . . . Wherever possible, we must lower the entry hurdles for those who advance the country," the CDU labor minister, Ursula von der Leyen, said. "Angela Merkel: German Multiculturalism Has 'utterly failed,'" *Guardian*, October 17, 2010.

11. Interior Minister Thomas de Maizière objected to any change and defended the status quo.

12. This unequal power balance between parties continued until the CDU and SPD formed their Grand Coalition in 2013. Since then, the issue of immigration, and particularly dual citizenship for immigrants, has been disputed.

13. For example, people of Turkish descent are insulted as *Knoblauch Fresser* (garlic munchers) and ethnic Germans as *Schinken Fresser* (ham gobblers). *Fressen* means "eat like an animal."

14. Note Merkel's statement about the failure of multiculturalism in Germany (citations at nn. 8 and 10 above). Her point is really not about the state's failure in implementing a multiculturalist policy, but rather the failure of immigrants to integrate into German culture.

15. Not only most ordinary Europeans and politicians but also the bulk of social research have been critical of "ethnic ghettos."

16. See, e.g., Özüekren and Ergöz-Karahan 2010; Özüekren and van Kempen 1997. In exploring the causes of urban segregation of immigrants, Özüekren and Ergöz-Karahan (2010) argue that "conservatism—especially when it takes its roots from Islamism—has played an important role in shaping the residential preferences and choices of individuals."

17. Grüner 2010: 276.

18. For in-depth analysis of the Turkish ghetto, see Erder 2006.

19. Logan, Zhang, and Alba 2002: 301.

20. Logan, Zhang, and Alba 2002.

21. Häussermann and Kapphan 2000: 211. See also Wacquant 2004 and 2008 on French *banlieue* and the ghetto as the result of ethnic and racial domination. But both of the perspectives—the one based on immigrants' choices and tastes and the one focusing on socioeconomic constraints fail to take into account the role of discriminatory policies, anti-immigrant sentiment, and, recently, rising Islamophobia in Europe, which reinforces spatial segregation (see Dikeç 2007: 6, 124–26, for an exception). Mustafa Dikeç argues that given the impossibility of imagining divisions and diversity within the unbreakable unity of the French Republic, urban policy is developed by imagining and constituting places of intervention, which are deprived, insecure, and problematic, transforming the Republic into a penal state.

22. Unsurprisingly, this trend can sometimes be observed by some third- and fourth-generation German Turks, but it remains marginal in the Turkish immigrant community at large.

23. For extensive debates and analysis of multiculturalism in Canada, see particularly Taylor 1993; Kymlicka 1996. In the Canadian case, various immigrant groups are *accommodated* by a state that supports and/or sponsors the survival and cohabitation of different immigrant cultures and their ways of life. This behavior of the state is largely reflected in granting the immigrants equal rights and freedoms in terms of lifestyle, education, housing, job market, and so on. "In contrast to many European countries, policy-makers in Toronto have not seen the spatial concentration of ethnic minorities as problematic. One reason for this is the success of pre-1980 European immigrant groups who remain residentially segregated but have achieved considerable mobility in the labor market and in housing" (Murdie and Ghosh 2010: 308).

24. France and Canada contrast strikingly here. Since the French Republic is conceptually indivisible, any notion of ethnic concentration, communitarianism, or ethno-religious difference is regarded as a threat to France's unity (Dikeç 2007). Conversely, since multiculturalism is a proud principle of the Canadian state (see esp. Murdie and Ghosh 2010), Canada recognizes and welcomes different immigrant communities, reinforcing democratic participation and political pluralism.

25. Painter 2006: 755.

26. See esp. Benedict Anderson 2006; Hall 1998; Brubaker 1992.

27. The literal definition of *kesin dönüş* is ultimate, final and definitive return of the immigrants to the homeland. The term has been largely identified with immigrants of Turkish descent in Germany, whom the German state expected to return to their homeland. In the age of heightened global mobility, this term has come to sound dated and almost ironic. Many mobile members of the Turkish diaspora question whether movement between the two countries can ever cease in a conclusive and absolute way.

28. Among many subfields of urban studies, geographers led the debate on the nature of the levels. They questioned if these levels were mere social constructs (Marston 2000) in the sense that they are avoidable for human geography and political processes (Marston, Jones, and Woodward 2005). Or did the levels have an unavoidably material character? Approaches to scale are also contested between the political and economic geographers, who see it as a material factor, and the constructivists, who see it as a discursive (hence constructed) entity (Moore 2008: 204). As the structure-agency dichotomy has long been contested in sociology, I shall not further engage in the debate. Many sociologists maintain that the structure-agency binary is a *continuum* (an axis) that is dynamic and always in the making rather than being fixed. Hence, this study uses scale to explore the political depth of democracy that is constantly negotiated between the material or physical aspects of space—sociopolitical structures and conditions—and the agency of people and places.

29. The prevalent question that has occupied social scientists, particularly political geographers, is what makes any of these levels more pivotal or popular at a given time and space? See esp. Brenner 1999, 2000; MacLeavy and Harrison 2010; Martin, McCann, and Purcell 2003; Swyngedouw 2000. The argument of the following two chapters is, however, that the interaction between levels makes them imperative for democracy. See also Brown and Purcell 2005; Purcell 2006. My ethnography shows that divisions on various levels meet and compete, but also compound each other, in ethnic neighborhoods in the host country.

30. Purcell 2006: 1921–22; emphasis added.

31. Ibid.: 1923; Moore 2008: 204. Scale fetishism does not stop with advocacies of the local or national, but there is a rapidly growing literature that idealizes global governance. Along these lines, global processes are seen as an "upscaling" of spatial politics. As with the romanticization of the local, there is also an abundant literature that ranks the importance of the (inter)national level over the others.

32. For example, in the summer of 2011, the Turkish legislature passed a law providing for restraining orders. But neither the debate nor information about the law reached the local, everyday level, and it failed to have any effect on the lives of abused women. This meant that the reform and contestations at the state level did not trickle down to everyday local life. If the link between these levels is not established, it is difficult to talk about a connection between the legislative and the local. Discontinuity of levels is also observable in the case of the Occupy movement, which remained largely local, although

it migrated internationally. The reason was that it skipped the national level by failing to engage and negotiate with the state, the site of most structural amendments and political reform. Such gapping between levels, sometimes called "scale skipping," is likely to lead to a decline in contestation.

CHAPTER 6. KREUZBERG'S DIVIDED DIASPORA

1. Founded in 1969 by the former Turkish prime minister Necmettin Erbakan (1926–2011), Millî Görüş is one of Europe's leading Turkish diaspora organizations. Since its ideology is Islamist, its national vision is devoutly Muslim.

2. Author's interview, July 20, 2012. On residential choices based on preference rather than socioeconomic necessity, see Logan et al. 2002: 319.

3. Author's interview, July 19, 2012.

4. Kreuzberg sits in the heart of downtown Berlin. It has a large green area, Görlitzer Park, and is bordered by the pretty river Spree.

5. Author's interview, July 2013.

6. Ismail 2000.

7. Dikeç 2007; Kuru 2009; Rottmann and Ferree 2008.

8. Carens 2010 analyzes the role of "passage of time" in making what was presumed to be a temporary immigrant community a permanent body of residents in Germany.

9. For the case of France, see Dikeç 2007: 73–74, 89. This primarily political conflict has been misunderstood and misportrayed in similar terms in the scholarly literature, which juxtaposes Islam with secular forms of politics. See Gellner 1981, 1996. See also, for critiques, Eickelman 1998; Zubaida [1988] 2009.

10. A similar concern with Muslim immigrants emerged and developed in France. Before the 1990s, Islam had been seen as a "good thing" to calm down the youth in the French *banlieue*, but since then, urban policy has moved "from a more socially oriented policy to one obsessed with security" in the *banlieue* (Dikeç 2007: 15, 74).

11. For example, the Turkish German feminist and social scientist Necla Kelek showcased Thilo Sarrazin's 2010 book *Deutschland schafft sich ab: Wie wir unser Land aufs Spiel setzen* [Germany abolishes itself: How we jeopardize our country]. Other Turkish German secularists such as Kenan Kolat and Ezhar Cezayirli have defended Kemalist ideas against public expressions of Islam.

12. Prominent public figures who have sought to mediate between the secularists and pious immigrant communities include the columnist Hilal Sezgin, the playwright Feridun Zaimoğlu, Cem Özdemir of the Green Party, the film director Fatih Akın, the DJ İpek İpekçioğlu, and the former director of the Ballhaus Naunynstraße theater, Shermin Langhoff.

13. Glaeser 1999: 18, 19.

14. Strom 2001: 3, 9.

15. Ibid.: 74.

16. This pattern is the opposite in the United States, where immigrants with higher education, income, and skilled professions move to suburban ethnic neighborhoods, whereas poor minority ghettos typify inner-city life (see, e.g., Logan et al. 2002).

17. Özüekren and Ergöz-Karahan 2010: 360. Many Turkish immigrants resided in Kreuzberg during the 1960s and 1970s. "In fact, the number of Turks living in Kreuzberg, Tiergarten and Wedding rapidly increased. In 1975, of the 87,900 Turks living in Berlin, about 65 per cent lived in these three districts" (ibid.).

18. Ibid.: 363.

19. Dikeç 2007: 10.

20. Kreuzberg became the geographical center of unified Berlin, since the north-south subway line (U8) intersects with the west-east subway line (U1) at the Kottbusser Tor (Kotti) station there.

21. Glaeser 2000: 1.

22. "Kreuzberg, a concentration area for Turkish workers in the past, gradually turned into a neighborhood inhabited by many welfare-dependent migrants. This is especially true for Kottbusser Tor, the center of Kreuzberg, where it is estimated that 80 per cent of the residents are not German in origin" (Özüekren and Ergöz-Karahan 2010: 365).

23. Administrative reform in 2011 combined Kreuzberg with Friedrichshain to form a new borough called Friedrichshain-Kreuzberg, but residents still regard Kreuzberg as a separate neighborhood.

24. On the "right to stay put," see particularly Weinstein 2014.

25. On the new middle class and gentrification, see Ley 1996. Debates about the gentrification of this former immigrant ghetto have caused the primarily political nature of these conflicts to be overlooked; the fault lines in Kreuzberg go far beyond class-based struggles and the discontents of neoliberalism.

26. For example, one outcome was increasing economic competition with newly merged East Germans. Another was the moving of major companies to other places where production costs were lower. These outcomes hurt the local economy and thus the job prospects of local Turkish German residents. There is an ongoing debate over whether Berlin (including Kreuzberg) is increasingly becoming a service-based economy by reason of the decline of its industrial base. Contra this view, see Krätke and Borst 2000.

27. For a similar assertion, see Kaya 2001.

28. Author's interview, August 30, 2011.

29. Turkey's consul general in Berlin, Mustafa Polat, told me in an interview on July 31, 2012, that Mutlu was one of the most successful and highly trusted Turkish politicians outside Turkey.

30. Mutlu explained to me that the police officer who had sued him for insult ten years before had lost the case after a fair hearing—which was made possible only after Mutlu had waived his immunity as a Bundestag member.

31. For an impressive analysis of the Alawite community in Turkish history and politics, see Tambar 2014.

32. Allen and Cochrane 2010: 1073–74.

33. See esp. Mann 1993; Painter 2006.

34. GLADT opposes discrimination, racism, and sexism and is inclusive of bi- and transsexuals, but for practical reasons it has retained its old name, Gays & Lesbians from Turkey. For further information, see www.gladt.de.

35. Pseudonym used for confidentiality.

36. Adam Moore (2008) suggested a shift from using scale as a category of analysis to a category of practice. Scale works as an analytical tool but must not be reduced to it, as scaling democratic contestations (practices) and analyzing the multiscalar nature of democratization (analysis) both strengthen our understanding of democracy.

37. Koenraad 2012: 256.

38. Nevertheless, being service (*hizmet*) oriented, the Gülen Movement still serves the Turkish community in Kotti, where it has opened a preschool. The Gülen Movement currently has one elementary school, one high school, one *Realschule* (junior high school), and four preschools in Berlin.

39. See Turam 2004, 2007.

40. See Özüekren and Ergöz-Karahan 2010: 360. This previous research explains the widening "social distance" among Turkish immigrants in Berlin as the result of "different interpretations of Islam." However, my findings on Kreuzberg contradict this. While I found no substantial disagreement about religious matters or interpretations of religious issues, the divides between and within the pious and secular immigrant populations were about worldviews, lifestyle, and struggles over power and status that had migrated from Turkey to Germany, as well as recognition in the host country.

41. The Religious Directorate (Diyanet İşleri Başkanlığı) is a branch of the Turkish state and operates under it. This is telling of the kind of secularism the Turkish state practices, since Diyanet enables the Republic to keep religion and religious affairs under its control rather than outside the realm of state affairs.

42. Owing to Germany's federal constitution, the sixteen states (*Länder*) constitute the federal level of governance.

43. Strom 2001: 8, 21 (quotation); emphasis added. "Unlike in US and British systems (in which municipalities are limited to functions described in their charters), [the German Basic Law] allows German municipalities to undertake any activity not elsewhere regulated" (ibid.).

44. Germany does not have a universal naturalization policy. Immigrants from European Union countries are treated differently from non-EU immigrants, and the rules applicable to the latter differ by country. For example, Iranian immigrants are allowed to keep their Iranian citizenship and acquire dual German citizenship because Iran does not allow its people to renounce their citizenship.

45. Author's field notes, August 28, 2011. The panel took place in Südblok, a lounge and bar in central Kotti that serves as a venue for community-related events.

46. Unlike the Turkish German candidates of the SPD, CDU, and Left Party, the Green Party's candidate had been born, raised, and educated in Turkey.

47. Partly because of their objection to "discrimination in both the housing and the labor markets" (Özüekren and Ergöz-Karahan 2010: 359), the leftists invest much more faith in ethnic neighborhoods than those who regard them as unsafe, problematic places. Studies correlate belonging to a Muslim group and discrimination in major European countries, including Germany. "Racist attacks against ethnic minority households, such as the one in Solingen against a Turkish household whose members were burnt to death in their house in 1993, also provides extreme evidence for the ethnic stratification theory. Such attacks and conflicts in mixed neighborhoods might lead some minority ethnic households to choose to live in their own segregated communities, in order to have a safer environment" (Özüekren and Ergöz-Karahan 2010: 359).

48. On violent places, see Davis forthcoming. Poverty, unemployment, widespread squatting, and treatment of immigrants as an underclass combined to give Kreuzberg its prior reputation as an unsafe, violent place.

49. Kuru 2009: 128.

CHAPTER 7. EMERGING SOLIDARITIES IN IMMIGRANT ZONES

1. Author's interviews with ethnic German residents of Kreuzberg, 2011–12.

2. The Autonomous Movement numbered some ten thousand anarchists by the late 1980s. In addition to being anti-system, anti-patriarchal—particularly against male violence and domination, the AM was also leftist, anti-capitalist, and "anti-German." The former anarchists also did not fail to highlight the paradox that they had been in a few violent protests despite their stance against violence.

3. Unlike the rest of the guests, Michael believed that the AM was still alive. He was still involved with squatting in the neighborhood, although he currently did not live in a squat. Michael told me that he had participated in three squatter activities in Kreuzberg over the past few years. He added that he did not stay in the occupied houses, but other squatters did.

4. Neco Çelik told me the same thing when I interviewed him in July 2013.

5. For an exception, see Schlueter 2012, whose findings show that the issue of friendship between German nationals and ethnic minorities in an ethnically segregated area is more complicated than previously thought. Schlueter highlights the role of education in facilitating new bonds and friendships across the national-immigrant dichotomy.

6. "Shermin Langhoff wird Leiterin des Gorki Theaters" [Shermin Langhoff to be the director of the Gorki Theater], *Tagesspiegel*, May 21, 2012. www.tagesspiegel.de/kultur /berliner-blut-shermin-langhoff-wird-leiterin-des-gorki-theaters/6657576.html

7. German law requires one to send one's children to the public schools in one's neighborhood, but Berliners found ways around it by using alternative addresses in other "white" neighborhoods.

8. Almost every Turkish immigrant I met in Kreuzberg had a different take on the issue and proposed different solutions. Some criticized Turkish parents for not putting enough effort into getting their children to learn German. Others blamed Germany's public education system. Many used the term "myth" to describe Turkish children's problems with German in elementary school. Several other interviewees of Turkish descent denied the degree of the problem, and some said that it existed only in the heads of anti-immigrant Germans.

9. Author's interview, 2011.

10. Author's interview, 2012. Language became a major problem in İpek's early schooling. İpek's mother took her to Turkey in her first years of elementary school so that she could learn Turkish. She defined herself as a *bavul çocuğu* (suitcase child) who was moved from one place to the other. "This is very typical of the second generation," İpek observed to me. "But the third generation are sent to Turkey only if they commit a crime." During her childhood in Wedding in Berlin, she was in a "class of immigrants," which became the underlying reason for why her German did not improve fast. İpek criticized the law that obliged residents to send their children to schools where they live.

11. More concretely, one can easily see the overlapping positive views of the politician Figen İzgi and of Hans, and conversely of the arguments between Inke and the DJ İpek. Also note the disagreement between Millı Görös and FID (pp. 140–41).

12. Bell and Binnie 2006: 869; emphasis added.

13. People who moved out of Kotti to other, more expensive residential parts of Kreuzberg said they had done so for reasons including safety, tranquility, and personal preference.

14. In her book *Stolen Honor* (2008), Kathrin Ewing suggests that the stigmatization of Turkish men as inherently oppressive and abusive to women masks anti-immigration discrimination against Turkish men.

15. White 1997: 757.

16. For a compelling piece on the racial profiling and perfunctory criminalization of immigrants in Sweden, see Jonas Hassen Khemiri, "Sweden's Closet Racists," *New York Times Sunday Review*, April 20, 2013; and see also Gezer 2013.

17. Hélie 2012: 2. Hélie warns us against essentializing "Muslim women" as victims, because there are many factors other than religion that lead to the oppression of women. Moreover, the policing of sexuality is not a unique characteristic of Muslim countries, and gender equality and reform are not inherent characteristics of the Western world.

18. Hélie and Hoodfar 2012.

19. Rottmann and Ferree 2008.

20. This group of anti-head-scarf Turkish immigrants includes well-known secularist figures and some Turkish members of the LGBT community.

21. İpek was born in Munich to parents who were first-generation immigrants. She has worked for SO 36 since 1998 and freelanced since 2001.

22. When I asked why women were asked at the entrance of the Club whether they were lesbians, İpek told me that this was to have a better gender balance, since lesbians are almost always a minority.

23. On debates that link emotional and political aspects of geographical mobility, see esp. Svašek 2010; Cresswell 2006.

24. Massey 1994.

25. Escobar 2001.

26. Tuan 1977: 52.

27. Existing works in the literature on democracy have mostly been based on quantitative and/or comparative analysis of transitory regimes and consolidation. See for ethnographic exceptions Bayat 2007; Wedeen 2008; Turam 2007. Rather than rejecting the existing literature that quantifies freedoms and rights in surveys, I propose an in-depth, qualitative inquiry into the spatial reach of contestation and depth of freedoms.

28. The NSU (National Socialist Underground) trials in Germany make one wonder whether advanced democracies could not be more efficient and forceful in protecting minorities. See, e.g., http://www.spiegel.de/international/germany/german-nsu-neo-nazi-trial-starts-in-munich-a-898287.html. Does being certified as a "consolidated democracy" guarantee that the accepted democratic rules apply? Or does a "certificate of consolidation" actually give a democracy leeway to violate civil rights? If this is the case, how do we capture, evaluate, and theorize the deterioration of the various dimensions of democracy? In light of these questions, I suggest that the term "consolidated democracy" may create more problems than it makes analytical contributions.

29. For analysis of overlaps between different levels of sovereignty and urban conflict, see also Davis and Libertun de Duren 2011; Brenner 2011.

30. Painter 2006: 770; emphasis added: "'[S]tateness' is the result of complex networks of prosaic practices of making, unmaking and remaking by actors *within* and *outside* state institutions." Some of Kreuzberg's most vocal residents work within state institutions, parliament, political parties, and local government.

31. Ibid.

32. The notion of belonging to the neighborhood while denying loyalties to the nation-state calls to mind the "postnational" citizenship theorized by Yasemin Soysal (1994), which calls for "universal personhood" rather than national belonging. Both ethnic German and Turkish German Kreuzbergers may be said to aspire to this.

33. Allen and Cochrane 2010: 1074.

34. This division disappears when the Turkish state persecutes Kurds in the homeland.

35. See also Dikeç (2007: 7) on the Muslim *banlieue* in France: "[W]hat the official policy discourse constitutes as 'badlands' also become the sites of organizing principles of political mobilization with democratic ideals."

36. Painter 2006.

37. Levi 1998.

38. See also Sassen 2006, 2012. Inasmuch as Turkish Germans have become "fixtures" in German society, I agree with Sassen (2008) and Carens (2010) on the increasing potential of cross-border mobility and immigration. However, I disagree with Sassen's claim that "in the post-1980 globalizing era . . . [the] state's 'right to control' loses its full formal vigor compared to what it was in the twentieth century" (2012: 119. While Sassen's work (1996, 2008) juxtaposes territorial state authority with globalization, ethnographic evidence in this book suggests that the interactions between the three levels—local, national, and global—reinforce one another.

CONCLUSION: UNIFIED OPPOSITION TO THE DIVIDED SUPREMACY OF THE AKP

1. "Merdiven devrimi" [Stair revolution], *Radikal*, August 31, 2013. The campaign was also called the "Rainbow revolution" or "Go get your paint prush" (Fırçanı kap gel). See www.sismec.org/2013/09/21/where-do-you-find-rainbows-in-turkey-up-in-the-skies -or-down-on-the-street.

2. See, e.g., Sedef Çakmak, "No Living on Land or in Air: Discourse of Public Morality and Human Rights Violations of Transgender Individuals in Turkey," *Turkish Policy Quarterly* 11, no. 4 (2013): 141–47. In September 2012, the police raided the Avcılar apartments of eleven transgender women, who had lived there for a decade. Along with neighborhood demonstrations by local residents against prostitution, transgender residents experienced aggression, including a fire in front of their building, forcing them out of their homes. Despite any lack of evidence of illegal prostitution, the police handcuffed the women during their raid on their homes. For minority groups, such as the LGBT community, "[H]uman rights violations consist of many aspects, ranging from right to live, right to education, right to housing, and right to work to right to form an association, as well as practices such as arbitrary detentions, arbitrary fines, and police brutality" (ibid., 142). LGBT individuals are *in theory* constitutionally protected, but like other excluded groups, they typically face discrimination at numerous sites in Istanbul. Most of the violations manifest themselves spatially.

3. Binnaz Saktanber, "The Voices of Turkish Protestors Have Been Heard," *Guardian*, June 2, 2013.

4. Şeyla Benhabib, "Turkey's Authoritarian Turn," *New York Times*, June 3, 2013.

5. John Stuart Mill calls this sort of government a "nanny-state" (Mill [1859] 1978: 9).

6. Coons and Weber 2013: 4.

7. "Kafası kıyak gençlik istemiyoruz."

8. Benhabib 2013.

9. Coons and Weber 2013.

10. Ahmet Hakan, "Kimse anlatamıyor, bari ben anlatayım" [Nobody can explain, let me explain], *Milliyet*, June 4, 2013; my trans.

11. Pınar Melis Yalsalı Parmaksız, "#resistankara: Notes of a woman resisting," *Jadaliyya*, June 16, 2003; emphasis added.

12. According to a KONDA survey conducted during the Gezi protests, the average age of the protestors was twenty-eight. http://t24.com.tr/haber/konda-gezi-parki -anketi-cikardi,231889 (in Turkish).

13. See Çağıl Kasapoğlu's interview with Tolga Göksu, "Çarşi neden Gezi eylemlerine destek verdi?" [Why did Çarşi support Gezi?], BBC Türkçe, June 14, 2013, www.bbc.co .uk/turkce/haberler/2013/06/130614_carsi_gezi_cagil.shtml (in Turkish). The reason given was "the government's encroachment on how we should have children, how we should give birth, what we should drink and eat. Its use of inappropriate qualifiers to refer to founders of Turkish Republic" (author's translation).

14. See "İki ayyaş sorusu: Ayyaşlıklarını nasıl tespit ettiniz?" [The "two drunkards" question: How did you diagnose their drunkardness?], *Radikal*, May 28, 2013.

15. Serhan Bali, "İngiliz modeli sanati kurtarır mı?" [Does the English model save art?], *Radikal*, May 28, 2013; also, my interview with a leading City Theater artist in Istanbul on May 25, 2013.

16. See esp. Tilly and Blockmans 1994.

17. Kerem Öktem, "Contour of a New Republic and Signals of the Past: How to Understand Taksim Square," *Jadaliyya*, June 7, 2013.

18. Hasson and Ley (1994) rightly differentiate between neighborhood organizations' materialist and postmaterialist aims—the former refer to housing- and gentrification-related matters, whereas the latter are understood as an issue of political participation.

19. Class is only one of the many factors in intersectional analysis, which include place, age, profession, religiosity, and gender.

20. See "Quick Thoughts: Cihan Tuğal on the Soma Mining Disaster," *Jadaliyya*, May 17, 2014. The CHP requested investigation of the most recent accidents in the Soma mines on April 29, 2014, but the AKP voted against this in parliament.

21. See esp. Hirschman 1970.

22. Sultan Tepe 2013.

23. Göle 2013b.

24. Sassen 2011: 574.

25. Weber differentiates power from domination, locating both in the monopoly of a coherent monolithic state. For Weberian sociology, both the state and the city are not only cohesive but also coherent (for critiques, see Migdal 2001; Zubaida 2006). Recent ethnographies of urban space (Dikeç 2007; Mills 2010; Turam 2012a) show, however, that both the city and the state consist of incoherent and separate parts, which often come into conflict.

26. Of great importance are Harvey's (2012) emphasis on the "right to the city," Sassen's (2011) highlighting of the importance of the "global street," and Benhabib's (2013) argument about the "huge 'democratic disconnect' between the street and the parliaments, the public square and the courthouse."

27. For exceptions, see Bayat 2007, [2010] 2013; Wedeen 2007; Turam 2007, 2012a.

28. Sennett 2012: 26.

29. Göle 2013a. Göle compares the "Gezi village" to the 1969 Woodstock rock festival, saying that "unlike political movements, [it was] open to improvisation, humor, and creativity."

30. The Gezi resistance brought the politics of lifestyle into the heart of political power and contestation. Predominant questions and perspectives in social movement and collective action literature fall short of—and obscure—the nonstrategic, unplanned, unintentional, and mundane aspects of urban politics.

31. Sassen 2011: 575.

32. Turam 2008b, 2012b.

33. Onur Erdoğan, interview with Murat Paker, "Soma'daki facia: Kendini kontrol etmek zorunda hissetmiyor" [Disaster in Soma: He does not feel obliged to control himself], *Al Jazeera*, May 20, 2014.

34. Turam 2012c.

35. Turam 2012c: 2, 3.

36. On Gülen-government relations, see esp. "Gülen: Kuvvet insani firavunlaştırır" [Gülen: Power could turn a human being into a pharaoh], *Radikal*, May 9, 2013.

37. "Leaders of Turkey and Israel Clash at Davos Panel," *New York Times*, January 29, 2009.

38. See Joe Lauria, "Reclusive Turkish Imam Criticizes Gaza Flotilla," *Wall Street Journal*, June 4, 2010; Turam 2012a, 2012b. It is noteworthy that Erdoğan, who is notorious for not taking criticism well, did not publicly respond to Gülen's objections.

39. Fethullah Gülen was the first Muslim leader to condemn the 9/11 terrorist attacks in in the United States.

40. Ruşen Çakır, "PKK Gülen ve hareketinden ne istiyor?" [What does the PKK want from Gülen and his movement?], *Radikal*, September 20, 2013.

41. On Atatürk's mausoleum as "a key site for ancestor worship," see Houston 2005: 107.

42. Author's interview with a follower of Gülen's in *hizmet* (service), September 2012. The AKP passed a new law changing the elementary-middle school system from eight continuous years of obligatory education into three periods of four years. This leaves the second and third periods of education to the choice of parents. This system facilitates the shift to religious education at a much earlier age and is likely to leave girls in underdeveloped eastern parts of Turkey with less education.

43. Several voters and adherents of the AKP, mostly businessmen, also told me that

the GM's economic power is overestimated, and that the AKP did not need their support, collaboration, or votes. Some compared the MÜSİAD, a Muslim businessmen's association associated with the AKP, with the TUSKON (Türkiye İş Adamları ve Sanayicileri Konfederasyonu; Confederation of Turkish Businessmen and Industrialists), an international organization linked with the GM.

44. Turam 2004, 2007.

45. On February 7, 2012, an Istanbul prosecutor summonsed National Intelligence Organization (Milli İstihbarat Teşkilatı; MİT) undersecretary Hakan Fidan, appointed by Erdoğan and reporting directly to him, to testify in an ongoing investigation (2009–present time) into the Kurdish Communities Union (KCK) and the Kurdistan Worker's Party (PKK). The AKP government thereupon introduced a new bill requiring the prime minister's permission for investigation of intelligence officials. The bill was quickly approved by the parliament and ratified by President Abdullah Gül, saving the intelligence undersecretary from being investigated. In a speech on February 19, Erdoğan claimed that he had acted to avoid infighting between the intelligence service, police, and judiciary, and to prevent *appointed* officials from dominating *elected* ones (who clearly included himself).

46. Skocpol 1979; Evans et al. 1985; Mann 1993.

47. Levi 1998.

48. See Gellner 1996: 26–28.

49. Meryem Atlas, "Kürtaja da karşıyım, yasağa da" [I am against both abortion and the banning of it," *Radikal*, June 4, 2012.

50. See, e.g., "Fethullah Gülen'den Gezi Parkı değerlendirmesi" [Fethullah Gülen on Gezi Park], *Hürriyet*, June 6, 2013. Gülen expressed important, albeit ambiguous, reactions to the Gezi protests. While he was consistent in his dislike of confrontation and blamed Turkey's educational institutions for turning the youth to rebellion, he condemned the government's handling of the situation and warned it that these protests should not be taken lightly.

51. "*Demokrasi sadece seçim değildir*" [Democracy is not just elections], *Habertürk*, June 4, 2013; "Gezi olaylarının başlangıcı ile grur duyarım" [I am proud of the beginning of the Gezi protests], *Hürriyet*, September 24, 2013.

52. Many devout Turks, particularly the less educated rural masses, who are more dependent on television for news, are left out of touch with corruption scandals and violations of rights and freedoms. Erdoğan not only cuts voters in the slums and periphery off from the voice and discontents of the opposition but provokes them to unite against it with his inflammatory speeches.

53. See esp. Erdoğan, interview with Paker, cited n. 33 above.

54. "Protesters Pray for Turkey's Hagia Sophia to Become a Mosque," NBC News, May 31, 2014, www.nbcnews.com/news/religion/protesters-pray-turkeys-hagia-sophia-become-mosque-n1119266. I thank Mehmet Cemalcılar for bringing this to my attention.

55. Benhabib 2013.

56. See, e.g., Timur Kuran. "Turkey's Electoral Dictatorship," *Project Syndicate*, April 10, 2014. www.project-syndicate.org/commentary/timur-kuran-warns-that-recent -local-elections-will-reinforce-recep-tayyip-erdo-an-s-authoritarian-turn.

57. Acemoğlu 2014.

58. Neither the actions nor the theories of civil society and collective action have sufficiently incorporated the politics of space/place. On this failure to grasp the importance of the spatiality of power, see esp. Leitner, Sheppard, and Sziarto 2008.

REFERENCES

Acemoğlu, Daron. 2014. "The Failed Autocrat: Despite Erdogan's Ruthlessness Turkey's Democracy Is Still on Track." *Foreign Affairs*, May 22.

Ağırdır, Bekir. Interview by Muhsin Öztürk. 2013. "Türkiye bu kutuplaşmayı kaldıramaz" [Turkey cannot survive this polarization]. *Aksiyon*, October 7.

Allen, John, and Allan Cochrane. 2010. "Assemblages of State Power: Topological Shifts in the Organization of Government and Politics." *Antipode* 42 (5): 1071–89.

Altınordu, Ateş. 2009. "The Debate on 'Neighborhood Pressure' in Turkey." *Footnotes* [newsletter of the American Sociological Association] 37 (2).

Anderson, Benedict. [1983] 2006. *Imagined Communities: Reflections on the Origins and Spread of Nationalism*. London: Verso.

Anderson, Betty. 2008. "Voices of Protest: Arab Nationalism and the Palestinian Revolution at the American University of Beirut." *Comparative Studies of South Asia, Africa, and the Middle East* 28 (3): 390–403.

———. 2011. *The American University of Beirut: Arab Nationalism and Liberal Education*. Austin: University of Texas Press.

Arat, Yeşim. 2010. "Religion, Politics and Gender Equality in Turkey: Implications of a Democratic Paradox." *Third World Quarterly* 31 (6): 869–84.

Arjomand, Said Amir. 1989. *The Turban for the Crown: The Islamic Revolution in Iran*. Oxford: Oxford University Press.

Aydınlı, Erşan. 2012. "Civil-Military Relations Transformed." *Journal of Democracy* 23 (1): 100–109.

Baiocchi, Gianpaolo, and Checa Sofia. 2009. "Cities as New Spaces for Citizenship Claims: Globalization, Urban Politics, and Civil Society in Brazil, Mexico and South Africa in the 1990s." In *Democracy, States and the Struggle for Global Justice*, ed. Heather Gautney, Omar Dahbour, Ashley Dawson, and Neil Smith, 131–53. London: Routledge.

Baran, Zeyno. 2008. "Turkey Divided." *Journal of Democracy* 19 (1): 55–69.

Barber, Benjamin R. 2001. "The 'Engaged University' in a Disengaged Society: Realistic Goal or Bad Joke?" Association of American Colleges and Universities Diversity Digest. www.diversityweb.org/digest/sm01/engaged.html.

Barnett, Clive, and Murray Low, eds. 2004. *Spaces of Democracy: Geographical Perspectives on Citizenship, Participation and Representation.* London: Sage.

Bartu, Ayfer C., and Biray Kolluoğlu. 2008. "Emerging Space of Neoliberalism: A Gated Town and a Public Housing Project in Istanbul." *New Perspectives in Turkey* 39: 5–46.

Bayar, Yeşim. 2014. *The Formation of the Turkish State, 1920–1938.* New York: Palgrave Macmillan.

Bayat, Asef. 1997. *Street Politics: Poor People's Movements in Iran.* New York: Columbia University Press.

———. 2007. *Making Islam Democratic: Social Movements and the Post-Islamist Turn.* Stanford: Stanford University Press.

———. [2010] 2013. *Life as Politics: How Ordinary People Change the Middle East.* 2nd ed. Stanford: Stanford University Press.

Belge, Ceren. 2012. "Dismantling Turkey's Juristocracy: AK Party and the Transformation of Political Power in Turkey." Conference paper, Middle East Studies Association Annual Meeting, Denver, CO, November.

Bell, David, and Jon Binni. 2006. "Geographies of Sexual Citizenship." *Political Geography* 25 (8): 869–73.

Benhabib, Şeyla. 2009. "Turkey's Constitutional Zigzags." *Dissent* 56 (1): 25–28.

———. 2013. "The Gezi Park Protests and the Future of Turkish Politics: An Interview with Şeyla Benhabib." Blog interview by Begum Adalet, Defne Over, Onur Ozgode, and Semih Salihoglu. *Dissent,* September 9. www.dissentmagazine.org/online_arti cles/the-gezi-park-protests-and-the-future-of-turkish-politics-an-interview-with -seyla-benhabib.

Berkan, İsmet. 2013. "Yargının zihniyet sorunu ve Ergin Saygun'un Durumu" [The mentality of the judiciary and Ergin Saygun's situation]. *Hurriyet,* February 8.

Berman, Sheri. 2006. *Primacy of Politics: Social Democracy and the Making of Europe's Twentieth Century.* New York: Cambridge University Press.

Bierman, Irene, A. Abou El-Haj Rifa'at, and Donald Preziosi. 1991. *The Ottoman City and Its Parts: Urban Structure and Social order.* New Rochelle, NY: Aristide. D. Caratzas.

Blokland, Talja, and Gwen van Eijk. 2010. "Do People Who Like Diversity Practice Diversity in Neighborhood Life? Neighborhood Use and Social Networks of Diversity Seekers in a Mixed Neighborhood in the Netherlands." *Journal of Ethnic & Migration Studies* 36 (2): 313–32.

Bluestone, Barry, and Bennett Harrison. 1982. *The Deindustrialization of America: Plant Closings, Community Abandonment and Dismantling of Basic Industry.* New York: Basic Books.

Bora, Tanıl. 1999. "Istanbul of the Conqueror: The 'Alternative Global City' Dreams of Political Islam." In *Istanbul Between the Global and the Local,* ed. Çağlar Keyder, 47–58. Lanham, MD: Rowman & Littlefield.

Boschman, Sanne. 2012. "Residential Segregation and Interethnic Contact in the Netherlands." *Urban Studies* 49 (2): 353.

Bourdieu, Pierre. 1987. *Distinction: A Social Critique of the Judgment of Taste.* Cambridge, MA: Harvard University Press.

Bozdoğan, Sibel. 2001. *Modernism and Nation-Building: Architectural Culture in the Early Republic.* Seattle: University of Washington Press.

Brenner, Neil. 1999. "Beyond State-Centrism? Space, Territoriality, and Geographical Scale in Globalization Studies." *Theory and Society* 28: 39–78.

———. 2000. "The Urban Question as a Scale Question: Reflections on Henri Lefebvre, Urban Theory and the Politics of Scale." *International Journal of Urban and Regional Research* 24: 361–78.

———. 2004. *New State Spaces: Urban Governance and the Rescaling of Statehood.* Oxford: Oxford University Press.

———. 2011. "Urban Locational Policies and the Geographies of Post-Keynesian Statehood in Western Europe." In *Cities and Sovereignty: Identity Politics in Urban Spaces,* ed. Davis Diane and Nora Libertun de Duren, 152–78. Bloomington: Indiana University Press.

Brenner, Neil, B. Jessop, M. Jones, and Gordon Macleod, eds. 2003. *State/Space: A Reader.* Oxford: Blackwell.

Brenner, Neil, David Madden, and David Wachsmuth. 2012. "Assemblages, Actor Networks, the Challenger of Critical Urban Theory." In *Cities for People, Not for Profit: Critical Urban Theory and the Right to the City,* ed. Neil Brenner, Peter Marcuse, and Margit Mayer, 117–37. London: Routledge.

Brenner, Neil, J. Peck, and N. Theodore. 2010. "Variegated Neoliberalization: Geographies, Modalities, Pathways." *Global Networks* 10 (2): 1–41.

Brown, J. Christopher, and Mark Purcell. 2005. "There's Nothing Inherent About Scale: Political Ecology, the Local Trap, and the Politics of Development in the Brazilian Amazon." *Geoforum* 36: 607–24.

Brubaker, Roger. 1992. *Citizenship and Nationhood in France and Germany.* Cambridge, MA: Harvard University Press.

———. 2005. "The 'Diaspora' Diaspora." *Ethnic and Racial Studies* 28: 1–19.

Bruch, Elizabeth E., and Robert D. Mare. 2006. "Neighborhood Choice and Neighborhood Change." *American Journal of Sociology* 112 (3): 667–709.

Burawoy, Michael. 1991. *Ethnography Unbound: Power and Resistance in the Modern Metropolis.* Berkeley: University of California Press.

———. 1998. "The Extended Case Method." *Sociological Theory* 16 (1): 4–33.

Çakır, Ruşen. 2008. *Mahalle baskısı* [Neighborhood pressure]. Istanbul: Doğan Yayıncılık.

———. 2013. "PKK Gülen ve hareketinden ne istiyor?" [What does the PKK want from Gülen and his movement?]. *Radikal,* September 20.

Çakmak, Sedef. 2013. "No Living on Land or in Air: Discourse of Public Morality and Human Rights Violations of Transgender Individuals in Turkey." *Turkish Policy Quarterly* 11 (4): 141–47.

Calhoun, Craig. 1993. *Habermas and the Public Sphere*. Cambridge, MA: MIT Press.

———. 2006. "The University and the Public Good." *Thesis Eleven* 84 (7).

Carens, Joseph H. 2010. *Immigrants and the Right to Stay*. Cambridge, MA: MIT Press.

Carothers, Thomas. 2000. "The End of the Transition Paradigm." *Journal of Democracy* 13 (1): 5–21.

Casanova, José. 1994. *Public Religions*. Chicago: University of Chicago Press.

———. 2001. "Civil Society and Religion: Retrospective Reflections on Catholicism and Prospective Reflections on Islam." *Social Research* 68 (4): 1041–81.

Cassano, Jay. 2013. "The Right to the City Movement and the Turkish Summer," *Jadaliyya*, June 1. www.jadaliyya.com/pages/index/11978/the-right-to-the-city-movement-and-the-turkish-sum.

Çelik, Zeynep. [1982] 1993. *The Remaking of Istanbul: Portrait of an Ottoman City in the Nineteenth Century*. Berkeley: University of California Press.

Charrad, Mounirra. 2010. "Women's Agency Across Cultures: Conceptualizing Strengths and Boundaries." *Women's Studies International Forum* 33: 517–22.

Chatterton, Paul. 2006. "'Give up activism' and Change the World in Unknown Ways: or, Learning to Walk with Others on Uncommon Ground." *Antipode: A Radical Journal of Geography* 38: 259–81.

Çınar, Alev. 2005. *Modernity, Islam and Secularism in Turkey: Bodies, Places and Time*. Minneapolis: University of Minnesota Press.

Clark, Janine. 2004. *Islam, Charity, and Activism: Middle-Class Networks and Social Welfare in Egypt, Jordan, and Yemen*. Bloomington: Indiana University Press.

Cohen, Robert, and Reginald E. Zelnik. 2002. *The Free Speech Movement: Reflections on Berkeley in the 1960s*. Berkeley: University of California Press.

Coons, Christian, and Michael Weber. 2013. "Introduction: Paternalism—Issues and Trends." In *Paternalism: Theory and Practice*, ed. id. New York: Cambridge University Press.

Craiutu, Aurelian, and Jeremy Jennings, eds. 2009. *Tocqueville on America after 1840: Letters and Other Writings*. New York: Cambridge University Press.

Cresswell, Tim. 2006. *On the Move: Mobility in the Western World*. London: Routledge.

Danzikyan, Yetvart. 2013. "Çığırından çıkan rejim" [The government out of control]. *Radikal*, June 17.

Daunton, Matthew, and Martin Hilton. 2001. *The Politics of Consumption: Material Culture and Citizenship in Europe and America*. New York: Berg.

Davis, Diane. 1994. *Urban Leviathan: Mexico City in the Twentieth Century*. Philadelphia: Temple University Press.

———. Forthcoming. "Socio-Spatial Inequality and Violence in Cities of the Global

South: Evidence from Latin America." In *Urban Inequalities Across the Globe*, ed. David Wilson and Faranak Miraftab.

Davis, Diane, and Nora Libertun de Duren, eds. 2011. *Cities and Sovereignty: Identity Politics in Urban Spaces*. Bloomington: Indiana University Press.

Dayaratne, Ranjith. 2012. "Landscapes of Nation: Constructing National Identity in the Deserts of Bahrain." *National Identities* 14 (3): 309–27.

Deeb, Lara, and Mona Harb. 2014. *Leisurely Islam: Negotiating Geography and Morality in Shi'ite South Beirut*. Princeton, NJ: Princeton University Press.

Desbiens, Caroline, Allison Mountz, and Margaret Walton-Roberts. 2004. "Introduction: Reconceptualizing the State from the Margins of Political Geography." Guest editorial. *Political Geography* 23: 241–43.

Diamond, Larry, Marc Plattner, and Daniel Brumberg. 2003. *Islam and Democracy*. Baltimore: Johns Hopkins University Press.

Dikeç, Mustafa. 2007. *Badlands of the Republic: Space, Politics and Urban Policy*. Malden, MA: Blackwell.

Dumitru, Diana, and Johnson Carter. 2011. "Constructing Interethnic Conflict and Cooperation: Why Some People Harmed Jews and Other People Helped Them During Holocaust in Romania." *World Politics* 63 (1): 1–42.

Eickelman, Dale. 1998. "From Here to Modernity." In *The State of the Nation*, ed. John A. Hall. New York: Cambridge University Press.

Erder, Sema. 2006. *Refah toplumunda getto* [The ghetto in a welfare society]. Istanbul: Bilgi Üniversitesi Yayıncılık.

Escobar, Arturo. 2001. "Culture Sits in Places: Reflections on Globalism and Subaltern Strategies of Localization." *Political Geography* 20 (2): 139–74.

Evans, Peter. 2002. *Livable Cities? Urban Struggles for Livelihood and Sustainability*. Berkeley: University of California Press.

Evans, Peter, Dietrich Rueschemeyer, and Theda Skocpol. 1985. *Bringing the State Back In*. New York: Cambridge University Press.

Evans, Sara M., and Harry C. Boyte. 1992. *Free Spaces: Sources of Democratic Change in America*. Chicago: University of Chicago Press.

Ewing, Kathrin. 2008. *Stolen Honor: Stigmatizing Muslim Men in Berlin*. Stanford: Stanford University Press.

Featherstone, Mike. 1987. "Lifestyle and Consumer Culture." *Theory, Culture & Society* 4 (1): 55–70.

Feldman, Saul D. 1979. "Nested Identities." *Studies in Symbolic Interaction* 2: 399–418.

Fisher, Bonnie, and John J. Sloan III. 1995. *Campus Crime: Legal Social and Policy Perspectives*. Springfield, IL: Charles C. Thomas.

Folch-Serra, Mireya. 1990. "Place, Voice, Space: Mikhail Bakhtin's Dialogical Landscape." *Environment and Planning D: Society and Space* 8 (3): 255–74.

Fraser, Nancy. 1993. "Rethinking Public Sphere: A Contribution to the Critique of

Actually Existing Democracy." In *Habermas and the Public Sphere*, ed. Craig Calhoun, 109–43. Cambridge, MA: MIT Press.

Freeman, Jo. 2004. *At Berkeley in the Sixties: The Education of an Activist, 1961–1965*. Bloomington: University of Indiana Press.

Gaffikin, Frank, Malachy McEldowney, Carrie Menendez, and David Perry. 2008. *The Engaged University*. CU2 Contested Cities—Urban Universities. Belfast: Queen's University.

Gamson, William A. 1989. "Safe Spaces and Social Movements." In *Perspectives on Social Problems*, ed. Gale Miller and James A. Holstein, 27–39. Greenwich, CT: JAI Press.

Gellner, Ernest. 1981. *Muslim Society*. New York: Cambridge University Press.

———. 1996. *Conditions of Liberty: Civil Society and Its Rivals*. New York: Penguin Books.

Genel, Sema, and Kerem Karaosmanoğlu. 2006. "A New Islamic Individualism in Turkey: Islamic Headscarved Women in the City." *Turkish Studies* 7 (3): 473–88.

Gershoni, Israel, and James Jankowski. 1995. *Redefining the Egyptian Nation, 1930–45*. New York: Cambridge University Press.

Gezer, Özlem. 2013. "Türkisiert: Warum ich nie zu einer richtigen Deutschen wurde" [Turkified: Why I can never be a proper German]. *Der Spiegel*, November 7, 74–75. www.spiegel.de/spiegel/print/d-119402601.html.

Giddens, Anthony. 1991. *Modernity and Self-Identity: Self and Society in the Late Modern Age*. Stanford: Stanford University Press.

Gieryn, Thoman F. 2002. "Give Place a Chance: A Reply to Gans." *City and Community* 1 (4): 341–43.

Glaeser, Andreas. 1999. *Divided in Unity: Identity, Germany, and the Berlin Police*. Chicago: University of Chicago Press.

Goffman, Erving. 1959. *The Presentation of Self in Everyday Life*. New York: Doubleday.

———. 1961. *Asylum: Essays on the Social Situation of Mental Patients and Other Inmates*. Garden City, NY: Anchor Books.

———. 1963. *Behavior in Public Places: Notes on the Social Organization of Gatherings*. New York: Free Press.

Gökarıksel, Banu. 2007. "A Feminist Geography of Veiling: Gender, Class and Religion in the Making of Modern Subjects and Public Spaces in Istanbul." In *Women, Religion & Space: Global Perspectives on Gender and Faith*, ed. Karen M. Morin and Jeanne K. Guelke, 61–80. Syracuse, NY: Syracuse University Press.

———. 2012. "The Intimate Politics of Secularism and the Headscarf: The Mall, the Neighborhood, and the Public Square in Istanbul." *Gender, Place, and Culture* 19 (1): 1–20.

Göle, Nilüfer. 2013a. "Bir kamusal meydan hareketinin anatomisi" [The anatomy of a public square movement]. *T24*, June 6.

———. 2013b. "The Gezi Occupation for a Democracy of Public Spaces. " *Open Democracy*, June 11. www.opendemocracy.net/nilufer-gole/gezi-occupation-for-democracy-of-public-spaces.

Gözler, Kemal. [1982] 2000. *Anayasasının Hazırlanması*. Bursa: Ekin Kitabevi Yayıncılık.

Grüner, Sabina. 2010. "'The others don't want . . .' Small-Scale Segregation: Hegemonic Public Discourses and Racial Boundaries in German Neighborhoods." *Journal of Ethnic and Migration Studies* 36 (2): 275–92.

Güçlü, Abbas. 1993. "Üniversitelere MGK emri" [The National Security Council order to universities]. *Milliyet*, April 13.

Gülalp, Haldun. 2010. "Rektor: Tebaasını kendisi oluşturan kral" [Rector: The king who established his own subjects]. *Radikal*, February 1.

Hall, John A. 1995. *Civil Society: Theory, History, Comparison*. Cambridge: Polity Press.

———. 1998. *State of the Nation: Ernest Gellner and the Theory of Nationalism*. New York: Cambridge University Press.

———. 2013. *The Importance of Being Civil: The Struggle for Political Decency*. Princeton, NJ: Princeton University Press.

Harb, Mona. 2009. "City Debates 2008: Spaces of Faith and Fun." *International Journal of Urban and Regional Research* 33 (4): 1073–8.

Harvey, David. 2003. "The Right to the City." *International Journal of Urban and Regional Research* 27 (4): 939–41.

———. 2012. *Rebel Cities: From the Right to the City to the Urban Revolution*. New York: Verso.

Hasson, Shlomo, and David Ley. 1994. *Neighborhood Organizations and the Welfare State*. Toronto: Toronto University Press.

Häussermann, Hartmut. 2005. "The End of the European City?" *European Review* 13 (2): 237–49.

Häussermann, Hartmut, and Andreas Kapphan. 2000. *Berlin—von der geteilten zur gespaltenen Stadt? Sozialräumlicher Wandel seit 1990*. Opladen: Leske + Budrich.

Hélie, Anissa. 2012. "Introduction: Policing Gender, Sexuality and Muslimness." In *Sexuality in Muslim Contexts: Restrictions and Resistance*. London: Zed Books.

Hélie, Anissa, and Homa Hoodfar. 2012. *Sexuality in Muslim Contexts: Restrictions and Resistance*. London: Zed Books.

Hinze, Annika Marlen. 2013. *Turkish Berlin: Integration Policy and Urban Space*. Minneapolis: University of Minnesota Press.

Hirschman, Albert O. 1970. *Exit, Voice, and Loyalty: Responses to Decline in Firms, Organizations, and States*. Cambridge, MA: Harvard University Press.

Horowitz, Donald L. 1993. "Democracy in Divided Societies." *Journal of Democracy* 4 (4): 18–38.

Houston, Christopher. 2005. "Provocations of the Built Environment: Animating Cities in Turkey as Kemalist." *Political Geography* 24: 101–19.

Howe, Marvin. 2000. *Turkey Today: A Nation Divided over Islam*. New York: Basic Books.

Işın, Engin, ed. 2000. *Democracy, Citizenship and the Global City*. New York: Routledge.

Işın, Engin F., and Patricia Wood. 1999. *Citizenship and Identity*. Thousand Oaks, CA: Sage.

Ismail, Salwa. 2000. "The Popular Movement Dimensions of Contemporary Militant Islamism: Socio-spatial Determinants in the Cairo Urban Setting." *Comparative Studies in Society and History* 42 (2): 363–93.

———. 2006. *Political Life in Cairo's New Quarters*. Minneapolis: University of Minnesota Press.

Jonker, Gordon. 2000. "What Is Other About Other Religions? The Islamic Communities in Berlin Between Integration and Segregation." *Cultural Dynamics* 12 (3): 311–29.

Kadıoğlu, Ayşe. 2012. "Limits of Conservative Change: Reform Choreography of the Justice and Development Party." In *Another Empire: A Decade of Turkey's Foreign Policy Under the Justice and Development Party*, ed. Kerem Öktem, Ayşe Kadıoğlu, and Mehmet Karlı, 33–59. Istanbul: Bilgi University Press.

Kafescioğlu, Çiğdem. 2009. *Constantinopolis/Istanbul: Cultural Encounter, Imperial Vision, and the Construction of the Ottoman Capital*. University Park: Pennsylvania State University Press.

Kaplan, İsmail. 1999. *Türkiye'de Milli Eğitim İdeolojisi*. Istanbul: İletisim.

Kasaba, Reşat. 1994. "A Time and a Place for the Non-State: Social Change in the Ottoman Empire During the 'Long Nineteenth Century.'" In *State Power and Social Forces*, ed. Joel Migdal, Atul Kohlı, and Vivienne Shue, 207–30. New York: Cambridge University Press.

Kaya, Ayhan. 2001. *Sicher in Kreuzberg, Constructing Diasporas: Turkish Hip-Hop Youth in Berlin*. Piscataway, NJ: Transaction Publishers.

Keyder, Çağlar. 1999. *Istanbul: Between the Local and Global*. Lanham, MD: Rowman & Littlefield.

———. 2005. "Globalization and Social Exclusion in Istanbul." *International Journal of Urban and Regional Research* 129 (1): 124–34.

Keyder, Çağlar, and Öncü, Ayşe. 1994. "Globalization of a Third-World Metropolis: Istanbul in the 1980s." [Fernand Braudel Center] *Review* 27 (3): 383–421.

Keyman, Fuat, and Ayşe Kadıoğlu, eds. 2011. *Symbiotic Antagonisms: Competing Nationalisms in Turkey*. Salt Lake City: University of Utah Press.

Koenraad, Bogaert. 2012. "New State Space Formation in Morocco: The Example of Bouregreg Valley." *Urban Studies* 49 (2): 255–70.

Krätke, Stefan, and Renate Borst. 2000. *Berlin: Metropole zwischen Boom und Krise*. Opladen: Leske + Budrich.

Kuru, Ahmet. 2007. "Passive and Assertive Secularism: Historical Conditions, Ideological Struggles, and State Policies Toward Religion." *World Politics* 59 (4): 568–94.

———. 2009. *Secularism and State Policies Toward Religion: The United States, France and Turkey*. New York: Cambridge University Press.

Kuru, Ahmet, and Alfred Stepan. 2012. *Democracy, Islam and Secularism in Turkey*. New York: Columbia University Press.

Kymlicka, Will. 1996. *Multicultural Citizenship: A Liberal Theory of Minority Rights*. New York: Oxford University Press.

Lefebvre, Henri. 1996. *Writings on Cities*. Oxford: Blackwell.

———. 2003. "Space and the State." In *State/Space: A Reader*, ed. Bob Jessop Brenner, Martin Jones, and Gordon Macleod, 84–100. Oxford: Blackwell.

Leitner, Helga, Eric Sheppard, and Kristin M. Sziarto. 2008. "The Spatialities of Contentious Politics." *Transactions of the Institute of British Geographers* 33: 157–77.

Levi, Margaret. 1998. "The State of Trust." In *Trust and Governance*, ed. V. A. Braithwaite and Margaret Levi, 72–102. New York: Russell Sage Foundation.

Ley, David. 1996. *The New Middle Class and the Remaking of the Central City*. New York: Oxford University Press.

Linz, Juan J., and Alfred Stepan. 1996. *Problems of Democratic Transition and Consolidation*. Baltimore: Johns Hopkins University Press.

Logan, John, and Harvey Molotch. 2007. *Urban Fortunes: The Political Economy of Place*. Berkeley: University of California Press.

Logan, John, Wenquan Zhang, and Richard D. Alba. 2002. "Immigrant Enclaves and Ethnic Communities in New York and Los Angeles." *American Sociological Review* 67 (2): 299–322.

Low, Setha M. 2000. *On the Plaza: The Politics of Public Space and Culture*. Austin: University of Texas Press.

MacKinnon, D., and J. Shaw. 2010. "New State Space, Agency and Scale: Devolution and the Regionalisation of Transport Governance in Scotland." *Antipode* 42 (5): 1226–52.

MacLeavy, J., and J. Harrison. 2010. "New State Spatialities: Perspectives on State, Space, and Scalar Geographies." *Antipode* 42 (5): 1037–46.

Majd, Hooman. 2008. *The Ayatollah Begs to Differ: The Paradox of Modern Iran*. New York: Doubleday.

Mandel, Ruth. 2008. *Cosmopolitan Anxieties: Turkish Challenges to Citizenship and Belonging in Germany*. Durham, NC: Duke University Press.

Mann, Michael. 1993. *Social Sources of Power*. New York: Cambridge University Press.

Mardin, Şerif. 2000. "The Social Construction of Scale." *Progress in Human Geography* 24 (2): 219–42.

———. Forthcoming. *A Muslim Imaginary*. Istanbul: İletisim Yayıncılık.

Marston, Sallie. 2000. "The Social Construction of Scale." *Progress in Human Geography* 24: 219–42.

Marston, Sallie, John P. Jones, and Keith Woodward. 2005. "Human Geography Without Scale." *Transactions of the Institute of British Geographers*, n.s., 30: 416–32.

Martin, Deborah G. 2003. "'Place-Framing' as Place Making: Constituting a Neighborhood for Organizing and Activism." *Annals of the Association of American Geographers* 93: 730–50.

Martin, Deborah G., E. McCann, and M. Purcell. 2003. "Space, Scale, Governance, and

Representation: Contemporary Geographical Perspectives on Urban Politics and Policy." *Journal of Urban Affairs* 25 (2): 113–21.

Martinovic, Borja. 2013. "Inter-ethnic Contact of Immigrant and Natives in Netherlands. A Two-sided Perspective." *Journal of Ethnic and Migration Studies* 39 (1): 69–85.

Massey, Doreen. 1994. "A Global Sense of Place." In id., *Space, Place, and Gender*. Minneapolis: University of Minnesota Press.

———. 1999. "A Space of Politics." In *Human Geography Today*, ed. Doreen Massey, John Allen, and Phil Sarre, 279–94. Oxford: Polity Press.

———. 2007. "The World We're In: An Interview with Ken Livingstone." *Soundings: A Journal of Politics and Culture* 36: 11–25.

McAdam, Doug, Sidney Tarrow, and Charles Tilly. 2001. *The Dynamics of Contention*. New York: Cambridge University Press.

McEldowney, Malachy, Frank Gaffikin and David C. Perry. 2009. "Discourses of the Contemporary Urban Campus in Europe: Intimations of Americanisation?" *Globalization, Societies and Education* 7 (2): 131–49.

McMillen, William. 2010. *From Campus to Capitol: The Role of Government Relations in Higher Education*. Baltimore: Johns Hopkins University Press.

Migdal, Joel. 2001. *State in Society: Studying How States and Societies Transform and Constitute One Another*. New York: Cambridge University Press.

Migdal, Joel, Atul Kohli, and Vivienne Shue. 1994. *State Power and Social Forces: Domination and Transformation in the Third World*. New York: Cambridge University Press.

Mill, John Stuart. [1859] 1978. *On Liberty*. Indianapolis: Hackett.

Mills, Amy. 2007. "Gender and *Mahalle* (Neighborhood) Space in Istanbul." *Gender, Place and Culture* 14 (3): 335–54.

———. 2010. *Streets of Memory: Landscape, Tolerance, and National Identity in Istanbul*. Athens: University of Georgia Press.

Moore, Adam. 2008. "Rethinking Scale as a Geographical Category: From Analysis to Practice." *Progress in Human Geography* 32 (2): 203–22.

Mumcu, Özgür. 2012. "ODTÜ yalnız değildir" [ODTÜ is not alone]. *Radikal*, December 27.

Murdie, Robert, and Sutama Ghosh. 2010. "Does Spatial Concentration Always Mean a Lack of Integration? Exploring Ethnic Concentration and Integration in Toronto." *Journal of Ethnic and Migration Studies* 36 (2): 293–311.

Nelson, E. D. 2001. "The Things That Dreams Are Made On: Dream Work and the Socialization of 'Stage Mothers.'" *Qualitative Sociology* 24 (4): 439–58.

Nørgaard, Helle. 2003. "The Global City Thesis—Social Polarization and Changes in the Distribution of Wages." *Geografiska Annaler* 85 (2): 103–19.

Norton, Richard August, ed. 1995. *Civil Society in the Middle East*. Vol. 1. Leiden: Brill.

Öktem, Kerem. 2012. "Projecting Power: Non-conventional Policy Actors in Turkey's

International Relations." In *Another Empire: A Decade of Turkey's Foreign Policy Under the Justice and Development Party*, ed. Kerem Öktem, Ayse Kadıoğlu, and Mehmet Karlı, 77–105. Istanbul: Bilgi University Press.

Öncü, Ayşe, and Petra Weyland, eds. 1997. *Space, Culture and Power: New Identities in Globalizing Cities*. London: Zed Books.

Ong, Aihwa. 2008. "Scales of Exception: Experiments with Knowledge and Sheer Life in Tropical Southeast Asia." *Singapore Journal of Tropical Geography* 29 (2): 117–29.

Öniş, Ziya. 2012. "The Triumph of Conservative Globalism: The Political Economy of the AKP Era." *Turkish Studies* 13 (2): 135–52.

———. 2013. "Sharing Power: Turkey's Democratization Challenge in the Age of the AKP Hegemony." *Insight Turkey* 15 (2): 103–22.

Öz, Özlem, and Mine Eder. 2012. "Rendering Istanbul's Periodic Bazaars Invisible: Reflections on Urban Transformation and Contested Space." *International Journal of Urban and Regional Research* 36 (2): 297–314.

Özbudun, Ergun. 2012. "Turkey's Search for a New Constitution." *Insight Turkey* 14 (1): 39–50.

Özüekren, Şule, and Ebru Ergöz-Karahan. 2010. "Housing Experience of Turkish (Im)migrants in Berlin and Istanbul: Internal Differentiation and Segregation." *Journal of Ethnic and Migration Studies* 36 (2): 355–72.

Özüekren, Şule, and Ronald van Kempen. 1997. *Turks in European Cities: Housing and Urban Segregation*. Utrecht: European Research Centre on Migration and Ethnic Relations.

Özyürek, Esra. 2006. *Nostalgia for the Modern: State Secularism and Everyday Politics in Turkey*. Durham, NC: Duke University Press.

Painter, Joe. 2005. "State: Society." In *Spaces of Geographical Thought: Deconstructing Human Geography's Binaries*, ed. P. Cloke and R. Johnston, 42–60. London: Sage.

———. 2006. "Prosaic Geographies of Stateness." *Political Geography* 25 (2): 752–74.

Perihan, Mağden. 2007. "Fazıl Say haksız mı?" [Is Fazil Say wrong?]. *Radikal*, December 16.

Peterson, Ruth D., and Lauren J. Krivo. 2010. *Divergent Social Worlds: Neighborhood Crime and the Racial-Spatial Divide*. New York: Russell Sage Foundation.

Pierce, Jennifer L. 2003. "Traveling from Feminism to Mainstream Sociology and Back: One Woman's Tale of Tenure and the Politics of Backlash." *Qualitative Sociology* 26 (3): 369–96.

Polletta, Francesca. 1999. "Free Spaces in Collective Action." *Theory and Society* 28: 1–38.

———. 2002. *Freedom Is an Endless Meeting: Democracy in American Social Movements*. Chicago: University of Chicago Press.

———. 2006. *It Was Like a Fever: Storytelling in Protest and Politics*. Chicago: University of Chicago Press.

Powell, Ryan. 2013. "Loïc Wacquant's 'Ghetto' and Ethnic Minority Segregation in the

UK: The Neglected Case of Gypsy-Travellers." *International Journal of Urban and Regional Research* 37 (1): 115–34.

Przeworski, Adam. 2003. "Minimalist Conception of Democracy: A Defense." In *The Democracy Sourcebook*, ed. Robert A. Dahl, Ian Shapiro, and José A. Cheibub, 12–17. Cambridge, MA: MIT Press.

Purcell, Mark. 2003. "Excavating Lefebvre: The Right to the City and Its Urban Politics of the Inhabitant." *GeoJournal* 58: 99–108.

———. 2006. "Urban Democracy and the Local Trap." *Urban Studies* 43 (11): 1921–41.

———. 2008. *Recapturing Democracy: Neoliberalization and the Struggle for Alternative Urban Futures*. New York: Routledge.

Purcell, Mark, and J. Christopher Brown. 2005. "Against the Local Trap: Scale and the Study of Environment and Development." *Progress in Development Studies* 5 (4): 279–97.

Putnam, Robert D. 1995. "Bowling Alone: America's Declining Social Capital." *Journal of Democracy* 6 (1): 65–78.

Read, Benjamin. 2012. *The Roots of the State: Neighborhood Organization and Social Networks in Beijing and Taipei*. Stanford: Stanford University Press.

Read, Benjamin, and Robert Pekkanen. 2009. *Local Organizations and Urban Governance in East and Southeast Asia: Straddling State and Society*. New York: Routledge.

Reynolds, Nancy. 2012. *A City Consumed: Urban Commerce, the Cairo Fire, and the Politics of Decolonization in Egypt*. Stanford: Stanford University Press.

Rose, Nikolas. 1999. *Powers of Freedom: Reforming Political Thought*. New York: Cambridge University Press.

Rottmann, Susan B., and Myra Marx Ferree. 2008. "Citizenship and Intersectionality: German Feminist Debates about Headscarf and Antidiscrimination Laws." *Social Politics: International Studies in Gender, State and Society* 15 (4): 481–513.

Saktanber, Binnaz. 2013. "The Voices of Turkish Protestors Have Been Heard." *Guardian*, June 2.

Sarrazin, Thilo. 2010. *Deutschland schafft sich ab: Wie wir unser Land aufs Spiel setzen* [Germany abolishes itself: How we jeopardize our country]. Munich: Deutsche Verlags-Anstalt.

Sassen, Saskia. 1991. *The Global City: New York, London, Tokyo*. Princeton, NJ: Princeton University Press.

———. 1996. *Losing Control? Sovereignty in an Age of Globalization*. New York: Columbia University Press.

———. 2006. *Territory, Authority and Rights: From Medieval to Global Assemblages*. 1st ed. Princeton, NJ: Princeton University Press.

———. 2011. "The Global Street: *Making* the Political." *Globalizations* 8 (5): 573–79.

———. 2012. "Borders, Walls and Crumbling Sovereignty." *Political Theory* 40 (1): 116–22.

Schlueter, Elmar. 2012. "Inter-ethnic Friendships of Immigrants with Host-Society Members: Revisiting the Role of Ethnic Residential Segregation." *Journal of Ethnic and Migration Studies* 38 (1): 77–91.

Schmitter, Philippe C. 2010. "Democracy's Past and Future: Twenty-Five Years, Fifteen Findings." *Journal of Democracy* 21 (1): 17–28.

Schwedler, Jillian. 2011. "The Radical Power of Just Showing Up." *Al Jazeera*, October 25. www.aljazeera.com/indepth/opinion/2011/10/201110257859154472.html.

Secor, Anna J. 2001. "Toward a Feminist Counter-Geopolitics: Gender, Space and Islamist Politics in Istanbul." *Space and Polity* 5 (3): 191–211.

———. 2003. "Citizenship in the City: Identity, Community, and Rights Among Women Migrants to Istanbul." *Urban Geography* 24 (2): 147–68.

———. 2007. "Between Belonging and Despair: State, Space, Subjectivity in Turkey." *Environment and Planning D: Society and Space* 25 (1): 33–52.

Sennett, Richard. 1998. *The Spaces of Democracy.* Ann Arbor: University of Michigan, College of Architecture and Planning.

———. 2012. "New Ways of Thinking About Space." *The Nation*, September 24.

Singerman, Diane. 1996. *Avenues of Participation: Family, Politics and Networks in Urban Quarters of Cairo.* Princeton, NJ: Princeton University Press.

Skocpol, Theda. 1979. "Introduction." In id., *States and Social Revolutions: A Comparative Analysis of France, Russia and China.* New York: Cambridge University Press.

Smith, Adam. [1759] 2011. *Theory of Moral Sentiments.* Seattle: Gutenberg Publishers.

Soja, Edward W. 2010. *Seeking Spatial Justice.* Minneapolis: University of Minnesota Press.

Soysal, Yasemin Nuhoğlu. 1994. *Limits of Citizenship: Migrants and Postnational Membership in Europe.* Chicago: University of Chicago Press.

Strom, Elizabeth A. 2001. *Building the New Berlin: Politics of Urban Development in Germany's Capital City.* New York: Lexington Books.

Svašek, Maruška. 2010. "On the Move: Emotions and Human Mobility." *Journal of Ethnic and Migration Studies* 36 (6): 865–80.

Swyngedouw, Erik. 2000. "Authoritarian Governance, Power and the Politics of Scale." *Environment and Planning D* 18: 63–76.

———. 2004. "Globalisation or 'Glocalisation'? Networks, Territories and Rescaling." *Cambridge Review of International Affairs* 17 (1): 25–48.

Taha, Akyol. 2013a. "AKP'nin yargı modeli" [The AKP's judicial model]. *Hürriyet*, February 7.

———. 2013b. "Yargı sorunu" [The problem of the judiciary]. *Hürriyet*, February 8.

Tambar, Kabir. 2014. *The Reckoning of Pluralism: Political Belonging and the Demands of History in Turkey.* Stanford: Stanford University Press

Tarhan, Erdem. 2007. "Gündelik yaşamda din laiklik ve türban" [Religion, laicism, and the head scarf in everyday life]. *Milliyet*, December 4–10.

Taylor, Charles. 1993. *Multiculturalism and the "Politics of Recognition": An Essay with Commentary by Charles Taylor and Amy Gutman.* Montreal: McGill-Queen's University Press.

Tepe, Sultan. 2013. "Democratic Conundrums in Turkey." *Review of Middle East Studies* 47 (1): 22–27.

Tetreault, Mary Ann. 1993. "Civil Society in Kuwait: Protected Spaces and Women's Rights." *Middle East Journal* 47 (2): 275–91.

Tilly, Charles, and Wim P. Blockmans, eds. 1994. *Cities and the Rise of States in Europe, A.D. 1000–1800.* Boulder, CO: Westview Press;

Tilly, Charles, and Sidney Tarrow. 2006. *Contentious Politics.* Boulder, CO: Paradigm Publishers.

Tocqueville, Alexis de. [1835–40] 2000. *Democracy in America.* Chicago: Chicago University Press.

———. [1856] 1955. *The Old Regime and the French Revolution.* New York: Anchor Books.

Tombuş, Ertuğ H. 2013. "Reluctant Democratization: The Case of the Justice and Development Party in Turkey." *Constellations* 20 (2): 312–32.

Toprak, Binnaz, İrfan Bozan, Tan Morgül, and Nedim Şener. 2008. "Türkiye'de farklı ölmak. Din ve muhafazakarlık ekseninde otekileştirilenler" [Being different in Turkey: Alienation on the axis of religion and conservatism]. Boğazici Üniversitesi, Bilimsel Arastirma Projesi.

Trouille, David. 2012. "Neighborhood Outsiders, Field Insiders: Latino Immigrant Men and the Control of Public Space." *Qualitative Sociology* 36 (1): 1–22.

Tuan, Yi-Fu. 1977. *Space and Place: The Perspective of Experience.* Minneapolis: University of Minnesota Press.

Tuğal, Cihan. 2009. *Passive Revolution: Absorbing Islam into Capitalism.* Stanford: Stanford University Press.

Turam, Berna. 2004. "The Politics of Engagement Between Islam and the State: Ambivalences of Civil Society." *British Journal of Sociology* 55 (2): 259–81.

———. 2007. *Between Islam and the State: The Politics of Engagement.* Stanford: Stanford University Press.

———. 2008a. "Turkish Women Divided by Politics: Secular Activism Versus Islamic Non Defiance." *International Feminist Journal of Politics* 10 (4): 475–94.

———. 2008b. "Between Kemalists and Islamists." *ISIM Review* 21 (Spring).

———. 2012a. "Primacy of Space in Politics: Bargaining Space, Power and Freedom in an Istanbul Neighborhood." *International Journal of Urban and Regional Research* 37 (2): 409–29.

———. 2012b. "Turkey Under the AKP: Are Civil Liberties Safe?" *Journal of Democracy* 23 (1): 109–18.

———. 2012c. "Introduction." In *Secular State and Religious Society: Two Forces in Play in Turkey*, ed. id. Basingstoke, UK: Palgrave Macmillan.

Ümit, Cizre. 2011. "Disentangling the Threads of Civil-Military Relations in Turkey: Promises and Perils." *Mediterranean Quarterly* 22 (2): 57–75.

Uitermark, Justus. 2014. "Integration and Control: The Governing of Urban Marginality in Western Europe." *International Journal of Urban and Regional Research* 38.

Vale, Lawrence. 2011. "The Temptations of Nationalism in Modern Capital Cities." In *Cities and Sovereignty: Identity Politics in Urban Spaces*, ed. Davis Diane and Nora Libertun de Duren, 196–209. Bloomington: Indiana University Press.

Yavuz, Devrim. 2012. "Capital, the State and Democratization: The Case of Turkish Industry." *Sociology* 46: 507–22.

Wacquant, Loïc. 2004. "Ghetto." In *International Encyclopaedia of the Social and Behavioural Sciences*, ed. Neil J. Smelser and Paul B. Baltes. London: Pergamon Press.

———. 2008. *Urban Outcasts: A Comparative Sociology of Advanced Marginality*. Cambridge: Polity Press.

———. 2010. "Designing Urban Seclusion in the Twenty-first Century." *Perspecta: The Yale Architectural Journal* 43: 164–75.

Warf, Barney, and Santa Arias, eds. 2009. *The Spatial Turn: Interdisciplinary Perspectives*. New York: Routledge.

Weber, Max. 1946a. *From Max Weber: Essays in Sociology*. Translated and edited by Hans H. Gerth and C. Wright Mills. New York: Oxford University Press.

———. 1946b. "Science as a Vocation." In *From Max Weber: Essays in Sociology*, trans. and ed. Hans H. Gerth and C. Wright Mills. New York: Oxford University Press. New ed., London: Routledge, 1991.

———. 1958. *The City*. Glencoe, IL: Free Press.

———. 1968. *Economy and Society: An Outline of Interpretive Sociology*. New York: Bedminster Press.

———. [1908] 1973. *On Universities: The Power of the State and the Dignity of the Academic Calling in Imperial Germany*. Translated by Edward Shills. Chicago: University of Chicago Press.

Wedeen, Lisa. 2007. "The Politics of Deliberation: Qāt Chews as Public Spheres in Yemen." *Public Culture* 19 (1): 119–32.

———. 2008. *Peripheral Visions: Publics, Power, and Performance in Yemen*. Chicago: University of Chicago Press.

Weinstein, Liza. 2009. "Democracy in the Globalizing Indian City: Engagements of Political Society and the State in Globalizing Mumbai." *Politics and Society* 37: 397–427.

———. 2014. *The Durable Slum: Dharavi and the Right to Stay Put in Globalizing Mumbai*. Minneapolis: University of Minnesota Press.

White, Jenny. 1997. "Turks in the New Germany." *American Anthropologist* 99 (4): 754–69.

———. 2002. *The Islamist Mobilization in Turkey: A Study in Vernacular Politics*. Seattle: University of Washington Press.

Whittier, Nancy. 1995. *Feminist Generations: The Persistence of the Radical Women's Movement*. Philadelphia: Temple University Press.

Wise, Amanda. 2010. "Sensuous Multiculturalism: Emotional Landscapes of Inter-Ethnic Living in Australian Suburbia." *Journal of Ethnic and Migration Studies* 36 (6): 917–37.

Yılmaz, Volkan. 2013. "New Constitution of Turkey: A Blessing or a Curse for LGBT Citizens?" *Turkish Policy Quarterly* 11 (4): 131–40.

Zubaida, Sami. 2005. "Max Weber's The City and the Islamic City." *Max Weber Studies* 6 (1): 111–18.

———. [1988] 2009. *Islam, the People and the State: Political Ideas and Movements in the Middle East*. 3rd ed. New York: I. B Tauris.

Zussman, Robert. 2004. "People in Places." *Qualitative Sociology* 27 (4): 351–63.

INDEX